Mark Edmonds

with illustrations by
Gary Wing

ROBERT NICHOLSON PUBLICATIONS

A Nicholson Guide

First published 1988

Design by Bob Vickers
Map by David Perrott

Robert Nicholson Publications
16 Golden Square
London W1R 4BN

Typeset by Rowland Phototypesetting Ltd,
Bury St Edmunds, Suffolk.

Printed in Great Britain by
Anchor Brendon Ltd, Tiptree, Essex.

ISBN 0 948576 12 X

88/1/110

Contents

1 The Soho Scene 5

2 Historic Soho 11
A Stroll Around Soho's Past 15
So Who Lived in Soho? 29

3 Eating 41
Restaurants 44
Cafés and Brasseries 91

4 Drinking 98
Pubs 99
Wine Bars 133
Drinking Clubs 140

5 Shopping 142
Designer Clothes and Accessories 144
Food and Drink 151
Specialist Shops 159
Markets 173

6 Entertainment 176
Casinos 176
Cinemas 180
Health Clubs 181
Live Music 183
Membership Clubs 188
Saunas 191
Strip Shows 191
Theatres 195
Nightlife 199
Nightclubs 202

7 Sex and Soho 209
Hostess Bars 211
Peep Shows 214
Prostitutes 215
Crime 217

8 Chinatown 222
Eating in Chinatown 230
Restaurants 231
Shops 241

9 Soho Services 245
Map 252
Index 254

Acknowledgements

This book would not have been possible without the help of a great many people who provided advice and information, in particular Roy Harrison of the Westminster City Archive and Bryan Burrough of the Soho Society. Thanks also to Louise Cavanagh, my editor, for all her encouragement and to David Avery, Jack Barrie, Clive Batty, Gaston Berlemont, Mike Berry, John Arthur Bryant, Alberto Camisa, Liam Carson, Paolo Crocetta, Robert Davis, Fiona Duff, Alan Frost, Jack Fuller, April Goodey, Reg Greenacre, Tony Jackson, David Key, Nick Lander, Agnes MacKenzie, Georgina Matthews, Flair Milne, Elizabeth Moody, Ed Morse, Criona Palmer, Philip Powell, Paul Raymond, Helen Steven, Angela Smyth, Gill Tan, Carla Tomasi, Les Waumsley, Nicholas Worger.

The author would also like to thank the following:
Curtis Brown Ltd, for permission to reproduce the verse by John Betjeman. Copyright John Betjeman.
W. H. Allen for permission to reproduce the extract from *Absolute Beginners* by Colin MacInnes.
Oxford University Press for permission to reproduce the extract from *Bohemia in London* by Arthur Ransome.

Mark Edmonds is a journalist based in London. He has contributed to a range of magazines and newspapers including *The Guardian*, the *Telegraph Sunday Magazine*, *Cosmopolitan*, *City Limits*, *She* and the *Islington Gazette*. He now works for *The Observer Magazine*.

1 The Soho Scene

For decades, Soho's cosmopolitan image as London's very own Quartier Latin has evoked thoughts of foreign restaurants, frothy Italian coffee, prostitutes, literary lions and inebriates. And Soho is currently enjoying a renaissance which harks back to its days as a society playground in the 18th century. Dozens of trendy, new restaurants have sprung up, fashion shops have taken over premises previously occupied by peepshows, and the nightclubs are buzzing like they've never buzzed before.

Yet it is still difficult to walk along Regent Street or Shaftesbury Avenue on a Saturday night during the football season without being approached by an embarrassed but lustful posse of pre- and post-pubescents asking 'Scuse me, mate, where's Soho?' In spite of Soho's fame this question is seldom met with an accurate reply. Most visitors to the capital are aware that it is somewhere in the West End, maybe near Piccadilly Circus, but it is unlikely that anyone but a genuine Sohoite (or Sohovian in Irma Kurtz parlance) would be able to pinpoint the area's boundaries. Soho does not in fact have any official boundaries, but the name is generally taken to mean that square mile of densely-packed streets bounded by four major thoroughfares; to the north Oxford Street, to the west Regent Street, to the east Charing Cross Road and to the south Coventry Street. Within these boundaries, if you look hard enough, you will certainly find prostitutes and peep shows, but contrary to popular belief, sex is not what Soho is about. True, the sex industry has always attracted more publicity than Soho's more traditional trades and crafts, but it has never been of prime importance.

The serious Soho aficionado will be aware of the area's unofficial sub-divisions. Wardour Street, one of the most important thoroughfares, is the traditional dividing line between east and west Soho. It also happens to mark the boundary between the two parishes which Soho embraces, St Anne's in the east and St James's in the west. Although both east and west have a cosmopolitan character, there are marked differences between the two halves. The architectural writer Ian Nairn described the land west of Wardour Street as 'Low Soho' and the land to the east as 'High Soho'. He was right in that west Soho has always been the poor relation. With the exception of Golden Square, Low Soho is a mish-mash of half-finished, ill-considered streets. Once you head west of Berwick Street Market, you are entering a no-man's-land of office blocks, car parks and grimy, unremarkable alleyways. There is a high concentration of housing (council blocks on Ingestre Place, Ganton Street and Dufour's Place), yet Low Soho always seems lifeless. Brewer Street and Beak Street offer some respite from the gloom but these are shopping thoroughfares which usually switch off at about 6pm. High Soho, however, has a raffish noisy charm of its own. Old Compton Street, bang in the middle, has always been the pumping heart of Soho, crossed by three main arteries – Dean Street, Frith Street and Greek Street – at its eastern end.

Old Compton Street is a bon viveur's dream. Restaurants jostle each other for space, while some of London's finest food shops provide a range of delicacies unequalled elsewhere. The Soho Brasserie, near the junction with Frith Street, is an important landmark. The Soho Revival more or less began here and the pavements outside are still chock-a-block with young and not-so-young trendies.

Greek Street, which leads up to Soho Square from Old Compton Street, was always one of Soho's more desirable residential thoroughfares. The houses here were grander than most, and in the 17th and 18th centuries provided city dwellings for the gentry who found it conveniently placed for London's nightlife, but also within easy reach of the country. This was a far cry from the pornographers and sleaze merchants who made their mark on Greek Street in the 1950s and 60s, but most of these have since disappeared. Greek Street is now dominated by some of London's most fashionable restaurants, one or two of the area's more interesting shops and that blight on contemporary London, office development.

On the other side of Shaftesbury Avenue (a thoroughfare not constructed until 1887, which served to divide old Soho), Gerrard Street forms the heart of London's Chinatown. Not always a centre for the Chinese who were comparatively late arrivals in the 1950s and 60s, for much of its life Gerrard Street was renowned as the haunt of literary and artistic characters. John Dryden was probably the first to arrive when he moved from Covent Garden in 1687. Since then the square mile has served as home to a long list of journalists and philosophers, poets and novelists. Shelley, Hazlitt, De Quincey and Burke all lived here in their time.

By the turn of the 20th century, Soho's coffee houses and restaurants had become a focal point for London's writers and artists and the area began to attract attention as a centre of literary life. In his book *Bohemia in London*, first published in 1907, Arthur Ransome recalled the atmosphere of the restaurants: '. . . the tradition is still current at the Soho dinner tables that there were a few grand years in which we rivalled the Quartier in costume and outdid the Montmartre in extravagant conversation . . . All down our long table there were not two faces that did not seem to me then to bear the imprint of some particular genius. Some were assuredly painters, others journalists, some very obviously poets, and there were several, too, of those amateur irregulars, who were always either exasperating or charming.'

The literary tradition established in Soho at this time was to continue for at least the next 50 years. The 40s and 50s saw a motley collection of writers, artists and layabouts adopt Soho as a stomping ground. Pubs such as the York Minster (now the French House), the Swiss (now Comptons) and the Helvetia were much-frequented by London's literary set. Under their roofs the likes of Dylan Thomas, Brendan Behan (who actually preferred the pubs of Fitzrovia), John Minton and Augustus John would cavort, before heading off for one of the after-hours drinking clubs such as the Colony, the Sunset or the Gargoyle. Of these only the Colony remains. Its habitués (who are very protective of the privilege and status which membership confers) would maintain that they represent all that's left of literary Soho. Yet only a few doors down Dean Street a young pretender seems as though it may soon become Soho's best-known literary rendezvous. The Groucho Club, which opened in 1985, is where authors, agents and publishers meet to discuss books, terms and, more likely, the gossip of the day. This is New Soho at its most self-conscious; but no more pretentious than Old Soho as evinced by the self-proclaimed 'bohemians' who stagger into the Colony every afternoon.

Inevitably, cliquey clubs like the Groucho and the Colony often come in for flak, and not just from those who have been denied entry. Some Sohoites consider these establishments to have about as much in common with the Real Soho as the tourists who crowd out the Shakespeare's Head under the false impression that the bard was born there. And it would seem that this dissatisfaction with Soho's literati is nothing new. John Keats, writing to Haydon at the beginning of the 19th century, asked:

> 'For who would go
> into dark Soho,
> To chatter with dark-haired critics,
> When he might stay,
> In the new-mown hay
> And startle the dappled prickets?'

However, it's not just the literary types who have adopted Soho as their own. For some years Britain's mediacrats have also been gaining a foothold in the area. It all started with the film industry. 20th Century Fox moved into Soho Square in the 1930s; soon afterwards they were joined by other American giants such as Rank, Warner Brothers and Columbia, many of whose offices still dominate Wardour Street and its environs. However, Cinematic Soho is now based around small production companies, cutting rooms and other attendant businesses. The biggies don't actually make any films here these days; their premises are merely administrative showcases. But it's not by coincidence that the British Board of Film Censors, the ACTT (production workers' union) and the British Film Institute all have their offices in Soho, and it's still possible to rent a preview room, make a voiceover for a commercial or even buy a clapperboard here.

In the last five years or so, a number of large advertising agencies have moved into the area, many of them refugees from Covent Garden. Those in charge at the agencies now feel that Soho has more to offer. It is very convenient, right in the centre of the West End and has the additional advantage of having a ready-made media support industry: film production companies, cutting rooms, printers, recording studios, colour laboratories, hordes of motorcycle messengers and some of the best opportunities in town for flexing the company Amex card. At lunchtime Soho's restaurants are stuffed with creative directors, art directors, copywriters and account executives, all eating out on expenses.

However, the noise the mediamen make in Soho is way out of proportion to their number. Recently, they've even spawned offshoots – they now have their own drinking clubs, and accessory stores where they can buy anything in matt black. One wonders which will be the first of Soho's restaurants to offer them a minding service for their portable telephones. This is indeed the Soho of the Filofax generation.

Soho may now be trendy, but many of its inhabitants are old-timers who care not a jot about who drinks at the Groucho Club or which of the new resident designers has just been lauded to the skies by *Fashion Weekly*. Despite the cosmetic changes a cosmopolitan, tolerant atmosphere still prevails. Little has changed, in fact, since the days when John Galsworthy, writing about Soho in *The Forsyte Saga* at the beginning of this century, described it: 'Of all quarters in this queer adventurous amalgam called London, Soho is perhaps least suited to the Forsyte spirit . . . Untidy, full of Greeks, Ishmaelites, cats, Italians, tomatoes, restaurants, organs, coloured stuffs, queer names, people looking out of upper windows, it dwells remote from the British Body Politic.'

It is this very 'remoteness' which gives Soho its distinct flavour and means that though much has changed, much has remained the same. The recent perception of Soho as nothing more than London's 'red-light' district makes a mockery of its identity as a genuine, functioning village at the centre of a great city. While sex ruled, rents soared and legitimate businesses found that competing with the petty criminals, wideboys and shysters who had made Soho their own, was extremely tough. The sex establishments were generating so much revenue that the freeholders of premises could demand excessively high rents. As a result, many of Soho's small bakeries, dairies and trattorias were forced to close down.

Fortunately, it seems Soho has at last emerged from those dark days. The pornographers are under control and only a few sex establishments still exist. Most of these are licensed by Westminster City Council; those that don't have licences will be forced to close down as soon as their lease expires. Meanwhile the Soho Revival continues apace. More and more shops are opening up, attempting to cash in on the boom. A new generation of young designers and entrepreneurs has arrived, aware that Soho is fast becoming London's trendiest spot.

But it is Soho's new-found popularity which may now prove a threat. Thankfully, up until now, the developers have been restrained by the planning laws and Soho has largely been spared the kind of high-rise concrete and glass structures which have spoilt so many other historic areas of London. Undoubtedly, however, more and more companies will be seeking premises in Soho, and local environmentalists will have to keep a watchful eye on planning applications. Large-scale office development would knock the guts out of Soho.

At the moment, though, the excitement of the district still has a fascination for thousands of people. If you are one of them, this book should help you appreciate the infinite charms, countless quirks and occasional chaos that somehow manage to combine to form London's most intriguing square mile.

2 Historic Soho

Soho is now so densely populated with offices, shops and houses that it is difficult to believe that this was once prime hunting territory; but development did not begin in earnest here until the 1680s. Before that time, a young man of titled provenance could ride from home and join the hunt on a rampage across the green blanket of fields which then covered Soho. The area in fact takes its name from a hunting cry of the time, 'So-ho', which the huntsmen would exclaim once they caught a glimpse of their quarry.

The hunts were organised by a number of aristocratic landlords, whose families had been given, leased, or sold slices of Soho (then known as St Giles's Fields) by Henry VIII. Henry's original intention had been to establish a Royal Park on the land, but this plan never reached fruition.

In 1686, the parish of St Anne was formed out of the parish of St Martin-in-the-Fields and some of the streets we know today were completed. (However, Soho west of Wardour Street, an area embracing streets such as Broadwick Street, Beak Street and Lexington Street, has always come under the parish of St James. St James's Church is in Piccadilly.) The layout of streets in the area was initially based on the old system of estate boundaries which separated the lands obtained by the aristocrats from Henry VIII. Both parishes, then as now, were bounded by public highways, the most important of which was The Waye to Uxbridge, to the north (later to become Oxford Street). These highways, and the small streets leading off them, were littered with poor dwellings; very different from the extravagant mansions that the aristocracy had in mind when they started developing the area in the 1680s.

Grand houses, such as Fauconberg House, Carlisle House and Monmouth House, were soon erected and by 1700 Soho had become one of the capital's most fashionable residential districts. Neither Mayfair nor Belgravia were quite the exclusive enclaves they are today and the aristocracy were not lured out of Soho until the latter part of the 18th century.

The titled classes from all over Britain and beyond would make the journey to this charming village for a taste of some of its pleasures. They would stroll around Soho Square and Golden Square (both very fashionable) and in the evenings enjoy some of London's most glittering nightlife. The most exclusive events were Mrs Theresa Cornelys' masked balls, held at Carlisle House in Soho Square. She rented this magnificent house, which even got a mention in Thackeray's *Barry Lyndon* (1844), from 1760 to 1772 and dukes, baronets and royalty were attracted to her splendid entertainments. For over a decade she was the undisputed queen of Soho society but gradually Carlisle House became less fashionable. In an attempt to attract trade from two competing places of entertainment, Almack's in St James's and the Pantheon in Oxford Street, Mrs Cornelys ended up penniless, having overstretched herself financially.

Her fall coincided with the demise of Soho as a fashionable spot. Bigger, grander houses would later be built in Mayfair and the upper classes slowly abandoned the streets and squares of Soho. Initially they went west to Mayfair, and later colonised Belgravia, owned largely by the Earl of Grosvenor, where residential development started in the 1820s.

Although the titled classes had dominated Soho since it became a residential district, another group was also making its mark upon the area. The Huguenots (French Protestants) formed Soho's first émigré population. For at least 20 years they had been the victims of religious persecution in France, where their rights and freedom had been gradually eroded. In 1681 many unsettled Huguenots came to England after Charles II offered them letters of denization, but the main wave of Huguenot migration did not take place until 1685 when the French King, Louis XIV, revoked the Edict of Nantes. Drawn up in 1597, this had guaranteed the Huguenots civil and religious rights which were now withdrawn.

About 40,000 Huguenots converged on London and many eventually found themselves in Soho. There had been a congregation of French Protestants in Westminster since the 1640s and as more and more Huguenots were arriving in London, the religious authorities agreed that a second chapel should be established. The vestry of St Martin-in-the-Fields allowed the Huguenots to take over a chapel in Hog Lane (now part of Charing Cross Road), which had been used by Greek Christian refugees. They had opened their chapel in 1680 but after only two years, financial pressures forced them to hand it over to the French.

The Huguenots were mainly of the artisan class, and soon set up small businesses in the area. They worked as gold or silversmiths, jewellers, engravers, weavers and clock and watchmakers. Figures collated by the vestry of St Anne's church indicate that in 1711, two-fifths of Soho's population of about 8000 was in fact French. The Huguenot population was concentrated in the south-eastern section of St Anne's parish in streets such as Moor Street, Romilly Street and Old Compton Street, all only a short walk from the French Protestant chapel on Hog Lane.

With the Huguenots already established, Soho was about to enter one of the most exciting phases in its cosmopolitan history. The late 18th century and much of the 19th was the age of revolution in Europe. In Paris, when the mob stormed the Bastille on 14 July 1789 led by the 'revolutionary monster' and former resident of Romilly Street, Jean-Paul Marat, it seemed that the old order was on the way out. The French revolutionaries were fanning the flames of dissent which were to sweep across much of the Continent in the next 60 years. In most countries, however, revolution did not succeed and governments imposed severe penalties upon the insurgents.

As a result, émigrés from all over Europe began to pour into Britain, a nation which had enjoyed relative stability while the rest of the Continent was in turmoil. Many of them arrived in Soho, which had a reputation for religious and political tolerance and, since the departure of the aristocracy, an abundance of cheap, if cramped, accommodation. (Many of the grand residences had been gutted and turned into lodging houses by the end of the 18th century.)

As the 19th century progressed, Soho earned its reputation as London's Quartier Latin. Writers, artists and musicians began to colonise the coffee houses and restaurants which were establishing themselves in and around Gerrard Street, and Soho soon became a popular spot for anyone whose ideas were at odds with the Establishment. An atmosphere of political intrigue hung heavy in the air, and Dickens used Soho as part of the setting for *A Tale of Two Cities* (1859). The taverns did a good trade, offering their erudite customers a range of entertainment to go with the beer. Verlaine and Rimbaud gave readings at their favourite bar in Old Compton Street, Marx beavered away in Dean Street, and Soho became about the nearest thing Britain ever had to an intellectual epicentre.

In the 1860s, two new groups of immigrants came to Soho from Europe: Germans and Italians. Many of the Italian émigrés were to find work in catering as waiters and cooks. Soho was becoming well known for its numerous foreign cuisines, and trained labour was required to run the restaurants and cafés that were opening up. Gerrard Street was at the centre of this culinary explosion, but there wasn't a prawn cracker in sight (the Chinese community did not become established in Soho until well after the Second World War) and the Mont Blanc in Gerrard Street was probably the first French restaurant in Soho to attract the English gourmand.

The late 19th century saw an influx of Swiss immigrants, many of whom settled in and around Golden Square and began to trade as textile merchants, dealing mainly in wool. Their influence remains today; many of the office blocks which look down upon Golden Square are leased by the textile trade.

Jews, who came originally from Eastern Europe, also began to arrive in Soho during this period and by 1900 they had established a thriving community – diminished in number now, but still vociferous. Many of them had come to Soho direct from Russia where they had experienced the brutality of the pogroms. Others had made a much shorter journey: they were tailors forced out of the East End after they had taken industrial action in 1891. Soho was conveniently placed for them, since the high-class outfitters in Savile Row (west of Soho across Regent Street) always required outworkers who would be prepared to make up clothes for piece rates.

The Soho of the early part of this century was therefore a cosmopolitan district. Many of the English residents had moved out, but more adventurous members of the English middle-class would come into the area to visit the restaurants after a trip to the theatre. Between the wars, a number of continental food shops were opened by émigrés, mainly in Old Compton Street, and most of Soho's restaurants enjoyed a good trade.

The Blitz left its mark on Soho. St Anne's Church was virtually demolished and there were a number of direct hits; the Swiss Hotel on Old Compton Street, for instance, was relieved of its upper floors. The most devastating attack, however, took place on 8 March 1941. Two 50-kilo landmines smashed through the roof of the Café de Paris, a well-known society haunt on Coventry Street, and 80 people were killed.

After the war, Soho began the slide which gave the district its sleazy image and which has only recently been reversed. An assortment of wideboys, cardsharps, tarts and spivs began to move into the area and soon the Vice had taken its hold. Soho was carved up by the mobs and occasionally a dispute over territorial rights would result in the local police having to drag a body out of an alley.

While the mob ran Soho, a new wave of bohemians (Dylan Thomas, Brendan Behan, Colin MacInnes *et al*) looked on, rendered oblivious by the powerful victuals served at the York Minster, the Coach and Horses and the Colony Room. Time was called on these gentlemen some time ago, but Soho remains compulsive and vibrant.

A STROLL AROUND SOHO'S PAST

Soho is only properly navigable on foot. Motorbike messengers who roar around the area would probably disagree, but only the pedestrian can breathe deep the smell of Soho's past without fear of obtaining a parking ticket. A tour of Soho should really begin in Soho Square. Walk into the centre of the square and look around: in the 17th century, this was the very heart of aristocratic Soho. None of the grand houses of that era remain, but both the French Protestant church (completed in

1893) and the Italianate Catholic church, St Patrick's (rebuilt 1891–3), are well worth a visit. The best examples of original Soho architecture in the square are number 10 (now a solicitor's office) and number 15 (headquarters of the Builders Merchants' Association).

A tourist reared on a diet of conventional international rubbernecking trips will find plenty to disappoint in Soho. Of those private houses of architectural merit which are still standing, only one, the House of St Barnabas in Greek Street, is open to the public. Yet Soho offers a wealth of history: some pubs date back to the 17th century, several shops have been here since the 18th century, and many of the residents are descended from the émigrés who arrived here hundreds of years ago and gave the village its unique character. Walk and you shall find.

Argyll Street

Named after the 2nd Duke of Argyll, John Campbell, who was one of the Duke of Marlborough's leading generals, Argyll Street was built in the 1730s on land belonging to him. The Duke's brother Archibald Campbell, later the 3rd Duke, set up his mistress, Mrs Shireburn, in Argyll House, a splendid mansion which dominated the street. The Earl of Aberdeen, a distinguished Victorian statesman and classicist, subsequently bought the house in 1808 but it was pulled down in 1864. Later a touring circus made its home on the site before the London Palladium was built here. The Palladium, which started out as a fashionable music hall, became known as one of London's most important variety theatres. It still packs 'em in, but the inter-box telephone system installed in 1910 is long gone. The Argyll Arms, a Victorian beauty, takes its name from a tavern which was established at the same time as the street.

Beak Street

A key Soho shopping and business thoroughfare, Beak Street was built in three parts. The main part of the street was known as Silver Street until 1883 when it was absorbed into the smaller Beak Street which opened out on to Regent Street. At number

Argyll Arms

40, on the corner of Upper James Street, there stood a tavern called the Crown. One of the characters in *Nicholas Nickleby*, Newman Noggs, frequented this establishment, and although Dickens does not mention Beak Street by name in his novel, historians maintain that he was referring to the thoroughfare when he wrote: 'In that quarter of London in which Golden Square is situated, there is a bygone, tumbledown street, with two irregular rows of tall meagre houses.' The Crown was knocked down in 1921.

Berwick Street

Now one of Soho's noisiest, most chaotic streets, Berwick Street was first colonised by French émigrés in the early 18th century. Two French churches were established here and, from 1838, St Luke's offered the indigenous population a place of worship. It has since been demolished. The market also dates back to the 18th century, although at first it was very much an *ad hoc* affair and did not receive official recognition until 1892. There were no formal pitches and traders merely sold their wares on the pavement. The Green Man at number 57 and the Blue Posts at number 22 both occupy sites on which taverns have existed since at least the late 1730s.

Brewer Street

Although this street was built in the 17th century, mostly on land belonging to Sir William Pulteney, it was known as Wells Street, after the builder who developed it, until the 18th century. Two competing breweries in the street, owned by Mr Thomas Ayres and Mr Henry Davis, gave it its present name. Both the breweries have since been demolished. The Tisbury Court end of the street has always had a raffish reputation. For decades it was known as Knaves' Acre.

Broadwick Street

One of the widest streets in Soho, Broadwick Street was also one of the most fashionable. During the first half of the 18th century the western end, then known as Broad Street, was full of gentry but the tradesmen were the main occupants in the latter half of the century. Although the layout of this part of Soho has scarcely changed since 1686 when building commenced on Broadwick Street (though that name did not exist until 1936 when Broad Street, in the west, and Edward Street, in the east, were renamed as such), little remains of the original houses and shops. The recently renovated listed houses on the north side, just east of Dufour's Place, are probably the best examples of original Soho architecture in the street. The Lion Brewery was demolished in 1937 and a police hostel, Trenchard House, built on the site; this is not a street in which to misbehave. Broadwick Street is famous for its water pump. In 1854 Dr John Snow discovered that cholera was a water-borne disease and the authorities promptly closed the pump down, thus preventing the deaths of countless Soho inhabitants. The pub at number 39 bears his name though it was known as the Newcastle-upon-Tyne until 1956.

Carlisle Street

Carlisle Street is one of the square mile's smaller thoroughfares and the site of Carlisle House, a grand mansion thought to be connected by underground passage to the even larger mansion, also called Carlisle House, in Soho Square in which Theresa Cornelys, a Viennese opera singer, held her magnificent masked balls. It is almost certain that in *A Tale of Two Cities* (1859), set partly in Soho, Dickens was describing the Carlisle Street House when he wrote of the home of Dr Manette: 'A quainter corner than the corner where the doctor lived was not to be found in London. There was no way through it, and the front windows of the doctor's lodgings commanded a pleasant little vista of street that had a congenial air of retirement on it.' Manette Street, named after the fictitious doctor in 1895, connects Greek Street with Charing Cross Road. Carlisle House was destroyed by a bomb in 1941.

Carnaby Street

Thanks to the London of the Swinging 60s, Carnaby Street is probably the most famous street in Soho. Its present incarnation, however, bears little resemblance to the thoroughfare which was laid out in the 1680s and soon became a Huguenot stronghold. In the 19th century small businesses flourished, including the tobacconist Inderwick & Co at number 45, which still survives. The first boutique, Lord John, was established in 1957 and for about 10 years Carnaby Street thrived: the phrase 'Carnaby Street' even became an entry in the *Oxford English*

Dictionary. Now, even though much of the Carnaby Street scene is laughably anachronistic, junior Mods still strut up and down on a Saturday afternoon, too young to ride a Lambretta, but old enough to wear a parka. The street is also full of European tourists, who seem to have been rubbernecking here *en masse* for the last 30 years. In the mid-60s, Ray Davies of the Kinks, who used to drink at the John Snow pub in Broadwick Street, wrote a song about the 'Carnabation Army' marching on and on. They still do, and they're mostly Danish.

Church of Our Lady of the Assumption and St Gregory

Warwick Street

Small Catholic church which was originally the chapel of the Portuguese Embassy. (In the second half of the 18th century, a number of European powers established their legations in Soho.) The chapel was destroyed during the Gordon Riots of 1780 when an anti-Catholic mob, probably from outside Soho, ran amok. It was rebuilt eight years later.

Dean Street

The very essence of bohemian Soho, Dean Street has attracted artists, writers and musicians since the 18th century when the aristocracy began to move out and the French began to move in. The street was built in the 1680s. The origin of the name is unknown but it may have been named after Dean Henry Compton, who gave his name to Old Compton Street. Distinguished former residents include the brilliant 18th century artists Francis Hayman and William Beechey, the sculptor Joseph Nollekens, and Karl Marx. Samuel Johnson and Oliver Goldsmith used Jack's Coffee House at number 33, a building which together with number 33a was Walker's Hotel from 1813–49. Admiral Lord Nelson stayed at number 33 before setting off for Trafalgar.

French Protestant Church

8 Soho Square

There has been a large French community in Soho since the

17th century when the Huguenots left France to escape religious persecution. For nearly 200 years they worshipped in a series of makeshift chapels. In 1893 this four-storeyed church, in the Flemish–Gothic style, was completed. Although Soho's French population has dwindled, services are still held regularly.

Frith Street

Named after Richard Frith, a successful local builder, Frith Street was developed in the late 1670s and early 1680s. Some 18th-century maps show it as 'Thrift Street', an inappropriate name since in its heyday Frith Street was one of Soho's most desirable addresses. Important society events were held at the house of the Venetian Ambassador who arrived in Frith Street in 1742. After the gentry had moved out, a number of distinguished residents lived here including Mozart, Hazlitt, the painters John Constable and Dante Gabriel Rossetti and, more recently, John Logie Baird who lived at number 22 between 1924 and 1926.

Gerrard Street

The street was developed between 1677 and 1685 by Nicholas Barbon on land belonging to Charles, Lord Gerrard. It was intended as a grandiose development and when the titled classes moved out in the 18th century, they left behind some fine houses with garrets (useful for the literary types who moved in later). Gerrard Street has always been cosmopolitan; some of the country's first foreign restaurants were established here in the late 19th century. For years, this part of Soho was much favoured by the intelligentsia. John Dryden was probably the first writer to arrive; he took dingy rooms here in 1687. Edmund Burke also lived in Gerrard Street and was a founder member of The Club (a literary talking shop) set up by Samuel Johnson and Sir Joshua Reynolds, which met at the Turk's Head in the 1760s. And it was over a meal at the Mont Blanc that G. K. Chesterton and Hilaire Belloc first met in 1900. Between the wars, Gerrard Street began to lose its artistic ambience and became a centre of dodgy dealings, shady night clubs and prostitutes. It is now dominated by the Chinese, who began to arrive in the 1960s.

Golden Square

Golden Square was completed at the turn of the 18th century. Like Soho Square, it started life as a residential square of elegant town houses owned by the aristocracy. Its name had nothing to do with the financial standing of its occupants but is probably a corruption of its original name, Gelding Close, referring to the geldings which grazed here before Soho was developed as a residential area. By the 1750s, the aristocracy had begun to move out and a number of foreign legations became established here, along with artists and medical men. Eventually, the diplomats joined the aristocrats in Belgravia and Mayfair. In the 19th century, small businesses gained a foothold here but the tone was lowered by a number of shoddy boarding houses and cheap hotels. In *Nicholas Nickleby*, first published in 1839, Dickens described the square's down-at-heel appearance: 'It is one of the squares that have been – a quarter of the town that has gone down in the world, and taken to letting lodgings . . . It is a great resort of foreigners. The dark-complexioned men who wear large rings, and heavy watch-guards and bushy whiskers, and who congregate under the Opera Colonnade, and about the box office in the season between four and five in the afternoon, when they give away the orders – all live in Golden Square or within a street of it.' In the second half of the 19th century, the square was home to a variety of businesses, including solicitors, makers of musical instruments, and architects. Then it was almost wholly taken over by textile merchants and manufacturers, some of whom still remain.

Great Marlborough Street

Great Marlborough Street runs parallel with Broadwick Street in the north-west corner of Soho. It was built at the beginning of the 18th century and named after John Churchill, 1st Duke of Marlborough, hero of the Battle of Blenheim (1704). Both streets are much wider than other Soho thoroughfares which may be why they lack character; elsewhere it's possible to carry out a conversation from opposite sides of the street. Its buildings are of little interest architecturally, but Great Marlborough Street has had some distinguished residents including Charles Darwin and, very briefly, Admiral Lord Nelson; he and his wife lodged at number 10. In 1716, five peers of the realm were living here. Nowadays Great Marlborough Street is probably best known for its magistrates' court, the London College of Music and the mock-Tudor façade of Liberty's. The court's colourful clientele includes Soho prostitutes, local spivs and the occasional errant pop star.

Greek Street

Named after the Greek Orthodox Church which stood in Hog Lane (now Charing Cross Road) on the site of St Martin's School of Art. Greek Street was laid out in the 1680s and although it has always had a slightly raffish air, encouraged by its taverns and coffee houses, it was nonetheless a desirable address in the 17th and 18th centuries.

Hospital for Women

29–30 Soho Square

Now part of the Middlesex Hospital, the Hospital for Women was established in 1843 in Red Lion Square, Bloomsbury, and moved to Soho in 1852. It was known originally as the Hospital for Diseases of Women, but the authorities felt a change of name was necessary because many people had assumed that it would only treat women suffering from venereal diseases.

House of St Barnabas

1 Greek Street W1. 01-437 1894.

Soho is not over-endowed with buildings of great architectural merit and the exterior of this house is merely run-of-the-mill Georgian. The interior, however, is a magnificent example of the mid-18th century English rococo style, with all its lavish ornamentation. After serving from 1811 as the administrative headquarters of the Westminster Commissioners of Sewers and later, the Metropolitan Board of Works, the house was bought by the House of Charity in 1861, for use as a hostel for 'as many destitute cases as possible'. Today it provides temporary shelter for homeless women. *Open to visitors 14.30–16.00 Wed, 11.00–12.30 Thur. Free (donations welcome).*

King Charles II

Soho Square

There are very few statues in Soho, and the state of this one probably reflects the indifference of Westminster City Council to their upkeep. Sculpted in 1681 by Caius Gabriel Cibber, it was owned at one time by W. S. Gilbert, who wrote the librettos to Sullivan's music. Gilbert's widow returned it to the square and it was erected in 1938.

King George II

Golden Square

This statue is attributed to John Van Nost and was erected in 1753 which is why it is said to be of George II since he was king then. It was donated to the public by an anonymous bidder, thought to have bought it at an auction at Canons Park, seat of the Duke of Chandos, in 1748. In *Nicholas Nickleby*, Dickens describes it as: 'a mournful statue of Portland stone, the guardian genius of a little wilderness of shrubs'.

London College of Music

47 Great Marlborough Street

Musicians including Mozart, Wagner and Haydn have spent time in Soho and in the 18th century a great many music-related businesses such as violin-makers and sheet-music publishers flourished in the area. The London College of Music was established in 1887 to cater for the increased demand for musical training. It first occupied number 42 and moved to number 47 in 1896. This building dates from the early 18th century.

Old Compton Street

Old Compton Street is probably the nearest thing Soho has to a high street. Completed in 1683, the street was named after Henry Compton, Bishop of London, and has always been Soho's main shopping thoroughfare. In the 17th and 18th centuries it was full of Huguenots who ran shops and other small businesses; thus the houses here were never as grand as those which had been built for the upper classes in Soho Square, Golden Square or Greek Street. The street has always been recognised as a meeting-place for exiles, and Italians also moved in, opening up shops and restaurants. French émigrés continued to arrive and after the failure of the Paris Commune (1871), Verlaine and Rimbaud, the poets, were often to be seen at a watering-hole here. Despite the proliferation of foreign shops and restaurants, Wheeler's, the English fish restaurant, is particularly well known. It opened at number 19 in 1929.

Poland Street

William Blake lived here from 1785 to 1791 and Shelley lodged in Poland Street in 1811, after being sent down from Oxford. In Shelley's time, the street was made up largely of artisans' workshops and small shops; but from the time when building finished in 1707 and throughout the 18th century it was a fashionable, residential street. The tradesmen who moved in had a choice of three taverns, the King of Poland (from which the street takes its name), the Kings Arms and the Star and Garter. The last two remain today, but the King of Poland (later known as Dickens Wine House) was flattened by a bomb in 1940. Jewellers and engravers predominated among the 19th century tradesmen; today the street is home to clothing, fashion and textile businesses.

St Anne's Church Tower

St Anne's Tower, which dominates High Soho, is one of the district's most famous landmarks. The church was built in the late 17th century to designs attributed to either Christopher

Wren or William Talman. The tower, however, was not added until 1717 and was rebuilt in 1803. The church was devastated during the Blitz but, miraculously, the tower survived. Ten thousand Soho residents are buried beneath the church, including King Theodore of Corsica, Hazlitt and the detective writer Dorothy L. Sayers. In 1976 the Poet Laureate, John

Betjeman, produced some lines in support of an appeal to restore the church:

> 'High in the air two barrels interlock
> To form the faces of this famous clock
> Reduced to drawing-room size this clock would be
> A Paris ornament of 1803.
> Let's make it go again, let London know
> That life and heart and hope are in Soho.'

St Patrick's Church

Soho Square

Most of Soho's 17th-century aristocrats worshipped at St Anne's, while most of the émigré communities used private chapels they had constructed themselves. The Catholic community, however, was without a place of worship until 1792, when a small chapel was built for them on Soho Square. The main impetus for St Patrick's came from a group of well-to-do Catholics who called themselves the Confraternity of St Patrick's. They felt that the itinerant Irish labourers who lived around Soho were in need of spiritual salvation, so they took out the lease on the rooms built by Theresa Cornelys at the rear of Carlisle House. The first chapel was knocked down in 1891 and replaced by the present Italianate church, designed by John Kelly and, architecturally, one of the most interesting buildings in Soho.

Soho Square

Richard Frith put up the first houses in Soho Square in the 1680s on land that had been known as Soho Fields and belonged originally to Charles I and Henrietta Maria. It was a very fashionable square and much has been written about its heyday in the mid-18th century. From 1760 to 1772 Mrs Cornelys ran Carlisle House, a grand mansion on the east side of the square. It had been the home of the 2nd Earl of Carlisle and the Neapolitan Ambassador (not at the same time) and was one of the most attractive private houses in London. It was demolished in 1791 and St Patrick's Church, built in the late 19th century, now covers part of the site. Carlisle House was

just one of the grand residences which were built in this square in the 17th century, when Soho was London's most fashionable district. Monmouth House, built for the Duke of Monmouth (illegitimate son of Charles II), was designed by Wren. It was demolished in 1773. Another grand house to be built in the 1680s was Fauconberg House where Arthur Onslow, Speaker of the House of Commons, lived from 1753 to 1761. (He could have practised his parliamentary techniques on William Beckford, Lord Mayor of London, who lived at number 22 from 1751 to 1770.) Fauconberg House, owned by Crosse & Blackwell from 1854, was demolished in 1924 to make way for new offices.

In the 18th century, as the aristocracy moved out, scientists, lawyers and architects moved in to be followed in the mid to late 19th century by publishers, booksellers and makers of musical instruments. The square became more commercial in the 20th century and in 1934 the film company Twentieth Century Fox moved into Twentieth Century House, a building designed by Sir Gordon Jeeves. The strange timbered lodge in the centre of the square is not a Tudor public lavatory, it merely covers the ventilation shaft of an electricity transformer station.

Wardour Street

Wardour Street has been the centre of the British film industry since the 1930s. Until recently it had a somewhat unsavoury reputation; someone once said it was the only street in Britain which was shady on both sides. The street started life as Commonhedge Lane, but was developed in the 1680s and the northern part was called Wardour Street after Edward Wardour, a local landowner. The southern part was known as Prince's Street until 1878. Most of the 17th-century houses were rebuilt in the 18th century. In the 19th century, Wardour Street was renowned for its antique trade though many of its wares, as patrons discovered to their cost, were of dubious origin.

SO WHO LIVED IN SOHO?

For centuries, Soho has attracted the eminent. Artists, writers, musicians and scientists have found the liberal, tolerant atmosphere of the square mile a stimulating environment in which to work. Some of these alumni, driven out of their own countries by political or religious differences, came here to join already established émigré communities; some arrived by accident; others merely knew that Soho was an agreeable place in which to get drunk.

The three parallel thoroughfares which cross Old Compton Street: Dean Street, Frith Street and Greek Street, probably have the largest concentration of distinguished former residents in the whole of the capital. But Soho is alive with history, and even the narrowest alleys and the dimmest backstreets have played their part.

Soho, in common with other historic parts of London, has its share of blue plaques. These may point out a particular person's home, but they don't tell the whole story. A famous person may have lived in a street briefly, but not long enough to merit a plaque; or he or she may have been denied one for political reasons (the decision to give Karl Marx a plaque in Dean Street was not reached without dissent).

Although great care has been taken in the compilation of this list of Soho's historic habitués, it is possible that Marat, for instance, may have lived a few doors further down Romilly Street than suggested here. Over the years houses have been combined or demolished and streets have been renamed and renumbered. As a result even the plaque-erecting authorities (some municipal, some private) have made mistakes. They rarely get the street wrong, however, since the names of the residents of a particular street at any given time can usually be traced back through the parish records.

Friedrich Accum (1769–1839)

33 Old Compton Street

Accum, a German chemist, was largely responsible for the introduction of gas lighting to the streets of Britain. He lived here from 1803 to 1822, a period in which Soho was attracting a large number of immigrants from central Europe. At his home, he would give lectures in chemistry and physics and sell laboratory equipment. His students included the Duke of Cumberland and Lord Camelford.

John Logie Baird (1888–1946)

22 Frith Street

This was the house where Baird first demonstrated television to members of the Royal Institution in 1926, in the attic which he'd rented for use as a laboratory. Although he had a house in Sydenham, Baird was obsessed with his work and would frequently stay overnight in his lab. Baird's rooms (and the blue plaque commemorating his work) are above the Bar Italia.

Sir Joseph Banks (1743–1820)

32 Soho Square

Banks was an eminent botanist and President of the Royal Society (1778–1819). With the money he inherited from his father, he bought an impressive town-house in what was then one of London's most desirable residential squares. Banks used his home to house his collection of natural history exhibits and scientific books, available to any scientist who cared to drop in. Invitations to regular 'philosophical breakfasts' were much sought after and academics from all over Europe would arrive to discuss current issues over a hearty meal. When he died, Banks left his house to his librarian, Robert Brown. It was demolished in 1936.

William Beckford (1709–1770)

22 Soho Square

Beckford was Lord Mayor of London in 1762 and 1769, and a tireless supporter of John Wilkes, the parliamentary reformer. He lived in the square between 1751 and 1770 and spent much of his time in Soho promoting Wilkes. In 1770 when Wilkes was released from gaol, Beckford hung a banner bearing the word 'Liberty' in three-foot-high white letters outside his home: a highly provocative act which would not have endeared him to his neighbours.

William Blake (1757–1827)

74 Broadwick Street

An office and residential development at 8 Marshall Street now stands on the site where this brilliant poet and painter was born and lived with his parents. In 1784, after serving an apprenticeship as an engraver, Blake opened a shop selling prints in the house next door to his old home (in the meantime he had married Catherine Boucher in 1782 and had been living in Green Street W1). The following year he returned to live in Soho, renting a house in Poland Street where he stayed until 1790, he then moved to Lambeth. The modernist plaque in honour of Blake, erected privately, is an insult to his memory.

James Boswell (1740–1795)

22 Gerrard Street

Boswell took lodgings here with a tailor in 1775, when Gerrard Street was becoming a fashionable address with writers and artists. The great biographer (author of *The Life of Johnson*) described his abode as 'a very neat first floor at sixteen shilling a week', but he soon moved out. Gerrard Street, full of coffee houses, taverns and restaurants, was to remain popular with the literary set until the Second World War.

Edmund Burke (1729–1797)

37 Gerrard Street

Burke, a free-thinking conservative philosopher and Whig statesman, lived at this address from about 1787 to 1790. He was no stranger to Soho, being a founder member of the Club (later known as the Literary Club) in Gerrard Street two decades earlier. Samuel Johnson and Sir Joshua Reynolds were also founder members. Burke's *Reflections on the Revolution in France*, written at the end of his time in Soho, was to become a blueprint for 19th-century conservative thinking.

Antonio Canal (Canaletto) (1697–1768)

41 Beak Street

Canaletto, one of the great Venetian landscape artists, was nearly 50 when he arrived in Soho, where he lived in a house owned by the cabinet maker Richard Wiggan between 1749 and 1751. He set up a studio which was to remain more or less intact until the 1920s. His skills as a painter were matched with an acute business sense; his work catered primarily to the taste of those members of English high society who had visited Venice, seen the Lagoon, strolled around St Mark's and wanted a souvenir of their trip. Some of his paintings can be seen at the Wallace Collection in Manchester Square or at the National Gallery in Trafalgar Square, both only a short walk from Soho.

Giovanni Giacomo Casanova (1725–1798)

Greek Street

While his exact address is not known, most of the great philanderer's biographers agree that he lodged in Greek Street, probably in about 1764. Casanova's sexual adventures and his activities as a professional gambler and sometime spy did not endear him to the European governments and monarchs of the day. This forced him to spend much of his life on the run. Somewhere on the Continent in the 1750s he fathered a child by the opera singer Theresa Cornelys, who was later to live in Carlisle House in Soho Square. This connection may account for his arrival in Soho.

Willy Clarkson (1861–1934)

41–43 Wardour Street

Clarkson was one of London's most famous theatrical costumiers and wig-makers. He moved into these premises in 1905. They were designed for him by H. M. Wakley; Sarah Bernhardt laid the foundation stone in 1904 and Sir Henry Irving the coping stone in 1905.

Theresa Cornelys (1723–1797)

Carlisle House, Soho Square

Theresa Cornelys (whose real name was Imer) played an important part in what some historians regard as the Golden Age of Soho, the mid-to-late 18th century. Theresa was a Viennese opera singer and erstwhile courtesan who hit upon the idea of offering the aristocracy nightly entertainment in Carlisle House, formerly the home of the 2nd Earl of Carlisle, in one of London's most fashionable squares. She held regular masked balls and concerts and soon earned a reputation as a particularly stylish hostess. For 10 years, she dominated London society and the glittering events she organised were well-documented by contemporary artists and writers.

However, she was soon to face competition; first from Almack's Assembly Rooms in St James's and then from the Pantheon in Oxford Street (which stood on the site of what is now Marks & Spencer). In an attempt to make her soirées more lavish and sumptuous than those of her competitors, she took out loans which she could not possibly repay. She was made bankrupt in 1772 and died, penniless, in Fleet Prison some years later. Carlisle House was demolished in 1791.

Thomas De Quincey (1785–1859)

58 Greek Street

De Quincey arrived in Soho in 1802, having run away from Manchester Grammar School. He lived a lazy, bohemian life, much of which he described in his most famous work, *Confessions of an English Opium Eater* (he bought his first dose of opium at a chemist in Oxford Street). He was more concerned about the state of his garret than might be expected from such an eminent member of the 19th-century demi-monde and described his quarters as having 'an unhappy countenance of gloom and unsocial fitfulness due in reality to long neglect of painting, cleansing and in some instances repairing'. There is some debate over the precise location of these lodgings. Some historians suggest that he lived at 27 Soho Square, in a large mansion house which backed on to Greek Street, while others maintain that the house had been divided before De Quincey arrived, thus creating number 58. Greek Street has since been renumbered. After his sojourn in Soho, De Quincey left to go up to Oxford.

John Dryden (1631–1700)

44 Gerrard Street

This celebrated English poet was probably the first member of the London literati to take rooms in Gerrard Street. In 1687 Dryden moved here from Covent Garden, where he had been living in Long Acre, and began writing in one of the ground-floor rooms overlooking the street. The Royal Society erected Dryden's plaque in 1875, but unfortunately they placed it on the wrong house (number 43).

William Hazlitt (1778–1830)

6 Frith Street

Hazlitt, essayist and philosopher, is still regarded highly by that dwindling band of British intellectuals whose allegiance lies with the Left. He had always remained a supporter of the French Revolution, which set him apart from many of his fellow Romantics who had abandoned the cause once the reality of 'The Terror' became known. In 1830 Hazlitt moved to Frith Street and wrote his last essays from number 6 where he died a particularly miserable death, from cholera, on 18 September. He was buried in St Anne's Churchyard.

John Hunter (1728–1793)

31 Golden Square

Hunter did not become well known as a surgeon until after he left Soho; his time in Golden Square in the 1760s was a period of relative obscurity when he was far from comfortably off. To supplement the income he received from his private practice, he taught anatomy in the evenings. His fortunes took a turn for the better in 1767 when he was elected a member of the Royal Society. He subsequently moved outside the area, to Jermyn Street. Number 31 was rebuilt in 1931.

Angelica Kauffman (1741–1807)

16 Golden Square

Angelica Kauffman was a talented Anglo-Swiss historical and portrait painter who moved to this house in 1767. The commissions soon rolled in, but cynics at the time said that this was more to do with her gender (female painters were few and far between) than her merits as an artist. However, she was a founder member of the Royal Academy and the first woman RA. She became known as 'Miss Angel' and the streets approaching Golden Square were frequently jammed with carriages transporting the vainer elements of 18th-century society to her studio. She lived in the square until 1781 when she went to Italy with her husband.

Fanny Kemble (1809–1893)

5 Soho Square

Daughter of the actor Charles Kemble, Fanny Kemble arrived at the family home from Paris where she had been a successful opera singer. She made a devastating debut at Covent Garden and revived its popularity in the early 1830s. She enjoyed a good living as a singer and an actress which is perhaps not surprising considering her theatrical connections. Her father, her uncle and her aunt, Mrs Siddons, were all successful on the stage. Kemble House, a block of flats in Dean Street, is named after the family.

Jean-Paul Marat (1743–1793)

31 Romilly Street

When Marat was living in Soho, few of the local residents would have had an inkling that he would turn out to be one of the chief architects of the French Revolution and an inspiration to his people. He led a quiet life, eschewing the coffee houses and taverns of the square mile, preferring instead to take refreshment in Old Slaughter's Coffee House in St Martin's Lane. His time in Soho was spent working as a doctor and from this address he produced a pamphlet entitled *An Enquiry Into the Nature, Cause, and Cure of a Singular Disease of the Eye*. He signed it J. P. Marat MD.

Karl Marx (1818–1883)

28 Dean Street

Arguably Soho's most famous inhabitant, Marx was forced to leave the Continent and come here because of his revolutionary activities. He arrived in Soho in 1850 and took rooms at number 64 Dean Street where he worked with Engels before moving to number 28. It was while he was at number 28 that he wrote most of *Das Kapital*. The squalid conditions in which he was living may account for the tome's dreariness. Marx would study every day at the British Museum in Bloomsbury and then make the journey south to Dean Street where he lived from 1851 to 1856 in two freezing rooms with his wife and children, three of whom died here. A visiting Prussian agent described Marx's rooms as being 'in one of the worst, therefore also the cheapest quarters in London . . . There is not one clean and good piece of furniture to be found; all is broken tattered and torn . . . everywhere is the greatest disorder.'

In 1926, the house became an upmarket Italian restaurant, Leoni's Quo Vadis. A museum in honour of Marx was established here in 1986, but regulars tend to be more interested in the saltimbocca.

Wolfgang Amadeus Mozart (1756–1791)

20 Frith Street

Mozart gave his first concert in Soho at Caldwell's Performing Rooms in Dean Street in 1763. His younger sister accompanied him on the harpsichord. Between 1764 and 1765, Mozart stayed with his father and sister in rooms owned by Thomas Williamson, a staymaker. Leopold Mozart served as manager and impresario, arranging private afternoon concerts for those among the local gentry who cared to buy a ticket. Mozart played at the Hickford Rooms in Brewer Street in 1765 and while staying in Soho he also taught music at 22 Soho Square, the home of Alderman William Beckford. During this period Mozart's father published his son's six sonatas K10–15, including the sonata for piano and violin, or flute, first published as Opus III number 1, dedicated to Queen Charlotte. Mozart also started work on the music which was to become part of his opera *Idomeneo*.

Joseph Nollekens (1737–1823)

28 Dean Street

Nollekens, a brilliant sculptor, was born in this house, which has since become one of the most famous addresses in Soho (Karl Marx took rooms here in the 1850s). Although Nollekens received numerous commissions for busts from British and foreign aristocrats over the years and became very rich, he was known in his early days more for his love of bell-ringing and meanness with money. He was reputed to keep his hall in darkness to save on candles and would wait for at least two knocks before illuminating the hall in case the caller turned out to be a local lad playing a prank. In 1770, having left Soho and spent some years in Italy, Nollekens returned to London and moved to Mortimer Street in Fitzrovia. A blue plaque was erected there in his honour in 1954.

Arthur Onslow (1691–1768)

20 Soho Square

Onslow, Speaker of the House of Commons between 1728 and 1761, lived here from 1753 to 1762 in Fauconberg House, one of the grand houses built in the square in the 17th century. Onslow's main claim to fame is the fact that he was always complaining about the late-night parliamentary sittings he was required to attend. He sold the lease in 1762 to the 4th Duke of Argyll and in 1771 John Grant, a Scottish lawyer, bought it. The house was then redecorated and embellished by the architect Robert Adam. Crosse & Blackwell took it over in the mid-19th century and built a jam and pickle factory at the back. The house was knocked down in 1924 and replaced with an office block.

Marquess of Pombal (1699–1782)

23–24 Golden Square

Between 1724 and 1747 these two fashionable houses in Golden Square made up the Portuguese Embassy. Sebastiao de Carvalho, the Marquess of Pombal, was Ambassador from 1739 to 1744. His main mission was to examine Britain's role as a burgeoning centre of commerce and trade and report back to his masters in Portugal, where the economy was in a slump. The Marquess was responsible for rebuilding Lisbon after the devastating earthquake of 1775.

Arthur Rimbaud (1854–1891) and Paul Verlaine (1844–1896)

5 Old Compton Street

Rimbaud and Verlaine, two of the first French symbolic poets, fled Paris in 1872 and arrived in Soho via Brussels. They took rooms in Tottenham Court Road, but accustomed as they were to Left Bank Parisian café society, this setting proved insufficiently bohemian so they made the short journey south to Soho with its then flourishing demi-monde. Here they found a cosy little bar on Old Compton Street with a suitably cosmopolitan clientele. Many of the regulars were, like themselves, refugees from France who'd fled their country after the fall of the Paris Commune. The pair spent much of their time in Soho drinking, talking and giving readings of their work.

William Roy (1726–1790)

10 Argyll Street

Major General Roy founded the Ordnance Survey, the Government-run cartographic body upon which most maps are based. Roy's map-making skills were first put to the test in Scotland during the Duke of Cumberland's campaign against Bonnie Prince Charlie. He produced maps of the Scottish mainland which opened it up to the English troops and later produced maps for the Duke of Brunswick to use in the Seven Years' War. He moved into the fine Georgian house at number 10 in 1779 and was there until he died. It was built on land which was originally part of the 2nd Duke of Argyll's estate. The house still remains, although much altered.

Percy Bysshe Shelley (1792–1822)

15 Poland Street

Shelley found the Soho of the early 19th century an altogether more tolerant place than the Oxford from which he had been expelled in 1811. At college, the poet had incurred the wrath of his ecclesiastical masters by producing a pamphlet entitled *The Necessity of Atheism* and was forced to seek lodgings elsewhere. For a few weeks, he lived in rooms above what is now the Marlborough Sandwich Bar, before eloping to Edinburgh with a schoolfriend of his sister.

Thomas Sheraton (1751–1806)

163 Wardour Street

Sheraton was one of the late 18th century's finest furniture-makers and designers and between 1791 and 1794 he lived in rooms on Wardour Street. In 1795, he moved to a more attractive address in Golden Square, although his quarters were less than luxurious; in common with many of Soho's characters over the years, he merely scraped a living. He moved back to Wardour Street in 1798 and stayed there until 1800.

John Christopher Smith (1712–1763)

6 Carlisle Street

One of Soho's privately erected blue plaques decorates the building in which John Smith worked as Handel's amanuensis after the composer's sight failed. Smith became established as a musician in his own right, however, with his operatic adaptation of *A Midsummer Night's Dream*, known as *The Fairies*, which was produced by Garrick at Drury Lane in 1754. This predates Benjamin Britten's version by over 200 years. The plaque was erected in 1958 by the Handelian Society.

Anne Louise de Staël (1766–1817)

30 Argyll Street

Dickins & Jones fashion store now stands on the site of the house in which Madame de Staël, a well-to-do French writer, spent one year of her ten years' exile after Napoleon banished her from France. She had been running a coffee house in Paris which had attracted a number of disaffected French intellectuals and they were beginning to question the diminutive dictator's judgement. She returned to France after the restoration of the monarchy in 1815. Her experiences in exile were recorded in *Dix Années d'Exil* published in 1821, four years after her death.

Richard Wagner (1813–1883)

52–53 Old Compton Street

In the early 19th century Old Compton Street was a major shopping thoroughfare, as it is today. Richard Wagner stayed here briefly in 1839 in a room in the Swiss Hotel which became the Swiss Tavern and is now Comptons pub. It is said that he started work here on his opera, *The Flying Dutchman*, which was first performed in 1843.

3 Eating

ENTRÉE

The cosmopolitan atmosphere of Soho has always attracted those in search of the unusual and the exotic. And for over a century, the square mile's eating houses have pandered to the palates of those with an interest in food and drink: small, family-run Italian cafés have flourished cheek by jowl with some of the grandest restaurants in London.

Soho's first foreign restaurants were those run for the benefit of the Huguenots, who began to colonise the area in the late 17th century. However, these were more like artisans' cafés than proper restaurants and it wasn't until the early 19th century that the area began to establish a reputation for good food. One of the earliest continental restaurants in the West End was the legendary Sablonière Hotel on the east side of Leicester Square. This opened in 1788, offering high-class French cuisine, and over the next 20 or 30 years established a business which a great many aspiring Soho restaurateurs were keen to emulate. Gradually, more and more foreign restaurants began to open up, spreading north across Leicester Square and finally into Soho proper via Gerrard Street.

Towards the end of the 19th century, Soho's restaurants were attracting bon viveurs by the carriageload. Word had spread that this raffish area, best known for its large population of down-at-heel disreputables, had spawned some of the best foreign eating houses in London. In 1869 a reader of *The Times* wrote to the newspaper praising Kettners, one of Soho's first grand French restaurants, for its excellent food and reasonable prices.

The turn of the century saw Soho's French restaurateurs consolidating their success. In 1900 the first meeting between G. K. Chesterton and Hilaire Belloc took place at a restaurant in Gerrard Street; elsewhere in Soho other writers, journalists and artists were switching their allegiance from the coffee houses (which traditionally had served execrable food) to the new-style restaurants.

These were boom years for Soho's restaurateurs. In 1885 *Baedeker's Guide to London* had listed only four restaurants in Soho; the 1923 edition, however, made reference to 25 different establishments, carefully noting the price of lunch or dinner and additional details such as whether ladies were allowed to eat there in the evenings! (Soho's seedy image prevailed long after John Galsworthy's remarks about the area in *The Forsyte Saga* had been forgotten.) Baedeker had obviously been won over by the enormous effort Soho's restaurateurs had gone to in establishing worthwhile eating houses. The 1923 edition offered what would, in Baedeker terms, amount to fulsome praise indeed: 'In Soho are innumerable foreign restaurants, many of which serve attractive table d'hôte meals with numerous courses at reasonable prices.' Lunch at Kettners in those days cost four shillings, dinner six and six.

Although the French had initiated the development of Soho as a gastronomic centre, the Italians were not far behind. They had started to move in towards the end of the 19th century. Within a few decades, these hard-working immigrants had carved up the Soho catering scene. They were prepared to accept long hours, low wages and undignified jobs as plongeurs and cleaners, in the hope that someday they would amass enough money to open their own restaurant. Through hard graft and sharp business sense many succeeded; by the 1920s and 30s, Italian food had developed a real following amongst London's gourmets and gourmands.

From then until the Second World War, the Italians continued to dominate the Soho catering scene. The French restaurants were still there and still popular, but even they began to hire Italian staff. Soho was the hub of an extremely efficient grapevine which stretched as far as the impoverished villages of southern Italy. This network ensured that the standards of cooking and service in Soho's restaurants remained high; any young Italian who did not work hard would face disgrace in the eyes of his family. The Second World War, however, brought the Italian hegemony to an end. Many of Soho's Italian waiters, chefs and restaurateurs were rounded up and packed off to internment camps in the country. Almost without exception, they went with good grace, aware that the war was but a temporary interruption.

The Italians' enforced departure from Soho allowed other nationalities to sneak in and steal a piece of the action. Greek establishments began to spring up around this time, along with restaurants owned by Hungarians, Indians, and Chinese. During the war, foreign restaurants enjoyed more popularity than their English equivalents, largely because their chefs were more imaginative in their use of limited ingredients. Careful trimming and cooking of meat, for instance, allowed them to make use of cheaper cuts, while traditional English chop and steak houses found that rationing and scarcities put paid to much of their trade.

The period after the war saw the number of restaurants in Soho increasing. The Italians were back, the Greeks were expanding (many Greek restaurateurs began to encroach on Fitzrovia, north of Oxford Street) and the French quietly got on with the business of making memorable meals and lots of money. The 50s were the heyday of eating out in Soho: the grand restaurants such as Kettners, Leoni's and the now defunct Chatelain packed in rich theatricals, politicians and musicians, while smaller establishments such as Kong Wah (a French and Italian house owned by one Mr Pang) and Pitta's (a Greek café) continued to serve poorer Sohoites with honest, less elaborate fare.

In the 60s and 70s many restaurants were driven out of business by the Vice. As neon signs and streetwalkers proliferated, Soho's public image degenerated. People became reluctant to bring their families to eat in an area which was rapidly becoming very sleazy. The smaller trattorias and family-run French restaurants in particular, began to feel the pinch. Many closed down, unable to stretch to paying the astronomical rents demanded by the freeholders of their premises. As more and more restaurants were serving their last plates of pasta, eagle-eyed developers saw their opportunity. Office buildings began to replace restaurants, topless bars the front rooms of friendly family-run cafés.

In spite of some recent casualties (Hostaria Romana, Bianchi's, Carrolls) the developers are now more or less under control. The licensing system introduced by Westminster City Council has driven out many of the porn merchants and hostess bars, and restaurateurs are once again clamouring for space within the square mile.

Baedeker's remarks of over 60 years ago are as relevant and apposite today as they were then. Soho is still the culinary capital of London; within this distinct yet disparate area you will find some of the best restaurants and food in town.

RESTAURANTS

The food now found in Soho's restaurants and cafés is undoubtedly far superior to that which would have been served up 20 or even 10 years ago. As the British palate has become more educated and accustomed to foreign food, restaurants have been forced to improve their standards. Although some establishments such as L'Epicure and Leoni's have made their names through offering traditional, rich fare, the new breed of Soho restaurateur is taking more care to provide food which is healthy and less damaging to the waistline.

The growth of the ethnic restaurants, particularly those serving food from South-East Asia, is an indication of the prevailing trend. Those who eat out are becoming more daring: they are willing to experiment with new flavours and textures, providing the ingredients are healthy and fresh. Soho's Indian restaurants are also becoming more adventurous; gone are the days of meat curry, boiled rice, flock wallpaper and soggy nan bread.

Nouvelle cuisine, which first appeared in the 70s, is no longer quite so fashionable, but many French restaurants in Soho still owe a great deal to its influence, as do the smart new restaurants serving the so-called 'New British cuisine'. The Italians, however, are more reluctant to innovate and still serve up Italian food as they perceive the British expect it. Notwithstanding the trattoria boom of the 60s, it is impossible to find simple, authentic food as it would be served in a trattoria in Italy. Any restaurateur who opened up a genuine trattoria in which he served a set meal consisting of pasta followed by simple grilled meat and cheese would surely find a guaranteed market among those Soho trendies who seek a reminder of their annual two weeks in Tuscany. Similarly, much custom must await the brave restaurateur who is prepared to dispense with those menacing pepperpots. This gimmick is unheard of in Italy.

There are fewer Italian restaurants in Soho than there were 20 years ago, and even fewer Italians working in them. Since Italy's phenomenal economic recovery after the Second World War, it has proved more and more difficult to recruit waiters from back home. Those who live in the poorer south are more likely to look to the teeming industrial cities of the north for work. Most of the Greek restaurants have also wound down their operations and headed north, to Fitzrovia, Camden Town and beyond, but those that remain offer excellent value.

Meal prices in Soho are, in general, highly competitive. The ethnic restaurants probably offer the best overall value; but watch out for the bill in some of the trendier Chinese, Indian or South-East Asian establishments. They are serving much more than basic food, so they won't be charging basic prices.

The restaurants and cafés listed here are only a selection from the dozens which line the streets of Soho. The food may not be superlative in every establishment (though in some it undoubtedly is) but every place with an entry has at least something – attractive surroundings, friendly service or even an intriguing history – which makes it worthy of recommendation. Bon Appetit!

The food prices quoted represent the cost of a three-course meal for one inclusive of VAT (and service where applicable) but without wine. All prices are approximate and should be used as a guide only.

The map reference which appears on the address line of each entry refers to the Soho Map on pages 252–253.

Alistair Little

49 Frith St W1. 01-734 5183. **M 6**

Few chefs would be bold enough to open a restaurant named after themselves, but Alistair Little seems to have got away with it. His small, austerely designed restaurant is one of the most popular eating places in Soho. Little, who first worked in Soho at L'Escargot, opened his own restaurant after a stint at 192 in Kensington. He has since become Soho's very own Superstar Chef, and his reputation spreads way beyond the boundaries of the square mile.

A meal at Alistair Little seldom disappoints. Along with Frith's and the Groucho Club, this is one of the few establishments in Soho to offer the so-called New British cuisine: traditional, indigenous fare pepped up with ingredients and cooking methods from abroad. Little is constantly striving to ensure that a meal here is a genuinely remarkable experience: he even has a way with jellied eels. The menu actually changes twice-daily, so there is little point in listing specific dishes, but recent menus have displayed a marked oriental influence, particularly in the seafood dishes.

The premises themselves are fashionably decorated, but understatedly so; there is little razzamatazz about Alistair Little. Customers are smart Filofax-toters from the record business and the more flamboyant sections of the media like magazine publishing, advertising and PR. Many people, however, regard the rubber chairs and minimalist layout of the place as a major drawback, and would sooner settle for less spectacular food in comfier surroundings.

Since the standard of Little's cooking has been praised to the heavens, it's impossible to eat here without having booked. Do so at least a day or two in advance, but see your bank manager first; it can be very pricey.

Alistair Little

Open: 12.30–14.30, 19.30–23.00 Mon–Fri. Closed Sat & Sun.
Booking: Essential.
Food: £20.00. *House wine:* £7.50.
Credit cards: Visa.

Amalfi

29–31 Old Compton St W1. 01-437 7284. **N 8**

Well-established Italian restaurant/café, which has not yet caught on with Soho's trendies. Washed down with half a carafe of vino rosso, a plate of Amalfi pasta (made on the premises) makes an excellent simple meal, in surroundings which are considerably more appealing than some of the local Italian greasy spoons. The waiters will not expect you to order anything more than pasta, but it is difficult to resist the splendid array of pastries and tarts in the window.

Another virtue of the Amalfi is that it is not a bad choice for a woman who wants to dine alone in Soho. Customers are generally older, more genteel types rather than boisterous businessmen, and the waiters aren't too obsequious. They are also notably restrained in their brandishing of the pepper mill.

Amalfi is open all day for coffee and cakes (take-aways are also available); for those who prefer not to stand at the bar, there are two tables on the right hand side of the restaurant. Order your coffee at the bar and bring it back to your table. There is no waiter/ess service in this part of the restaurant, but the blonde girl who makes the cappuccino and espresso behind the bar has one of the sweetest smiles in Soho.

Amalfi

Open: 12.00–14.45, 18.00–22.45 Mon–Sat; 12.00–22.00 Sun.
Patisserie open 10.00–22.30 Mon–Sun.
Food: £10.00. *House wine:* £5.30.
Credit cards: Access, Amex, Diners, Visa.

Andrea Doria

17 Beak St W1. 01-734 6615. **E 8**

Charming, unpretentious restaurant on the corner of Kingly Street. Small, cosy and decorated in typical anglicised Italian style – complete with hanging flasks of chianti – the interior is very dark. But the crisp linen tablecloths and sparklingly clean glasses assuage any suggestion of seediness. There is a tiny bar at one end of the dining room, from which aperitifs and espresso are dispensed with courteous aplomb. This is easily one of the best Italian eating places in Soho, yet one of the least known.

The small menu reflects Italian regional cuisine, but does not concentrate on any particular area. Saltimbocca is a good choice, but vegetarians with qualms about the fate of calves are also catered for; try the pasta stuffed with spinach and ricotta cheese, usually available in a variety of sauces. Starters, however, can be disappointing. Avoid the antipasto since much of it is fresh from the tin.

Atmosphere is relaxed and informal. The staff are extremely helpful and you will not be pressured into leaving as soon as the clock strikes three. And since the new licensing laws have taken effect, the chances are that you will be actively encouraged to order a strega or amaretto; what better way to prepare for an afternoon's work.

Andrea Doria

Open: 12.00–15.00, 18.00–23.00 Mon–Sat.
Closed Sun.
Food: £12. *House wine:* £5.20.
Credit cards: Access, Amex, Diners, Visa.

Ashley's

2 St Anne's Court W1. 01-434 9941. **L 4**

Stuffier sister of the phenomenally successful Last Resort wine bar, Ashley's has yet to find its feet. The menu is shortish and straightforward, aimed very much at the expense account set. Few concessions have been made to food fads: the cuisine here is mainly trad French, with the odd surprise such as steamed vegetables with sesame seeds and tofu. Those with a particularly conservative palate might choose a dish from the grill list, which includes chicken breast, sole and fillet steak.

The restaurant opened in 1987 and has not yet built up a following. The vast dining room, with its camp pastel decor and ghastly muzak, is not intimate enough to attract couples and not masculine enough to attract the moguls.

Ashley's

Open: 12.00–14.30, 18.00–23.00 Mon–Fri; 18.00–23.00 Sat. Closed Sun.
Booking: Advisable at lunchtime.
Food: £18.00. *House wine:* £4.95.
Entertainment: Pianist every lunchtime and four evenings a week.
Credit cards: Access, Amex, Diners, Visa.

Au Jardin des Gourmets

5 Greek St W1. 01-437 1816. N 4

Long-established French restaurant (reputedly a favourite of Noël Coward's) which is fighting hard to stem the onward march of arrivistes such as La Bastide and L'Escargot. Although he has sold off the rest of his Genevieve chain of restaurants, Joseph Berkmann is still the owner of this cosy yet passé wood-panelled establishment, which he bought in 1977.

Food is modern French, prepared by Paul Kay, a young chef trained by Paul Bocuse. The menu is particularly strong on seafood and the wine superb. Berkmann is in charge of what must be among the finest cellars in London. This is a claret-enthusiast's nirvana and Americans frequently come here just to sample Berkmann's extensive list. Some vintages are pre-1900.

Unless you come with a large wad of travellers' cheques, this is very definitely one for the expense account – particularly if you have a taste for vintage claret. The rooms upstairs can be hired, for buffet or bouffe.

Au Jardin des Gourmets

Open: 12.15–14.30, 18.30–23.30 Mon–Fri; 18.30–23.30 Sat. Closed Sun.
Booking: Advisable.
Food: £13.50 set menu; £22.50 à la carte.
House wine: £5.75.
Credit cards: Access, Amex, Diners, Visa.

Bahn Thai

21a Frith St W1. 01-439 0340. **N 6**

Much-hyped Thai restaurant popular with Soho's media set but not worthy of much recommendation. The tables are too close together and the decor too kitsch for comfort (the ceiling is covered with multi-coloured paper parasols).

The exterior of Bahn Thai promises much: a glass façade topped with an intriguing Bahn Thai logo offers a glimpse of what is normally a very full restaurant, particularly at lunch-time. However, once you are in, the place is too dark. The service can also leave a lot to be desired; at peak times it can be maddeningly slow. The owner, who also owns another Bahn Thai in Kensington, would be well-advised to take on a few more staff. A lesson in PR would not go amiss either; when you ring up to book your table, an answering machine records your requirements, and at the end of your meal, you are presented with a slip of paper marked 'Invoice'. Presumably everyone who comes here is on expenses.

The food is traditional Thai fare with a few Chinese-style surprises. The hot and sour duck is an interesting variation on Peking Duck, but some dishes such as the beef in oyster sauce (or was it Lancashire hotpot) can be downright boring. However, the seafood, particularly the crab and lobster, can make a meal here a worthwhile experience.

Bahn Thai

Open: 12.00–14.45, 18.00–23.15 Mon–Sat; 12.00–14.30, 18.30–22.30 Sun.
Booking: Advisable.
Food: £12.00. *House wine:* £5.95.
Credit cards: Access, Amex, Visa.

La Bastide

50 Greek St W1. 01-734 3300. **N 5**

This building was originally the home of Richard Frith (Soho's first property speculator) and subsequently became a restaurant called Romano Santi. Although Santi's started out in life as a straightforward, Italian restaurant, it was eventually taken over by a Turkish proprietor who presided over its decline. Romano Santi closed for good in the early 1980s after a fire gutted the premises.

La Bastide, which opened in 1986, has succeeded where a number of other French restaurants in the area have failed. During its short life, the restaurant has managed to attract a loyal core of regulars – mainly middle-aged theatricals and publishers – who can be relied upon to come here once or twice a week.

Nicholas Blacklock, who moved here with his partner, Susan Warwick from the D'Artagnan restaurant in Marylebone, is one of Soho's few genuine chef/proprietors. He devises all of La Bastide's menus, which change regularly; at present they concentrate on a different region of France each month, offering a set-price menu of dishes peculiar to that area. The system is similar to that in operation at Frith's across the road: for a fixed price, you can choose two or three courses from a wide selection; it is possible to order three starters, or even three puddings. However, for obvious reasons the management does not encourage people to order three main courses from the set-price menu.

There is also an à la carte menu offering nouvelle-style dishes, but served in much bigger portions: typical dishes might be duck terrine with layers of ox tongue, red mullet with crab pancakes or veal medallions with lime and shallots. A third menu, known as the Soho Menu, consists of straightforward, brasserie-style fare such as onion soup, mussels and black pudding. The wine list is extensive and entirely French; however the main attraction for many people is the splendid array of Armagnacs. You can choose from over 40 different varieties, none of which are more than about 25 years old. (At that point, they cease to improve with age.)

La Bastide's interior is perhaps a little too formal for modern, media-minded Sohoites; the trend at present is away from heavy velvet curtains and traditional wallpaper, yet apparently this is very popular with the Americans, who presumably can afford to sample the Armagnac. (A single measure of some of those served here can cost more than your meal.) Levi 501's (even matt black ones) would probably seem out of place in the main restaurant, but a private function room is available upstairs.

La Bastide

Open: 12.30–14.30, 18.00–23.30 Mon–Fri; 18.00–23.30 Sat. Closed Sun.
Booking: Essential.
Food: £17.00. *House wine:* £6.00.
Credit cards: Access, Amex, Diners, Visa.

Bengali Spice

11 Greek St W1. 01-434 4177. **N 4**

Formerly a sister branch of the immensely popular and successful Bengal Lancer in Kentish Town, Soho's Bengal Lancer never quite fulfilled its early promise or justified the brouhaha which surrounded its opening. When it was launched, the Bengal Lancer was touted as Britain's first Indian brasserie. Now, with new management and a change of name, its hours are in keeping with the rest of Soho's Indian restaurants; apparently the demand for breakfast kedgeree and mid-morning tiffin was insufficient to merit opening before lunchtime.

Although it is no longer such a novelty, the Bengal Lancer is still worth a visit. It is a clean, well-run establishment which offers a variety of Indian dishes, mainly 'new-wave' in style. Decor is subtle, seats comfortable; in Soho it seems that the traditional curry house with wall-to-wall flock and dingy red candle lamps has well and truly had its day. Dishes worth sampling include a daily chef's special (usually a good bet), mogaz masala (marinaded lambs' brains) and charcoal-grilled trout. A very cheap set lunch is also available, presumably to woo trade from local offices. For less than a fiver you can enjoy a starter followed by curry and rice in surroundings which make some of Soho's long-established French restaurants seem shabby. Wash your meal down with potent Indian beer.

Bengali Spice

Open: 12.00–15.00, 18.00–23.30 Mon–Sun.
Food: £10.00. *House wine:* £5.50.
Credit cards: Access, Amex, Diners, Visa.

Bill Stickers

18 Greek St W1. 01-437 0582. **N 5**

The campest eating house in Soho, darlings, and if your taste runs to a zebra-striped bar, mock-Greek statues and what purports to be Marilyn Monroe's dining table, this is the place for you. Bill Stickers opened in 1986 on the site of what was the Establishment Club. The decor has about as much style as that of a Blackpool boarding house: kitsch wall decorations leer down at diners seated in tacky scarlet and gilt chairs. The high-camp waiters are even more outrageous. Clad in tuxedos, they mince from table to table serving drinks, taking orders and mopping the fevered egos of the diners.

Since it opened, Bill Stickers has earned a reputation as something of a theatrical hangout, Soho's equivalent of the classier and starrier Joe Allen's in Covent Garden. (Late opening hours may have something to do with this.) Second-rate thespians come here regularly, swapping gossip and bitchery while waiting for the part they've always wanted to arrive in their laps. No one's here for the food, which veers between acceptable and execrable. Traditional school canteen staples such as bangers and mash, along with more elaborate dishes such as lemon chicken and sole fried in matzo meal. Most are as tasteless as the decor. Good range of cocktails, however; not all of them come complete with half a pineapple.

Bill Stickers

Open: 12.00–03.00 Mon–Fri; 19.00–03.00 Sat; 19.00–23.00 Sun.
Booking: Advisable Thur, Fri & Sat evenings.
Food: £14.00. *House wine:* £6.25.
Credit cards: Access, Amex, Diners, Visa.

Le Bistingo

57–59 Old Compton St W1. 01-437 0784. **L 7**

Bistingo is a reliable London-wide chain of bistros serving unpretentious French fare such as escargots, onion soup, stuffed mushrooms and boeuf bourguignon. This branch, on the site of the legendary 2 i's coffee bar, offers excellent value in homely, comfortable surroundings. Well worth a visit, but don't expect haute cuisine.

> *Le Bistingo*
>
> *Open:* 12.00–14.30, 18.00–23.30 Mon–Sat; 19.00–22.30 Sun.
> *Booking:* Essential for large parties.
> *Food:* £15.00 (à la carte). *House wine:* £5.35.
> *Credit cards:* Access, Amex, Diners, Visa.

Braganza

56 Frith St W1. 01-437 5412. **N 5**

Vast, much-hyped establishment owned by the Kennedy Brookes conglomerate who took over the Wheeler's Chain, of which this was part, in 1984. Unfortunately this restaurant is one of many trying desperately hard to cash in on the Soho boom.

Yet Braganza does have its plus points. The decor and layout of the place, for instance, would serve as a useful conversational standby at a dreary business lunch. Different artists were commissioned to decorate each floor. The idea was to give each section a separate identity. The ground floor is a straightforward brasserie wherein trendy Sohoites can hold breakfast meetings over cappuccino and croissants. The first floor is more restrained: decor is softer, clientele older, food more sophisticated and it affords an excellent view of the brasserie below. The second floor is altogether more bourgeois: linen tablecloths and napkins, parquet flooring and dark wood panelling combine to give this part of the restaurant a more established and grown-up air. Diners here are unlikely to be regulars at the Wag Club.

The food at Braganza is acceptable, but not spectacular. The menu is best termed 'international' – French/Italian with a touch of the New British and American. Many of the sauces are nouvellish in origin, but thankfully portions are robust. Emphasis is on meat and game, but there is always a wide selection of seafood starters and main courses on the menu, and at least one dish suitable for vegetarians. The menus in the brasserie and in the restaurant change once every three months and half a dozen or so 'specials' are available each day. The wine list is equally international featuring bottles from France, Spain, Chile, Australia, California, New Zealand, Portugal, Italy and even England.

Braganza

Open: Restaurant 12.00–15.00, 17.30–23.30 Mon–Fri; 17.30–23.30 Sat. Brasserie 10.00–23.00 Mon–Fri; 17.30–23.30 Sat. Closed Sun.
Booking: Advisable for the restaurant.
Food: Restaurant £15.00. *House wine:* £5.50.
Entertainment: Pianist on first floor every evening.
Credit cards: Access, Amex, Diners, Visa.

Café Loire

12 Great Marlborough St W1. 01-434 2666. **F 3**

Formerly an American restaurant called Surprise, Café Loire is a big, brightly-lit brasserie with a wine bar at the front. Its position, just south of Oxford Street, suggests that it might have difficulty attracting a passing trade in the evenings, although the Palladium's more monied patrons may well see fit to drop in here for a meal before or after the show. Café Loire is not one of Soho's better known French restaurants, but it does offer competent food, agreeable surroundings and efficient service.

The dishes should appeal to most tastes: elaborate, labour-intensive main courses such as chicken supreme stuffed with vegetable mousse, or duck breast with pink peppercorn sauce are usually available along with more straightforward fare such as plain grilled Dover sole.

The menu is perhaps too long for comfort: apart from the standard à la carte and the plats du jour, diners can also take their pick from a selection of regional dishes. All of these originate from the Loire, as do most of the wines. The wine bar is well worth a visit, particularly if you're laden with carrier bags from Marks & Spencer, next door. A cool glass of Café Loire's Saumur is enough to convince anyone that there is life after the checkout queue.

> *Café Loire*
>
> *Open:* 12.00–15.00, 17.30–23.30 Mon–Fri.
> Closed Sat & Sun.
> *Booking:* Essential at lunchtime.
> *Food:* £15.00–£18.00. *House wine:* £6.25.
> *Credit cards:* Access, Amex, Diners, Visa.

Chez Victor

45 Wardour St W1. 01-437 6523. **L 10**

Unusual to find a French restaurant in this Chinese-dominated corner of Soho, Chez Victor opened in 1901. It has always cocked a snook at contemporary eating trends and still does very nicely thank you. Both the exterior and the interior have scarcely changed since the restaurant first opened: the paintwork and typography on the outside seems straight out of pre-war Paris and service is old-fashioned too; Leon, one of the waiters, who looks like Donald Pleasance, has been here for years.

An original poster of the exiled de Gaulle's proclamation to the Free French still hangs on the wall and the air is often heavy with the smell of Gauloise. Well-fed, middle-aged Frenchmen are regular patrons and the atmosphere is not unlike those formal yet relaxed establishments one finds in the Marais district of Paris. However, for food which is by no means devastatingly exciting (onion soup, coquille St Jacques, cassoulet) prices can be very high. Stick to the dishes of the day. Small, but very acceptable wine list. The clarets are usually a good bet.

Chez Victor

Open: 12.00–14.30, 18.00–23.15 Mon–Fri; 18.00–23.15 Sat. Closed Sun.
Booking: Advisable.
Food: £14.00. *House wine:* £7.00.
Credit cards: Access, Amex, Diners, Visa.

Chiang Mai

48 Frith St W1. 01-437 7444. **N 5**

Soon after it opened in 1983, Chiang Mai began to establish its reputation as one of Soho's best ethnic eateries. Thai food suddenly became fashionable and the expense account set would snap up tables as fast as you could say Saatchi and Saatchi. Fortunately, Chiang Mai now has a more stable clientele, who care less about the kudos of eating here and more about the quality of the food. That said, it remains popular and booking is essential.

The Chiang Mai is an extremely pretty restaurant. The main dining room on the ground floor is designed to represent a traditional Thai stilt-house; the soft tones of the walls and lighting convey a relaxed, colonial atmosphere. Bring a battered Somerset Maugham and a Panama hat.

The food is excellent, but expect to pay more than you would at an Indonesian or Malaysian establishment. The long menu is made up mainly of dishes from Chang Mai province in northern Thailand (the restaurant has a sister branch over there) but there are some more obvious Far Eastern specialities available, such as satay.

Those unfamiliar with Thai cuisine should perhaps opt for one of the set meals, supplementing the owner's choice with one more dish from the à la carte menu (portions are not enormous); the hot and sour seafood salad, containing fresh prawns, crab and squid on a bed of beansprouts and ginger would be an excellent choice. And Chiang Mai's version of spring rolls, stuffed with wonderfully light 'vermicelli' serves as a tasty appetiser. Each of the set meals has been chosen with traditional Thai eating habits in mind: Thais normally start with a soup, a fried or grilled dish, followed by curry and salad. The dishes should not be mixed, but eaten one at a time with rice. Thai food is similar to that served elsewhere in the Far East; however, flavours tend to be more subtle and presentation more important. A visit to Chiang Mai would serve as a splendid introduction for anyone wanting to sample this delicious cuisine, widely regarded as South East Asia's finest.

Chiang Mai

Open: 12.00–15.00, 18.00–23.00 Mon–Sat.
Closed Sun.
Booking: Advisable.
Food: £15.00. *House wine:* £5.95.
Credit cards: Access, Amex, Visa.

Cho Won

27 Romilly St W1. 01-437 2262. **N 6**

Sandwiched between Kettners and Rugantino, Cho Won is an elegant restaurant serving authentic Korean specialities. The dark exterior gives way to a very bright, almost garish interior decorated in the Japanese style with traditional wall-coverings. The ground floor is an ordinary dining room, with Western tables. Upstairs, however, you'll find the Korean version of the Japanese tatami mat room where diners crouch at low tables, having first removed their shoes. This room can be rented for private parties and is particularly popular with Far Eastern businessmen. The trendies have yet to discover it.

The food at Cho Won is influenced by Japanese styles of cuisine, but there is less emphasis on presentation. Most of the dishes are served spicy hot, with sauces made from garlic, ginger, spring onion and soya beans. Those unfamiliar with Korean food won't go wrong if they choose one of the two excellent-value set meals. These start with a soup of the day (the dumpling soup, similar to, but more delicate than Chinese wun tun is first class) and continue with a range of Korean dishes such as bul gal bee (strips of raw beef with sugar and sesame seeds) grilled corvina (fish) and chap che (mixed vegetables with vermicelli). All of this is accompanied by kim chee, a very spicy cabbage pickle, and Korean rice. To the uninitiated, the rice may seem overcooked, but it is served sticky so that it can be scooped up on the delicate silver-plated chopsticks which the Koreans use. One appetiser which doesn't appear on the set menu but is worth ordering is the bracken stalks with sesame. It is only available between March and August when bracken stalks from the English countryside are apparently at their best.

Service here is exemplary and the staff are more than happy to explain each dish; lessons in Korean chopstick-wielding are also available. At the end of your meal, you will be served Polo mints in a heart-shaped dish; a nice touch and typical of this agreeable, welcoming little restaurant.

Cho Won

Open: 12.00–15.00, 18.00–23.00 Mon–Sat; 17.00–22.00 Sun.
Food: £10.00. *House wine:* £4.50.
Credit cards: Access, Amex, Diners, Visa.

Christy's Healthline

122–126 Wardour St W1. 01-434 4468. **J 4**

This was the first of Soho's trendy veggie establishments, and although the food is good, the surroundings are reminiscent of the lobby of an American bank. However, the minimalist decor (that's what it's called apparently) attracts a large number of Soho's young poseurs. They seem to enjoy eating in a room decorated throughout in white tiles, the monotony only interrupted by a handful of potplants.

The restaurant was opened (oops, conceived) by Keith Christy Murray, a disenchanted former Cranks employee who felt that there was more to vegetarian food than nut rissoles, onion loaf and toasted baps. The menus at Christy's are reasonably inventive – starting with lentil, basil and tomato soup followed by casserole – but rely too much on trad veggie fare. Wholemeal pizzas and quiches are staples. The wine bar offers the usual range of trendy snacks, salads etc, and even serves a wholemeal cream tea. (If you prefer, substitute cappuccino for tea.)

> *Christy's Healthline*
>
> *Open:* 09.00–24.00 Mon–Fri, 10.30–24.00 Sat, 12.30–23.00 Sun.
> *Booking:* Advisable.
> *Food:* £8.00. *House wine:* £5.75.
> *Credit cards:* Access, Amex, Diners, Visa.

Compton Green

14 Old Compton St W1. 01-434 3544. **O 6**

Second of Soho's 'new wave' vegetarian eateries, Compton Green is roomy and well designed. It was opened in 1987 by Robert Martinez who previously owned a vegetarian restaurant in the City. The food here is light years ahead of the stolid, stodgy fare served up in traditional, complacent veggie establishments. Sauces are light, ingredients imaginative. The menu changes once a month: typical main courses might be Tagliatelle Germano with salad (suitable for vegans), marinated vegetable and tofu kebabs with rice and peanut sauce or savoury cream cheese tart of the day. Traditionalists will appreciate the restaurant's wide selection of old-fashioned puddings which include summer pudding and hot, rich chocolate cake.

> *Compton Green*
>
> *Open:* 11.30–22.45 Mon–Sun.
> *Food:* £7.50. *House wine:* £4.95.
> *Entertainment:* Pianist every evening.
> *Credit cards:* Access, Amex, Diners, Visa.

Cranks

8 Marshall St W1. 01-437 9431. **F 5**

Cranks is one of the more disappointing restaurants in Soho. The secret of its success defies conventional commercial wisdom: why on earth are people prepared to pay quite high prices for boring salads and leaden hot dishes which seem to have been on the menu since the place opened in the early 60s? Only the soups, thick, warm and filling, are worthy of serious praise.

There is no waiter service here at lunchtime; you have to join the self-service scrum (and usually a very long queue by 1pm). An evening meal, however, can be more relaxing: Cranks' 'Wine & Dine' nights offer food which is marginally better than that served at lunch in a much more civilised, candlelit environment. The dishes are more elaborate, the tables less crowded. The disadvantage is that dinner is likely to cost you twice as much as lunch.

Cranks

Open: Buffet 08.00–19.00 Mon–Fri, 09.00–19.00 Sat. Closed Sun. Restaurant 18.30–22.30 Mon–Sat. Closed Sun.
Booking: Advisable (restaurant only).
Food: £9.00. *House wine:* £5.75 (Wine & Dine).
Credit cards: Access, Amex, Diners, Visa (restaurant only).

La Cucaracha

12 Greek St W1. 01-734 2253. **N 4**

Given the popularity of Mexican food, it is surprising that there are no other Mexican restaurants in Soho. La Cucaracha opened in 1967, but seems to have failed to cash in on the public's passion for tacos and burritos. Its main problem is that it is much too big; this does not bode well for a lively atmosphere when half-empty. Service is frequently over-attentive (presumably because the waiters aren't rushed off their feet) and the deathly hush does not engender exuberant chat.

The decor might well have been attractive in the mid-70s, but by now it seems terribly hackneyed; the white walls and huge windows evoke one of those hastily built villas which can be found all over the Costa del Sol. The wooden sculptures are no doubt typical examples of Mexican art.

The food, however, is more than acceptable. If you are a fan of chilli con carne and its umpteen variations you'd be hard pushed to find better anywhere else. The menu concentrates on traditional Mexican food but there is the occasional speciality. Newcomers should throw caution to the wind and sample the turkey in chocolate and chilli sauce or opt for a carnitas à la Cucaracha, the Mexican equivalent of an Indian thali: guacamole, barbecued pork (with crackling), refried beans, mixed salad, all served on one plate with pancakes. The wine list is predominantly Hispanic in origin, but drink tequila (available in two grades, silver or gold). Its hallucinogenic effects will be a great help when it comes to stumping up for the bill. La Cucaracha is not cheap.

La Cucaracha

Open: 12.15–14.30, 18.00–22.30 Mon–Sat. Closed Sun.
Food: £15.00. *House wine:* £6.80.
Entertainment: Live music every evening.
Credit cards: Access, Amex, Diners, Visa.

Delhi Brasserie

44 Frith St W1. 01-437 8261. **M 5**

Pretentiously-named Indian restaurant with little to distinguish it from dozens of similar establishments which have opened in the last few years. This is not a brasserie, and neither the food nor the proprietor comes from Delhi. However, Delhi Brasserie and its sister restaurant in South Kensington have both developed a considerable following in the relatively short time they have been in business.

Food is mostly traditional tandoori fare, perfectly acceptable, but far from innovative. The tandoori trout and quail are the most unusual items on the menu, but you'd be hard-pressed to find an upmarket Indian restaurant in Soho which didn't offer these dishes. Decor, however, in pastel pink and green is very much in the new style. As is the attractive engraved-glass window which tempts potential diners in from Frith Street.

Cocktails are served, copiously adorned with maraschino cherries, oranges and teeny parasols. If it weren't for the accoutrements the Soho Classic, a mixture of two vermouths, gin and orange, would make an agreeable drink.

At the end of your meal the best is yet to come. The waiter suddenly appears wielding a miniature vacuum cleaner with which to remove the grains of pilau rice – and any other disasters – from your table cloth before offering you coffee and kulfi.

Delhi Brasserie

Open: 12.00–14.30, 17.30–24.00 Mon–Sun.
Booking: Advisable.
Food: £11.00 (set menu). *House wine:* £5.25.
Credit cards: Access, Amex, Diners, Visa.

Desaru

60–62 Old Compton St W1. 01-734 4379. **L 7**

Garish Indonesian/Malaysian restaurant which is typical of the new wave of ethnic eateries which came to Soho in the late 70s and early 80s. This one, however, offers service which is much more refined than similar establishments, even though the menu itself is fairly predictable. Choose from a standard range of Far Eastern dishes including the by-now ubiquitous satay, prawns in hot sambal sauce and kalio kental. Singapore laksa (a huge bowl of noodle soup with coconut, prawns and fish cakes) can make a filling one-course meal if you are in a hurry. However, since Desaru is not that cheap, the budget diner would be better off crossing Shaftesbury Avenue and heading for Chinatown.

Like many of the newer Indian restaurants in the area, Desaru has jumped on the cocktail bandwagon. These are dispensed from the bar, designed in the shape of a beach hut, at the front of the restaurant. The cocktails normally go down well with the poorer members of Soho's media set, who have patronised Desaru from the moment it opened.

Desaru

Open: 12.00–15.00, 18.00–23.45 Mon–Fri; 12.00–23.45 Sat; 13.00–22.00 Sun.
Booking: Advisable.
Food: £15.00. *House wine:* £5.40.
Credit cards: Access, Amex, Diners, Visa.

L'Epicure

28 Frith St W1. 01-437 2829. **M 6**

One of the few restaurants left in Soho offering solid Cuisine Bourgeoise. L'Epicure specialises in traditional, stodgy, rich food, mainly French but with the occasional dish from Italy or elsewhere in Europe. The proprietor, Nigel Tarr, has a Swedish wife, which explains why Potage St Germain à la Suèdoise (Swedish-style pea soup) appears on the menu.

Nigel Tarr took over the premises in 1977. Though there has been a restaurant on this site since 1921, it wasn't called L'Epicure until 1953 when it was bought by a Greek Cypriot. He gave the menu its international flavour and introduced flambé cooking, which has since become the hallmark of the restaurant. At least half the dishes on the menu are flambéed at the table, cooked on lamps fuelled by methylated spirits.

The flaming gas lamps which decorate the outside of the restaurant serve as a useful landmark for taxi drivers. Some regulars are prepared to bet a lobster thermidor (very good here and at a set, rather than market, price) that the lamps date back to the 1950s, but in fact they weren't introduced until 1978.

L'Epicure has a predominantly middle-aged clientele. Customers tend to be managing directors rather than Paul Smith-clad junior execs. Also popular with politicians, it is the Right's equivalent of the Gay Hussar, although in the 60s this was

Labour Prime Minister Harold Wilson's favourite restaurant. At times of crisis he would chair emergency inner sanctum meetings in an upstairs room, which has since been converted to a gents lavatory. Nowadays, prominent Tory Ministers eat at L'Epicure along with a few renegades from the Left such as David Owen and Roy Jenkins. And even though L'Epicure has fallen out of favour with the Left, Roy Hattersley, Labour's shadow spokesman on eating out, is still a regular.

L'Epicure

Open: 12.00–14.30, 18.00–23.15 Mon–Fri; 18.00–23.15 Sat. Closed Sun.
Booking: Advisable.
Food: £20.00–£25.00. *House wine:* £5.20.
Credit cards: Access, Amex, Diners, Visa.

L'Escargot

48 Greek St W1. 01-437 2672. **M 6**

L'Escargot enjoys a reputation as one of London's trendiest eateries. Since the restaurant reopened in 1981 on the site of an old, yet fading Soho favourite, L'Escargot Bienvenue, the gossip columnists have elicited more than a few choice paragraphs from the literary launches, press beanos and showbiz parties which frequently take place behind the impressive 18th-century façade of what was once the Duke of Portland's town house.

Perhaps the restaurant's greatest publicity coup occurred when Clive Ponting, the Ministry of Defence civil servant cleared of offences under the Official Secrets Act chose to hold his acquittal party here. The TV cameras covering the event for the news filmed the exterior, thus giving L'Escargot a priceless prime-time plug.

For a restaurant with such an intimidating reputation, the atmosphere is unusually friendly. Elena, the charming maître d', whom owner Nick Lander lured from the now-defunct Bianchi's across the road, offers a warm welcome to the portly publishers who pack the restaurant on the first

floor. The young staff who run the downstairs brasserie are equally accommodating.

The food is not outrageously expensive. The brasserie offers reasonably-priced starters and main courses, plus an excellent pudding menu. The restaurant is more formal (and more expensive) but the food is much the same as that served downstairs – mainly French and nouvellish in style. However, chef Martin Lam has incorporated dishes from other cuisines (such as Italian and Indian) into his menus, which change every two months. The wine list is comprehensive and selected by wine critic Jancis Robinson, who is married to Nick Lander.

L'Escargot

Open: Brasserie 12.15–15.00, 17.30–23.15 Mon–Fri; 18.00–23.15 Sat. Restaurant 12.15–14.30 Mon–Fri; 18.30–23.15 Sat. Closed Sun.
Booking: Essential for the restaurant; not accepted for the brasserie for less than six at lunchtime.
Food: Brasserie £15; Restaurant £25.
House wine: £5.50.
Entertainment: Jazz singer and pianist every evening in the brasserie.
Credit cards: Access, Amex, Diners, Visa.

Frith's

14 Frith St W1. 01-439 3370. **M 6**

One of Soho's finest eateries, and one of the first to raise the flag for New British Cuisine. NBC betrays the influence of French nouvelle cuisine, but portions are larger and vegetables presented in a less pretentious way. The emphasis at Frith's is on fresh, indigenous ingredients, prepared imaginatively on the premises by chef(ette) Carla Tomasi.

The menu changes monthly which gives Carla the opportunity to produce dishes which make the most of seasonal specialities; Frith's is particularly strong on game and fish. Sauces, such as red cabbage and orange or red wine and tarragon are light and adventurous, and puddings, while unmistakably British in origin offer few throwbacks to old-style stodge. How many schools ever served up lemon and honey ice-cream with tangerine sauce and shortbread?

Decor is dark and sleek high-tech; a little contrived perhaps, but intimate nonetheless. The design-conscious will not approve of the distinctly outré Habitat knives and forks; a surprising faux pas, since so much thought has gone into every other aspect of the restaurant.

Pricing policy here is novel: you pay a flat fee for four courses: starter, middle, main and pudding or cheese. There is only a handful of dishes on the menu, which ensures that Carla does not spread her considerable talents too thinly. The cheeses, in particular, are remarkable: no mass-produced Cheddar or Wensleydale here, only obscure home-made farmhouse cheeses, shipped in fresh from the provinces.

Frith's is a very popular (and small) restaurant so booking is essential. You'll probably find at least one or two minor celebs eating here at lunchtime (clientele is predominantly media/theatrical, with some famous political faces); while the evenings attract Soho's beautiful people. Serious food lovers maintain that Frith's is worth a visit for its bread rolls alone.

Frith's

Open: 12.00–14.30, 18.00–23.30 Mon–Fri; 18.00–23.30 Sat. Closed Sun.
Booking: Essential.
Food: £18.00. *House wine:* £4.50.
Credit cards: Access, Amex, Diners, Visa.

Fuji

36–40 Brewer St W1. 01-734 0957. **H 8**

One of four Japanese restaurants on the street which is fast becoming known for its Far Eastern influence. Even the butchers (European) boast that their steak is so tender that it is suitable for teriyaki.

Japanese cuisine has been available in London now for over 20 years, yet it has failed to win mass acceptance. Fuji is a very elegant, very authentic restaurant but the prices it charges may explain why the Japanese take-away has never caught on. A set meal for two costs more than you'd pay anywhere else in Soho, even in the ritzy French establishments. It is possible to skimp, selecting just a few items from the sushi list, but that does not make for a satisfactory night out. And besides, there is a minimum charge.

For those who can afford to splurge, a full range of Japanese delicacies is available including tempura, teriyaki and sashimi. All are beautifully cooked; it is virtually impossible to have a bad meal at a Japanese restaurant. The staff are extremely obliging and will help a novice through the more mysterious corners of the menu. Drink saké or beer.

Fuji

Open: 12.30–14.30, 18.00–22.45 Mon–Fri; 18.00–22.45 Sat; 18.00–22.15 Sun.
Booking: Advisable.
Food: £25.00. *House wine:* £6.00.
Credit cards: Access, Amex, Diners, Visa.

Gay Hussar

2 Greek St W1. 01-437 0793. **N 4**

Celebrated politicians' haunt owned by Victor Sassie, one of Soho's most publicity-conscious restaurateurs. He never advertises; for over 30 years he has relied upon the gossip columnists to keep his restaurant's name in the papers. And they do, usually penning barbed accounts of tired and emotional left-wing MPs staggering out of the restaurant's portcullis-like doors after a large lunch. For years, the Gay Hussar has been a favourite with the Left. The food, while not cheap, is inexpensive and hearty enough to assuage the doubts of the helpers back in the constituencies.

The restaurant is probably a little too crowded at lunchtime for any serious politicking. The tables, which are very close together, allow for easy eavesdropping. And besides, this is the unofficial canteen of the parliamentary press lobby. Middle-aged publishers can also be found here scouting for talent: many a political biography originated at the Gay Hussar over a bottle of Tokay and a bowl of cold cherry and beetroot soup.

The Gay Hussar has fallen from favour of late, possibly because the Labour Party has spent so long out of office. However, the food remains excellent value for money; the Gay Hussar offers what must be the most substantial and filling set-price lunch in Soho. The menu is firmly mid-European (Sassie trained as a chef in Budapest), and includes classics such as Serbian chicken with peppers and tomato, veal goulash with dumplings, and smoked goose.

> ### Gay Hussar
> *Open:* 12.30–14.30, 17.30–22.30 Mon–Sat. Closed Sun.
> *Booking:* Essential.
> *Food:* £9.50 lunch, £16 dinner (set menu).
> *House wine:* £5.50.
> *Credit cards:* Not accepted.

Grahame's Seafare

38 Poland St W1. 01-437 3788. **F 2**

Upmarket though unpretentious fish and chip restaurant, popular with the Jewish community; the fish is cooked in matzo meal. Regulars come mainly from north London, but the restaurant's proximity to Oxford Street attracts lots of shoppers. Food is simple fried or grilled fish (plaice, cod, Dover sole) served with delicious chips. Take-aways are available too, but those who take their fish home miss out on being mothered by Grahame's posse of friendly waitresses.

> ### Grahame's Seafare
> *Open:* 12.00–14.45 Mon; 12.00–14.45, 17.30–20.45 Tue–Thur & Sat; 12.00–14.45, 17.30–19.45 Fri. Closed Sun.
> *Booking:* Advisable.
> *Food:* £7.00. *House wine:* £5.50.
> *Credit cards:* Visa.

Jimmy's

23 Frith St W1. 01-437 9521. **N 6**

Long-established Greek restaurant, popular with students, budget-conscious tourists and impecunious Sohoites. The atmosphere in this dark, smoky basement is seedily bohemian, the food filling but unremarkable. The standard range of Greek starters and main courses – tzatziki, taramasalata, kleftico, moussaka – should be complemented by retzina or what must be the roughest house red in Soho, which comes in a label-less bottle. And in typical Greek style you drink out of tumblers rather than wine glasses.

In spite of its obvious failings, Jimmy's is worth a visit. The food is excellent value for money, and portions are huge. Big fat chips are served with every main course and if you ask for bread you'll receive a huge doorstep of fresh white; few concessions are made to healthy eating here. Another advantage of Jimmy's is that this is not the kind of tourist-orientated Greek restaurant wherein the waiters will suddenly drop the plates and perform a folk dance. You'll be lucky if they remember to take your order.

Jimmy's

Open: 12.30–15.00, 17.30–22.45 Mon–Sat. Closed Sun.
Booking: Essential for large groups.
Food: £7.00. *House wine:* £4.00.
Credit cards: Not accepted.

Kettners

29 Romilly St W1. 01-437 6437. **O 7**

One of Soho's oldest and most architecturally interesting eating houses, Kettners opened in the mid-19th century as the Restaurant du Pavilion. In 1869 it was bought by an Alsatian named Kettner; for over a century Kettners thrived, serving high-class French cuisine. Now the restaurant is owned by Pizza Express magnate Peter Boizot and the food and atmosphere is altogether different.

Today, in the house to which Edward VII was known to bring Lillie Langtry (he opted for one of the private rooms upstairs) junior advertising executives talk shop over 'Round Plate Specials' (hamburger, chips and salad) and Peroni beer. Thankfully, the enormous dining rooms have been well preserved even if the food is a pale shadow of its formerly glorious self; lobster used to be a Kettners speciality. The nearest the restaurant gets to that nowadays is pizza with anchovy.

Nonetheless, Boizot should be congratulated on his acumen. He transformed a famous yet fading restaurant into a going concern and Kettners is probably the swishest pizza joint in Europe. The red leather armchairs are extremely comfortable. The food represents very good value if you like American/Italian roadhouse fare, and the service is always polished. Disadvantages: it is impossible to book, the braying poseurs in the Champagne Bar can be unbearable and the massed ranks (if you can call them that) of the Parliamentary Liberal Party hold regular lunches here.

If you want a seat at lunchtime in the main restaurant it is advisable to arrive by about 12.45. Otherwise you'll be ushered towards the 'white room', a high-tech mistake in chrome and smoked glass which clashes horribly with the rest of the decor.

Kettners

Open: 12.00–24.00 Mon–Sun.
Booking: Not accepted.
Food: £10.00. *House wine:* £6.25.
Entertainment: Pianist every evening.
Credit cards: Access, Amex, Diners, Visa.

Laline

69–70 Dean St W1. 01-734 3224. **L 6**

Laline opened in early 1987 amid a flurry of publicity, which concentrated mainly on the elegance of the building. Undoubtedly, the builders and designers who revamped what was once one of Soho's best-loved Italian restaurants, Hostaria Romana, have done an excellent job. Laline exudes elegance, from the art nouveau pennants flapping in the wind outside to the attractive bar which dominates the restaurant as you enter.

Laline is in fact both wine bar and restaurant; the wine bar section at the front of the building, which divides into several rooms, serves the usual range of French wine bar-type fare

(Laline is owned by the Chez Solange group) while the restaurant proper provides more substantial food. The emphasis is on modern, flour-free French cooking. Laline, along with L'Escargot, is one of the few French restaurants in Soho to offer entertainment; a pianist performs here every night. Given how much it must have cost to do the place up, prices are very reasonable.

> ***Laline***
>
> *Open:* 12.00–14.30, 19.00–23.30 Mon–Fri; 19.00–23.30 Sat. Closed Sun.
> *Food:* £20.00. *House wine:* £5.85.
> *Entertainment:* Pianist performs every night.
> *Credit cards:* Access, Amex, Diners, Visa.

Last Days of the Raj

42 Dean St W1. 01-439 0972. **M 6**

Soho branch of Covent Garden's famous Last Days of the Raj which opened in 1986. The restaurant has not yet attracted a following as committed as the Red Fort's, but the food is of a uniformly high standard. And service is much better than in its Covent Garden counterpart. All that's lacking in fact is a little atmosphere; at present the restaurant often seems less than half-full, particularly at lunchtime and on midweek evenings.

The menu is very similar to that at Covent Garden, dishes such as murgei masala (tandoori chicken cooked in a cream and nut sauce) along with more traditional curries. Vegetables are excellent and the lassi most refreshing. In common with most new-wave Indian restaurants it is possible to drink cocktails here, before, during and after the meal.

> ***Last Days of the Raj***
>
> *Open:* 12.00–15.00, 18.00–23.30 Mon–Sun.
> *Food:* £12.00–£15.00. *House wine:* £5.50.
> *Credit cards:* Access, Amex, Diners, Visa.

Leoni's Quo Vadis

26–29 Dean St W1. 01-437 4809. **M 5**

Perhaps the most famous restaurant in Soho. Superb traditional Italian food and an intriguing history combine to make a visit to Quo Vadis essential for anyone who has an interest in Soho's development as the culinary centre of the capital.

This building is one of the oldest surviving in Soho. It was erected in 1692 but did not become a restaurant until 1926 when Peppino Leoni sank his life savings (about £800) into buying the freehold of the building. Leoni's reputation as one of London's leading restaurateurs soon became established. The menu, decor and standards of service have changed little over the last 60 years; Leoni, who died in the early 70s, always believed that it would be foolish to interfere with a formula which had proved so successful. The current owners, Messrs Lahoud and Khallil, concur.

The main dining room is very pretty; starched pink linen and soft, traditional dining chairs give off a discreetly affluent ambience. Leoni's still specialises in dishes dripping with rich sauces made from calorie-laden ingredients. Try polpettine con pinoli (meat balls with pine kernels cooked in red wine with garlic and mushrooms) or bistecca arrabiata, peppered sirloin flamed in whisky.

The pasta dishes, as you'd expect from a restaurant of this standing, are impeccable. Leoni always claimed the credit for introducing fettucine to Britain and his Fettucine Quo Vadis (noodles with cream, tomato and fresh basil) remains one of the most popular items on the menu. Pasta is also available as a main course, which helps to keep the bill down; Leoni's is not cheap.

Fortunately, the restaurant does not demand any money for showing diners Karl Marx's room on the top floor. The founding father of communism lived here in penury between 1850 and 1856 while he was writing *Das Kapital*, and his tiny, spartan room has scarcely been altered since he left. A waiter will gladly escort you upstairs if you ask, but it might be best to go before your meal, the climb could well prove too much later on!

Leoni's Quo Vadis

Open: 12.00–14.30, 18.00–23.15 Mon–Fri; 18.00–23.15 Sat; 19.00–22.30 Sun.
Booking: Advisable.
Food: £16.00–£18.00. *House wine:* £5.95.
Credit cards: Access, Amex, Diners, Visa.

Matono

25–27 Brewer St W1. 01-734 1859. **J 8**

Soho's only proper sushi bar, and an excellent starting point if you've never tried Japanese food before. You sit on stools at a brightly-lit bar and watch the chef prepare the ingredients, mainly titbits of raw fish, rice and shellfish, usually wrapped in seaweed. Garish signs on the door should help you discover the precise contents of each sushi 'parcel' but do not be afraid to ask. As in most Japanese restaurants, the service here is swift and efficient and the staff are only too happy to explain.

Other dishes such as sashimi, salads and teriyaki are generally available, but this is primarily a sushi bar; you should eat nothing else. Take-aways too.

Matono

Open: 12.00–14.30, 18.00–23.00 Mon–Sat; 18.00–23.00 Sun.
Booking: Advisable.
Food: £15.00–£25.00. *House wine:* £9.80.
Credit cards: Access, Amex, Diners, Visa.

Melati

21 Great Windmill St W1. 01-437 2745. **J 9**

Once connected to the Melati on Peter Street, this branch has now gone its own way. Prices are much the same, although this restaurant boasts a better selection of dishes. House specialities include fish head curry, prawn fritters in a sweet and sour sauce and incredibly hot mutton dishes which are cooked with what seems like mountains of chilli.

The young, sweat-shirted staff are always happy to explain any of the dishes to those unfamiliar with Malaysian/Indonesian food and they certainly don't oversell. They'll even warn you if they think you're ordering too much in the way of rice, noodles or vegetables. The satay is uniformly good and veggies are well-catered for; dishes suitable for vegetarians are indicated on the menu. Drink jasmine tea, wine, beer or cocktails.

> *Melati*
>
> *Open:* 12.00–23.00 Mon–Thur & Sun; 12.00–24.30 Fri & Sat.
> *Booking:* Advisable.
> *Food:* £12.00. *House wine:* £5.75.
> *Credit cards:* Access, Amex, Diners, Visa.

Melati

31 Peter St W1. 01-437 2011. **K 7**

Arguably the cheapest of Soho's Indonesian restaurants, Melati serves excellent, café-style Malaysian food. Solo diners are made welcome and it is possible to order a simple soup and noodles without the waiters getting annoyed. Service at Melati's is usually charming, much better than you'd find at some of Soho's inexpensive Chinese restaurants.

Since many people are unfamiliar with Indonesian food, the waiters are always keen to explain dishes and ensure that you don't over-order. The satay (beef and/or chicken), served with rice cakes and cucumber is usually delicious, but a trifle overpriced given the size of the portions. A consistent winner from the main courses is the kalio kental, chicken cooked in a coconut sauce. The mixed vegetables are also of a high standard; crisp, tasty and fresh.

> *Melati*
>
> *Open:* 12.00–14.45, 18.00–23.00 Mon–Sat. Closed Sun.
> *Booking:* Essential.
> *Food:* £12.00. *House wine:* £5.50.
> *Credit cards:* Access, Amex, Diners, Visa.

Mykonos

17 Frith St W1. 01-437 3603. **M 4**

A throwback to the period immediately after the war when Soho was *the* place to go for Greek food, Mykonos is an airy, traditional restaurant which offers the usual Greek specialities, plus a few extras. The vegetable moussaka, in particular, is well worth sampling. Otherwise, stick to dolmades (succulent and not at all greasy) or deep fried kalamares (tasty and unrubbery).

Lunchtime clientele is the usual mixture of Soho media execs out on expenses. Those who come here for dinner are more likely to have travelled into the area for a play or a film. Service is polished and friendly, even when waiters are confronted with a large party. This is a favourite venue for degenerate office functions: set meals can be ordered in advance and the boss usually receives a bottle of Metaxa as a public relations gesture at the end of the meal.

Mykonos

Open: 12.00–14.30, 17.30–23.30 Mon–Fri; 17.30–23.30 Sat. Closed Sun.
Booking: Essential for large parties.
Food: £11.00. *House wine:* £5.00.
Credit cards: Access, Amex, Diners, Visa.

Pasta Fino

27 Frith St W1. 01-439 8900. **N 7**

Acceptable if inauthentic pasta place with a useful late-night delicatessen upstairs. The pasta, made on the premises, is cooked well and served with a variety of interesting sauces, but no marks for ambience. The red-white-green decor is obviously designed to evoke an Italian trattoria but fails dismally. And the clientele – a ragbag of tourists and poseurs who'd probably feel more at home in Covent Garden than Soho – don't help.

However, service, carried out by camp waiters and cute

waitresses who look as though they might well be resting dancers, is fast and efficient and it's difficult to have a bad meal here. The food is far superior to that served in similar establishments elsewhere in Soho (Fatso's Pasta Joint on Old Compton Street for instance) and it can be spectacularly good. The puddings and sorbets in particular are enough to make you forget the naffness.

> *Pasta Fino*
>
> *Open:* 12.00–23.00 Mon–Sat. Closed Sun.
> *Booking:* Essential for large parties.
> *Food:* £7.00. *House wine:* £5.75.
> *Credit cards:* Access, Visa.

Pavilion

15 Poland St W1. 01-437 8774. **G 3**

When the Academy Cinema on Oxford Street showed its last film in 1986, movie buffs weren't the only people to mourn its demise. Regular customers of Vasco and Piero, the partnership who ran the Pavilion restaurant upstairs were equally disappointed. However, the pair soon found this alternative site less than a hundred yards from their previous restaurant; by the summer of 1987, they were back in business. Although the decor at the new Pavilion is less garish than that of its predecessor, everything else is much the same. The menus are still inventive, the service still courteous and the prices still excessive.

Very much a film industry 'canteen', the Pavilion has an amazingly loyal core of regulars who are prepared to pay the high prices for what they regard as well-above-average Italian food. The cuisine is quite unlike that served in Italian restaurants elsewhere in Soho. There are no trattoria clichés about the menu, the decor or the service; no obsequious waiters hovering over tables clutching pepper mills, no flasks of Chianti hanging from the ceiling and it is impossible to order spaghetti bolognese.

The menu changes once a day and it rarely features more

than one pasta dish. The sauces are always unusual (taglierini with cream and rucola – a salty herb – for instance) and serve as an excellent alternative to the standard trat fare. The main courses are dominated by seafood dishes (brochette of king prawns, bream in tomato and basil sauce) though carnivores can get their teeth into plainly cooked steaks and lamb if they wish. Portions are huge; regular customers have spare tyres to prove it. The pudding menu (spoken rather than written), however, may be disappointing. The profiteroles can seem a bit tired, the rest pretty ordinary. Opt for the magnificent zabaglione – you may have trouble persuading them to serve this at lunchtime but given the likely size of your bill you have every right to insist.

Pavilion

Open: 12.30–15.00, 18.00–23.00 Mon–Fri; 18.00–23.00 Sat. Closed Sun.
Booking: Advisable, especially at lunchtime.
Food: £20. *House wine:* £6.50.
Credit cards: Access, Amex, Diners, Visa.

La Perla

28 Brewer St W1. 01-437 2060. **J 8**

An Italian restaurant has stood on this site since the early 50s, and in the 10 years of its existence La Perla has managed to maintain the tradition of value for money and excellent service. The restaurant was redecorated in 1986 and although regulars bemoan the disappearance of the chrome and plastic booths which gave the place the appearance of a restaurant in New York's Little Italy, it is now much more comfortable. Unfortunately, the revamp has also meant that La Perla can become very crowded, particularly at lunchtime.

Soups and pasta are the best bet here if you want to keep the bill down. All the pasta (with the exception, curiously, of the spaghetti) is made on the premises and a plateful of tortellini or ravioli is usually enough to fill up even the most hungry diners. Those in need of further sustenance can always opt for a meat-and-two-veg-style main course; a wide selection of specials is available each day, and prices are very reasonable. Service is thoughtfully maternal without being obtrusive.

La Perla

Open: 12.00–15.00, 17.30–23.15 Mon–Sat. Closed Sun.
Booking: Advisable.
Food: £9.00. *House wine:* £4.95.
Credit cards: Access, Visa.

Pizza Express

10 Dean St W1. 01-437 9595. **L 3**

Any pizza enthusiast will concur that the Pizza Express chain offers easily the best and most authentic pizzas in London. They are crisp, imaginative and remarkably good value. This branch is as good as any in the chain; there is plenty of room, service is friendly and atmosphere relaxed. You have to like pizza though, since there are few alternatives. Puddings are disappointing: skip the gâteaux and make for one of Old Compton Street's patisseries. There you'll also find genuine cappuccino, an astonishing omission on Pizza Express's part.

The chain's owner, Peter Boizot, is one of the organisers of the annual Soho Jazz Festival and this is one of only a handful of venues in Soho offering live jazz all year round. Played in the basement, you will have to pay an extra charge if you sit down here. This can be quite steep, but the acts are usually of a high standard and the food is infinitely superior to Ronnie Scott's. The door policy, however, can be censorious. Groups of males, in particular, are often discouraged.

Pizza Express

Open: 11.30–24.00 Mon–Sun.
Booking: Essential for jazz room.
Food: £8.00. *House wine:* £5.25.
Entertainment: Jazz bands Tue–Sat evenings.
Credit cards: Not accepted.

Red Fort

77 Dean St W1. 01-437 2410. **L 5**

Red Fort, opened by Amin Ali, formerly part of the Camden Council-backed collective which set up Last Days of the Raj in Covent Garden, is now widely regarded as one of the best Indian restaurants in London. It's trendy too. Dedicated poseurs will insist on lingering in the bar for a cocktail before the meal. Here you get a great view of other diners, many of whom are famous or beautiful; the Red Fort has a loyal following among young Indian actresses with long lustrous locks and complexions as perfect as a Kashmir sunset.

The food is memorable. The Curry Club, a band of Indian food enthusiasts based in Haslemere, Surrey, puts the Red Fort in its Top Ten British Indian Restaurants. The menu is varied and imaginative. Fave treats at the Red Fort include momo (spicy minced meat parcels from Nepal) and quail dishes. In all, a first-rate restaurant which more than justifies its somewhat steep prices. Booking is essential if you don't want to be escorted to the rather dreary basement room. The action's upstairs.

Red Fort

Open: 12.00–14.45, 18.00–23.15 Mon–Sun.
Booking: Advisable.
Food: £18.00. *House wine:* £5.95.
Credit cards: Access, Amex, Diners, Visa.

Rasa Sayang

10 Frith St W1. 01-734 8720. **M 5**

Probably the best-known Singaporean restaurant in London, the Rasa Sayang is finding it hard to compete with the plethora of new-wave Indonesian and South East Asian eating houses currently springing up all over Soho.

The food is acceptable; satays and kalio kental are usually faultless but some of the seafood dishes are in need of attention. Nondescript chunks of fish swimming in a greasy chilli sauce cannot be anyone's idea of the perfect Singaporean meal. Most regular diners are either record producers or those who long to become record producers. They obviously find the kitsch, grotto-style decor appealing; no doubt those fibreglass stalactites and stalagmites looked very novel in 1973. Tourists are also drawn here, initially by the smart blue and white frontage and thereafter by the reasonable prices; the set meals are a good bet for those with no experience of Indonesian/ Malaysian food. They include a selection of the more unadventurous items from the main menu and a bottle of house wine.

Rasa Sayang

Open: 12.00–14.45, 18.00–22.45 Mon–Thur; 12.00–14.45, 18.00–23.45 Fri & Sat. Closed Sun.
Booking: Advisable at lunchtime.
Food: £12.00. *House wine:* £4.60.
Credit cards: Access, Amex, Diners, Visa.

Rugantino

26 Romilly St W1. 01-437 5302. **N 7**

Many of the family-run Italian restaurants in Soho have either closed down or sold out to the conglomerates. Not so Franco Carraro's Rugantino, which he opened in 1965; it remains a favourite with those after traditional Italian fare as it's been served in Soho since before the Second World War. The restaurant enjoys a reputation as one of Soho's more upmarket Italian eateries; its prices reflect this. However, standards are high: all ingredients are fresh and service is friendly without being fawning.

The menu, devised by Franco and his chef, is well thought out; dishes from all over Italy are included, although the emphasis is on Venetian specialities (Franco learned his trade at the Hotel Danieli in Venice) such as tonno con fagioli. The standard menu has the usual selection of ubiquitous Italian starters (melon with prosciutto, insalate tricolore) but those with more adventurous tastes are also catered for: try the fennel stuffed with spinach and cheese or the quail's eggs Fiorentina. The daily specials are also worth investigating; venison in thyme with a Guinness sauce is one of the more unusual dishes which crops up from time to time. Overall the accent is on large portions and rich sauces; this is not the place to take a calorie-conscious food faddist.

Although Rugantino has a firm following among local office workers, clients in the evening tend to be visitors, mainly theatre-goers. Many of them are tempted by Rugantino's fixed price menu which offers three courses. Do not be disheartened if the upstairs room seems chock-full, particularly after the theatres have turned out: there is usually space downstairs. Book if you'd prefer to sit upstairs (the upstairs room is much more attractive and offers a better view of Soho).

Rugantino

Open: 12.00–15.00, 18.00–23.30 Mon–Fri; 18.00–23.30 Sat. Closed Sun.
Food: £12.95. *House wine:* £5.25.
Credit cards: Access, Amex, Diners, Visa.

Saigon

45 Frith St W1. 01-437 7109. **M 6**

Saigon is one of the more upmarket Vietnamese restaurants in London. It is fashionable and does not resort to Far Eastern kitsch (traditional dancers etc) to pull in the punters. A cool, spacious building, this elegant restaurant is ideal for a romantic night out.

The food, in common with most establishments of this type, is fresh and very imaginative. Choose from a vast menu, which ranges from simple, familiar fare such as spring rolls stuffed with prawns and pork, to green papaya salad. Set meals are available at a reasonable price for those who prefer to entrust their palate to the management. The clientele is predominantly local media-types, always keen to demonstrate their knowledge of far-flung cuisines.

Saigon

Open: 12.00–23.30 Mon–Sat. Closed Sun.
Booking: Advisable.
Food: £9.50. *House wine:* £4.90.
Credit cards: Access, Amex, Diners, Visa.

Satay & Wine

10 Old Compton St W1. 01-437 3950. **O 6**

The unappealing frontage belies this restaurant's considerable charm. The menu is mainly made up of satay dishes (prawn, beef, lamb, chicken) but there is also a list of daily specials which includes interesting seafood dishes and fiery Malaysian soups. Service is impeccable. These premises were once the home of a short-lived Alsatian restaurant, and the present owners took over in the hope of cashing in on the popularity of Old Compton Street as an eating area. However, Satay & Wine is seldom full – quite surprising given the excellent quality of the food.

The basement is something of a curiosity, even in these parts. This is London's only Malaysian wine bar, and a great venue for a party. (Book a table or the whole bar.) Surroundings are not too plush, so any guests inclined towards moderate rowdiness shouldn't feel too intimidated. Wines are the usual mix of French, Italian and German, but it is possible to buy Singaporean Tiger beer. Only satay dishes are available in the wine bar.

Satay & Wine

Open: Restaurant 12.00–23.00 Mon–Sat. Closed Sun.
Wine bar 18.00–23.00 Thur, Fri & Sat only.
Booking: Advisable for large parties.
Food: £5.95 (set menu). *House wine:* £5.50.
Prices increase in evening.
Credit cards: Access, Amex, Diners, Visa.

Soho Pizzeria

16–18 Beak St W1. 01-434 2480. **E 8**

Useful pizza establishment at the quieter end of Beak Street. Restaurants in this part of Soho have a habit of closing down (the New Orleans Jazz Café was a notable casualty) but this one seems here to stay.

Formerly the Pizza Pomodoro, it offers the usual selection of Italian-style pizzas plus calzone (a pasty-shaped pizza made of folded-over dough). The salads are worthwhile too, and if pizzas pall, a daily pasta dish is available. Unforgivably, it is always made from dried rather than fresh pasta; anathema to anyone with a half-serious interest in Italian food.

Although some diners are drawn from the Regent Street shopping brigade, this is a favourite spot for local office-based media trendies who want to continue the evening after they've left the pub. Service is fast, efficient and friendly and there's a grand piano. Live music in the style of BillyJoel/Elton John/ Randy Newman is played every night from 8.30pm.

Soho Pizzeria

Open: 10.00–24.00 Mon–Sun.
Booking: Essential to reserve at lunchtime.
Food: £8.00. *House wine:* £5.95.
Entertainment: Live music every evening.
Credit cards: Access, Amex, Diners, Visa.

Soho Soho

11–13 Frith St W1. 01-494 3491. **M 6**

Formerly the home of tapestry-maker Joshua Morris, this is now the site of one of the most contrived eating houses in Soho. The tapestry which follows the stairs up to the restaurant is supposed to commemorate Morris's work (he was the best known of the 18th-century Soho tapestry-makers), and if we are to believe Soho Soho's handout, the paintings of famous Sohoites on the wall attempt 'to reflect Soho's deep artistic and French heritage'.

Soho Soho was set up in October 1987 by two former directors of Kennedy Brookes, the property and restaurant combine who conspired to revamp Braganza. This place is cast in the same mould. The exterior, in particular, is a triumph of tackiness; even the telephone number (494 exchange) is parvenu.

Food both in the restaurant, and in the wine bar downstairs is uninspiring. Choose from standard brasserie items (salads, terrines, roulades) or more overblown dishes such as the Aiguillette de Canard 'Soho Soho'; duck served with a demi-glace sauce and garnished with mousse of carrots.

The wine bar is open all afternoon for those who have the time, or the inclination, to linger. One can only hope that Soho Soho will get the customers it deserves.

Soho Soho

Open: Restaurant 12.00–15.00, 18.00–23.00 Mon–Fri; 18.00–23.30 Sat. Wine bar 11.30–23.00 Mon–Sat. Restaurant & wine bar closed Sun.
Food: £12.00. *House wine:* £6.00.
Credit cards: Access, Amex, Diners, Visa.

Le Tire Bouchon

6 Upper James St W1. 01-437 5348. **F 8**

A bustling, pretty bistro in a corner of Soho normally ignored by the discerning gastronome. Tire Bouchon is phenomenally popular with executives from Granada Television (office on Golden Square), publishing people and the occasional journalist on expenses. Food is reliable brasserie fare such as cassoulet, salade niçoise, or Toulouse sausages plus more elaborate dishes of the day. A meal here seldom disappoints.

At lunchtime booking is essential, since this cosy but cramped little restaurant fills up fast. The best tables are those at the window which afford a splendid view of those poseurs who pointedly stroll past after they've had their hair cut next door. Service is efficient, but genuinely Gallic, the white-aproned waiters are in no doubt about their station in life. Although the dishes are robust and very filling, it's worth leaving room for some cheese. The selection is truly comprehensive; it is unlikely that you will find a better range of French fromage anywhere in London.

Tire Bouchon's early closing times mean that it is not somewhere to go for a long, leisurely dinner. However, soup, salad and an assiette de charcuterie would make for an excellent pre-theatre supper. And if you're up early enough they'll also serve breakfast: croissant, pain au chocolat and brioche; smoked salmon or bacon and scrambled eggs with lots of good strong coffee and orange juice.

Le Tire Bouchon

Open: 08.00–21.30 Mon–Fri. Closed Sat & Sun.
Booking: Advisable.
Food: £10.00. *House wine:* £5.80.
Credit cards: Access, Amex, Diners, Visa.

Topo Gigio

46 Brewer St W1. 01-437 8516. **H 9**

Cavernous basement restaurant, much favoured by the admen. Bustling atmosphere at lunchtime gives way to a more restrained, laid-back pace in the evening. Popular with foreign tourists, particularly Americans, who seem to appreciate the waiters' efforts to please. It's a shame that the food is unremarkable. Topo Gigio is afflicted with an extraordinarily long menu. The problem with this type of all-encompassing establishment is that the food can never be as fresh as you might find in a restaurant with a shorter menu. The huge range of fish dishes, for instance, suggests that the owner of the Topo Gigio is also the owner of a very large deep freeze. And although the prices charged here are cheaper than those of the grander Italian restaurants in Soho, for frozen food they are a bit steep.

Obviously some ingredients are fresh: the pasta, for instance, is of a high standard and vegetables (which, maddeningly, are charged for individually) are usually tasty and not overcooked. The daily specials are normally a safe bet too. Salads, however, can look distinctly tired, and by the end of the evening the pudding trolley is in need of a refit. Cappuccino and espresso are acceptable.

Topo Gigio

Open: 12.00–23.30 Mon–Sun.
Booking: Essential for large parties.
Food: £10. *House wine:* £5.70.
Credit cards: Access, Amex, Diners, Visa.

Van Long

40 Frith St W1. 01-434 3772. **N 7**

Formerly Nam Long, the restaurant changed its name in 1987 after the chef's wife gave birth to a baby daughter which they called Van. An elegant, attractive Vietnamese restaurant, Van Long is typical of the well-thought-out, new-wave of South East Asian eating houses which have caught the imagination of trendy London foodies.

This establishment is particularly popular with post-Big Bangers from the City anxious to spend some of the proceeds of their latest Golden Hello. (Two varieties of champagne are available.) The modern prints on the walls also reflect yuppie taste; like muzak, they merge into the background. The service, though helpful, is perhaps a little too anodyne and matches the soft pastels of the decor. Unless you request chopsticks, you'll be given a spoon and fork.

The menu is extraordinarily long, but those bewildered by the sheer variety can always opt for one of the set menus. The set seafood menu is a good bet, but beware, the food is deceptively filling; what seems to be a paltry portion would usually satisfy all but the hungriest of diners. At lunchtime a special, cheaper, set meal is available with optional soups.

The food here is rarely disappointing. Many of the dishes utilise herbs native to Vietnam but now grown here. Lemon grass, in particular, is a favourite; the golden crispy fish with lemon grass in a pancake with pickles and cucumber is widely regarded as Van Long's pièce de résistance. That alone is a good enough reason to come here, but do try the hot and sour fish soup and the beef with scallions and lemon grass as well.

Van Long

Open: 12.00–15.00, 18.00–23.15 Mon–Sun.
Food: £12.00. *House wine:* £5.00.
Credit cards: Access, Amex, Diners, Visa.

Verde Valle

74 Wardour St W1. 01-437 3519. **K 6**

Cosy, old-fashioned Italian restaurant which might be suitable for an intimate meal for two if the tables weren't so close together. Standard range of anglicised Italian food: pastas, veal dishes, steak and fish. The minestrone and ravioli in brodo are noticeably good and it is usually worth trying one of the daily specials.

A few tourists venture here in the evenings after a visit to the theatre or one of the cinemas on Leicester Square, but otherwise it's strictly for the locals, mainly the expense account set from Wardour Street's film cutting and editing rooms. At lunchtime in particular, the small dining room can become very crowded; booking is advisable. Prices are reasonable, but for an economy meal, stick to the pasta. Do leave room, though, for VV's excellent zabaglione and a cappuccino or espresso.

Verde Valle

Open: 12.00–15.00, 18.00–23.30 Mon–Fri; 18.00–23.30 Sat. Closed Sun.
Booking: Advisable at lunchtime.
Food: £12.00. *House wine:* £5.00.
Credit cards: Access, Amex, Diners, Visa.

Wheeler's

19–21 Old Compton St W1. 01-437 2706. **O 6**

This was always the most louche of the Wheeler's chain of fish restaurants, established in London in 1856. As much a part of the 1950s Soho scene as the York Minster and the 2 i's, Wheeler's no longer attracts the fashionable and the bohemian; possibly because the food is no longer what it was.

The Wheeler's chain was recently taken over by Kennedy Brookes, a London-wide restaurant combine which is expanding at an alarming rate. Although Kennedy Brookes turned Braganza (formerly part of the Wheeler's chain) into something which looks more like a branch of Next for Men, they haven't interfered much with this place. Much of the original design remains the same, and thankfully the oyster bar is still intact. The oysters just about make a visit to Wheeler's worthwhile; they are always fresh (the company has its own oyster beds) and there are a number of sizes to choose from. However, the sauces with which the sole and lobster are served are often uninspired, so it may be best to order your fish plain.

Bon Viveur in London, a restaurant guide published in the 50s, contained a paean to Wheeler's of Old Compton Street, conjuring up a delightful post-war image of what was then one of Soho's best and most-loved restaurants: 'This is a temple devoted to shell fish . . . Oysters in season are whipped open, hundreds to the hour, by Jack, once a wrestler, now a renowned oyster opener. In the cool, quiet interior oyster lovers consume dozens, excellent and fresh . . .' Unfortunately, few restaurant critics today would be prepared to offer praise half as fulsome. Wheeler's is well and truly out; it's about time Kennedy Brookes did something about it.

Wheeler's

Open: 12.30–14.30, 18.00–23.15 Mon–Sat; 12.30–14.30; 18.30–22.00 Sun.
Booking: Advisable.
Food: £16.00. *House wine:* £6.50.
Credit cards: Access, Amex, Diners, Visa.

CAFÉS AND BRASSERIES

Bar Italia

N 6

22 Frith St W1. 01-437 4520. A glorious establishment and easily the most authentic Italian café in Soho. Unfortunately our idiotic licensing laws prevent the sale of alcohol. If it were possible to buy an Amaretto, a Peroni or a Campari here no Sohoite would ever need take a holiday in Italy. Clientele is 90 per cent Italian, 10 per cent trendy. During the season, satellite broadcasts of Italian football matches are shown every Sunday on the huge TV screen which dominates one end of the bar. This is Italian Soho at its most vibrant.

Bar Italia has been run by the Polledri family since 1950. Originally the customers all came from Soho, but now that Soho's Italian population has decreased and the community has spread itself across London, many of the regulars come in from elsewhere. The decor and atmosphere, however, have changed little since the 50s. The original mirrored walls are a narcissist's dream and Rocky Marciano still stares aggressively down from one wall. (The poster was borrowed by the producers of *Absolute Beginners*, who used it in the film, along with a mock-up of the café's exterior.) Bar Italia has always attracted a low-life element; this adds to its charm, but Tony Polledri knows where to draw the line. A sign, in Italian, on the wall beneath the Marciano poster reminds customers that undesirables will be ejected for 'any reason or no reason'. *Open 07.00–23.00 Mon–Sun.* No credit cards.

Barocco Espresso Bar **O 6**

13 Moor St W1. 01-437 2324. Tiny family-run café specialising in very cheap pasta and very strong espresso. Cramped, but cosy, Barocco is ideal for a pre-theatre light meal or a fast solo lunch. Standard range of pastas, are available but don't expect superlative food; the Barocco is run on very tight profit margins. However, the home-made minestrone is delicious and the trifle sensational. As they don't have a licence, a meal here may turn out to be cheaper than anywhere else in Soho. If you like, bring your own wine or beer; Barocco's friendly waitress will gladly supply glasses. There is no charge for corkage. *Open 12.00–23.00 Mon–Sat. Closed Sun.* No credit cards.

Ed's Easy Diner **O 6**

12 Moor St W1. 01-439 1955. An authentic American diner right down to the tabletop jukeboxes which allow 50s nostalgia freaks to play The Chiffons all evening if they feel so inclined. Ed's opened at the end of 1987 on a prime site at the end of Old Compton Street previously occupied by a series of greasy

burger bars. The menu, while still burger-dominated, is immeasurably superior to its predecessors, fries are crisp, salads are fresh and the burgers are about the best in Soho. This is definitely a fast-food joint with only limited seating and diners are not encouraged to linger over their American beers, but it would be a shame to leave without sampling the superb pecan pie. Be warned though, the extras can certainly bump up the bill. *Open 11.30–24.00 Mon–Thur & Sun, 11.30–01.00 Fri & Sat.* No credit cards.

Harry's D 7

19 Kingly St W1. 01-734 3140. Celebrated Soho café, and the only all-nighter in the area. Harry's is decked out in posters of contemporary Americana, but is far too clean to offer even a reasonable impression of a Stateside roadhouse. The walls, floors and boring furniture are spotless. In fact the only discomfort is the atmosphere; Harry's can get very stuffy indeed.

Night-time clientele includes taxi-drivers, nightclubbers, policemen and insomniacs. The smoked salmon and scrambled eggs served here are a legendary pick-me-up. And after a night at the Valbonne across the road, you'll need one. The rest of the breakfasts (mainly fry-ups), served throughout the night, are not-half-bad either. *Open 21.30–16.00 every day/night except Sun.* No credit cards.

Maison Bertaux O 7

28 Greek St W1. 01-437 6007. Genteel French patisserie which has served coffee and cakes here since the late 19th century. This establishment has the feel of those refined coffee shops run by fearsome madames in little market towns in rural France. Tables, chairs and counters are always disconcertingly spotless. The pace is a lot less frenetic and the atmosphere much less pretentious than many of Soho's cafés. *Open 09.00–18.00 Tue–Sat, (09.30–13.00 Sun, take-aways only). Closed Mon.* No credit cards.

New Piccadilly

J 11

8 Denman St W1. 01-437 8530. Authentic 50s diner as yet uninvaded by Soho's trendier fraternity. However, given the popularity of Bakelite telephones and baseball caps, it is surely only a matter of time before they stake their claim.

Like many of the smaller, unpretentious little cafés in Soho, New Piccadilly offers excellent value, and you are encouraged to bring your own booze (no corkage charge). Standard range of grills and fry-ups plus Italian specials such as basic spaghetti and lasagne. Furniture – wipe-clean booths in bright red plastic and Formica-topped tables – is straight out of *American Graffiti*. It is a shame that they haven't got round to installing a Wurlitzer. *Open 10.00–22.00 Mon–Sun.* No credit cards.

Pasticceria Cappucetto

O 6

8–9 Moor St W1. 01-437 9472. Busy, bustling Soho café overshadowed somewhat by Patisserie Valerie but still worth a visit for the pastries. Service can be a little irksome and the two rooms a little crowded. If it gets too hot, order an ice cream. This is one of the few places in Soho where you can buy a proper Italian-style cone. Clientele more touristy than trendy, largely because of the café's proximity to the Palace Theatre. *Open 07.30–20.00 Mon–Sat. Closed Sun.* No credit cards.

Patisserie Valerie

N 8

44 Old Compton St W1. 01-437 3466. Famous Hungarian-owned café, long-established as a favourite place for romantic trysts over breakfast. The stark wooden tables and chairs make for an atmosphere redolent of one of the more bohemian cafés in Madrid or Paris. Unfortunately, the croissants are greasy and flavourless. Opt for a slice of toast instead, or, if you have a strong stomach at 9am, one of Patisserie Valerie's superb cakes. A selection is placed on each table and you tell your waitress what you've consumed when you leave. The authentic Continental atmosphere extends to the preserves which are charged for by the tiny portion.

Overall, Pat Val's is strong on ambience but weak on value. Even the coffee is insipid. All cakes, including large ones suitable for celebrations, can be bought to take away. *Open 08.30–19.00 Mon–Sat. Closed Sun.* No credit cards.

Phil Rabin's Salt Beef Bar J 10

39 Great Windmill St W1. 01-434 9913. Phil Rabin opened his restaurant here in 1944; although it was much patronised in its heyday by artistes, staff and audiences from the Windmill Theatre, this charming establishment is no longer fashionable. It is to be hoped that it will not go the same way as two other Great Windmill Street salt beef bars – Carroll's and the Nosh Bar (a favourite haunt of the boxers who trained in Jack Solomon's gym).

This restaurant is Soho's equivalent of Katz's, the Jewish deli in New York. Here, as there, you are guaranteed to strike up a conversation with your fellow diners the moment you walk through the somewhat scruffy front door. Although Rabin's has not achieved as much international fame as Katz's its sandwiches are known way beyond the bounds of the parish of St James.

Available on rye, brown or Mother's Pride white, Rabin's salt beef is an essential ingredient of any gastronomic tour of Soho. Eat it plain, with mustard, pickled cucumber (sweet and sour or haimische), a mixed salad or coleslaw. Other Jewish specialities are also available – gefilte fish, matzos, lockshen pudding etc – but surprisingly Rabin's is not recognised by the Beth Din authorities as a kosher restaurant. This is partly because Rabin's has never applied for a licence and partly because they serve milk with meat. *Open 11.00–23.00 Mon–Sat, 11.00–22.30 Sun.* No credit cards.

Pho M 10

2 Lisle St W1. 01-437 8265. Tiny Vietnamese café serving unusual snacks, lunches and dinners. Fast service, cheap prices. Surroundings can seem a little cramped, but good-value food, in particular the spicy Singaporean-style noodle dishes,

makes a visit worthwhile. The Vietnamese spring rolls should also be sampled. Unlicensed, but the Falcon and Blue Posts are both nearby. *Open 12.00–22.00 Mon–Sat, 11.00–22.00 Sun.* No credit cards.

Pollo **O 6**

20 Old Compton St W1. 01-734 5917. Quintessential Soho café, busy and bohemian and usually full of arty poseurs from Saint Martin's on Charing Cross Road. Over the last few years, this café has developed something of a cult following among young Soho trendies which makes it very difficult for anyone else to get a seat, particularly in the evening. The booths downstairs are usually the best bet.

Pollo's food is at best acceptable, at worst appalling. A good guide is that the pasta dishes are far superior to the more expensive chicken cordon bleu/veal escalope-type numbers. Avoid the salads unless you are particularly fond of limp lettuce and tired tomatoes. Despite its erratic quality, the food at Pollo's is normally wolfed down (and seldom sent back) by the hep cats who hang out here.

For atmosphere, and the chance to immerse yourself in 50s nostalgia (espresso is served in authentic low slung Pyrex cups) Pollo's can't be beaten. But if you are at all interested in food, head elsewhere. *Open 09.00–23.30 Mon–Sat. Closed Sun.* No credit cards.

Star Café **K 2**

22b Great Chapel St W1. 01-437 8778. Inexpensive Soho institution, presided over by Mario Forte (emphatically no relation). The Star Café is one of the best traditional cafés in the area: its breakfast fry-ups are a delight (those watching their cholesterol levels can opt for muesli instead) and at lunchtime the grills and salads are complemented by a selection of fresh daily specials. These might include boeuf bourguignon, spaghetti bolognese or leeks with ham and cheese sauce.

The small upstairs dining room leads down to a basement

section which can usually be relied upon to provide seats. Turnover is high, so you shouldn't have to wait long anyway. Clientele is a typical mixture of new and old Soho. The Star is popular with local shopkeepers and tradesmen and the media-men always turn out in force. (Unusually for a café, the Star is licensed, which may help to explain the attraction.) The film business in particular, is well represented here: copies of *Screen International* as well as *Campaign* and most of the national dailies are available for the use of patrons. *Open 07.00–16.30 Mon–Fri. Closed Sat & Sun.* No credit cards.

Soho Brasserie — N 6

23–25 Old Compton St W1. 01-439 9301. This symbol of new Soho opened in 1984 on the site of the Helvetia pub. An unashamed poseur's paradise, the Brasserie attracts a ragbag clientele, ranging from impecunious students from St Martin's School of Art who will spin one drink out over an evening, to international jetsetters who settle their dinner bills with gold Amex cards. But is all the fuss justified? In its early days, the Brasserie was of interest because it numbered genuine celebs (Jagger came here) among its regulars. Yet now it seems a shadow of its former self, almost as passé as the Hippodrome round the corner.

The food has always been acceptable but seldom spectacular. The fish dishes are usually inventive (Soho is lacking a serious, modern fish restaurant) but the rest of the menu seems strangely predictable, a kind of cobbled together encyclopaedia of trendy eating. How many brasseries these days don't offer fresh pasta, poached eggs, mozzarella salads and French sausages? The decor and fittings are equally clichéd, right down to the stainless steel beer pump on the bar. You will not find many French people drinking here and even the waiters tend to have Preston rather than Parisian accents.

Prices, inevitably, are high. But you may consider them worth it if you manage to bag a seat in the window. These offer a prime vantage point from which to view Old Compton Street, plus a chance to look languid in the process. *Open 10.00–23.30 Mon–Sat. Closed Sun.* Access, Amex, Diners, Visa.

4 Drinking

In the last five years, the drinking scene in Soho has changed dramatically. Many of the seedier bars in which down-at-heel bohemians shared rounds with out-and-out gangsters have disappeared, to be replaced by thickly-carpeted 'theme' pubs, all part of the corporate plans put into motion by the breweries' marketing departments. Some drinking houses, such as the French on Dean Street and the Coach & Horses on Greek Street retain a raffish clientele, still given to splurging the last of their cash on a half bottle of Mumm. The hangover is overcome the next morning with an espresso at the Bar Italia.

The rest, however, have fostered a new generation of Soho habitué: the bright, upwardly mobile under 30s who work locally in advertising, journalism, graphic design or all three. You'll spot this type, Filofax in one hand, spritzer in the other at the Soho Brasserie on Old Compton Street. It seems impossible-

ible for anyone else to get a table in the window. To them, Dylan Thomas was the author of a set book on the A-level syllabus, not a fellow drinker at the French.

Although Soho has lost a large number of its characters – its watering holes may have something to do with that – the area still has plenty to offer the discerning drinker. The beer, thanks to the efforts of the Campaign for Real Ale, has improved immeasurably. And it's now possible for a lone woman to order a drink in a wine bar (if not one of the local pubs) without being disturbed by reprobate males unsatisfied by the local peep shows.

And then there are the clubs. You'll need friends in the demi-monde if you wish to drink at one of the handful of establishments which serve alcohol in the afternoons; if you don't you may just get in at one of the new-style membership clubs. Tell them you're in publishing.

PUBS

Admiral Duncan

54 Old Compton St W1. 01-437 5300. **L 7**

Nautical kitsch is the theme of this friendly Younger's house, one of four in the immediate vicinity; the long, low-ceilinged, wood-panelled bar resembles the deck of an 18th-century warship. Fortunately, the bar staff don't have to wear sailor suits. Although the staff are helpful, the pub always seems very dark and can make for a very depressing night out. Head here if you wish to wallow in self-pity. Food OK, but very much in the curry/chilli/cottage pie mould.

Admiral Duncan

Open: 11.00–15.00, 17.30–23.00 Mon–Fri; 11.00–15.00, 18.30–23.00 Sat; 19.00–22.30 Sun.
Brewery: William Younger.
Beer: IPA, Younger's.
Food: Bar snacks and meals lunchtime and evening.

Argyll Arms

18 Argyll St W1. 01-734 6117. **C 2**

On the northernmost fringe of Soho just south of Oxford Street, this establishment offers a contrast to the tin-pot take-aways, ropey restaurants and plastic pubs which have made Argyll Street one of the most unappealing thoroughfares in the area.

The Argyll is a triumph of Victorian pub architecture, which its owners have left more or less intact; most of the fittings are original including the carefully-preserved plasterwork on the ceilings. Their good taste, however, does not extend to the uniform they've chosen for their bar staff. They have to dress up in silly Highland waistcoats and dresses of Argyll tartan.

It can get crowded early in the evenings with suburban theatregoers who've come up for a show at the Palladium. However, they usually down their sherries by about half past seven, thus making room for more serious drinkers. Five real ales are available in the downstairs bar. The upstairs Palladium Bar is more sedate (pint glasses not allowed) and less busy than the two bars downstairs; its sofas are good for relaxing on. The food, much of it microwaved, is acceptable, but if you choose to eat upstairs you'll have to take it up yourself.

Argyll Arms

Open: 11.00–15.00, 17.30–23.00 Mon–Sat. Closed Sun.
Brewery: Free House.
Beer: Dorset IPA, Charrington IPA, Tetley's, Adnam's Southwold, Wadworth 6X, Boddingtons.
Food: Meals and snacks lunchtime and evening.

Bath-House

96 Dean St W1. 01-437 3805. **K 2**

Formerly the Sound & Vision, there has in fact been a pub here since 1738. Also previously known as the Bath House, the Green Man and the French Horn, its present incarnation came about because the owners, Whitbread Inns, had been unhappy about the clientele the pub had been attracting and felt a change of name and image was necessary. The marketing department aimed to transform a rather seedy Soho hostelry, much frequented by those in the lower echelons of the music industry, into a wholesome, family establishment in which you could happily buy your granny a pre-theatre sherry.

Unfortunately the brewery's choice of name was not entirely appropriate. Although reviving one of the former appellations – Bath House was a Georgian mansion on Piccadilly which had given its name to an earlier pub on this site – they overlooked the present-day connotations of the word. In North American cities, 'bath-houses' are notorious homosexual pick-up joints.

The new interior is standard brewery mock-Victorian. Not bad for a quick drink after work (it doesn't get too crowded) but the taped middle-of-the-road chart hits grate after a while. Fellow-drinkers will be predominantly lower-to-middle management – spot the suits from Burton's – plus shoppers seeking respite from the Oxford Street scrum.

Food is very imaginative for a pub of this type. The emphasis is on home-cooked, healthy fare and at least one vegetarian dish is available each day. The upstairs wine bar (even more chintzy than the pub) is open only at lunchtimes, but is available for hire in the evenings.

Bath-House

Open: 11.00–15.00, 17.30–23.00 Mon–Sat. Closed Sun.
Brewery: Whitbread.
Beer: Flower's, Wethered.
Food: Large selection always available.

Blue Posts

22 Berwick St W1. 01-437 5008. **J 5**

There are three 'Blue Posts' pubs in Soho, each named after the blue posts which stood outside taverns in the 18th century to advertise the local sedan chair service, which would pick up from there.

Of the trio, the Berwick Street pub has perhaps the most loyal regulars. At lunchtimes the majority of drinkers occupying the tables which surround the small bar are from Wardour Street's filmland; this is the place to come if you want work as a lighting technician, a production assistant or even as an extra. Deals are struck over large gin and tonics; some of the mini-moguls who come here bring their secretaries who make notes of technicians' names on booking sheets. No union card, however, means no job. In the evenings, particularly on Saturdays, the pub is often deserted. At least you can find a seat without being elbowed in the ribs by a cheroot-puffing sound-recordist, but the atmosphere is not the same.

Blue Posts

Open: 11.00–15.00, 17.30–23.00 Mon–Sat; 12.00–14.00, 19.00–22.30 Sun (summer only).
Brewery: Watney Combe Reid Truman.
Beer: Yorkshire, Combes.
Food: Snacks always available.

Blue Posts

28 Ganton St W1. No phone. **E 6**

Smallest and least interesting of the three pubs in Soho which bear this name. Catering predominantly for the tourist trade, the pub enjoys the patronage of countless Burberry-clad Americans throughout the year, all clutching, it seems, Hamley's carrier bags. However, there are a reasonable number of local regulars and of a winter's night it can be quite cosy. Food is always freshly made and above par for pub fare.

Blue Posts

Open: 11.00–14.00, 17.30–23.00 Mon–Fri; 11.00–14.00, 17.30–21.00 Sat. Closed Sun.
Brewery: Whitbread.
Beer: Brakspear's, Flower's.
Food: Meals and snacks lunchtime and evening.

Blue Posts

28 Rupert St W1. 01-437 1415. **L 10**

Unusual atmosphere and decor harking back to the Soho of the 50s. The interior is reminiscent of a set from the film *Dance With a Stranger*. After a gin and tonic or three, it's quite possible to imagine a young blonde strolling across the bar in seamed silk stockings to dispense cigarettes from a tray hanging from her neck. Indeed the upstairs bar was the scene of many a dispute involving local spivs and their molls in the 50s.

There is an exceptional selection of drinks including, in winter, hot toddies and hot buttered rum (made on the premises from a recipe which includes cloves and spices) and glühwein. Proper cocktails are also available, at a very reasonable price. You won't find fruit salad-laden, arriviste aberrations like pina coladas or Harvey Wallbangers on the list, but the bar staff do churn out an excellent dry martini. Good, home-cooked food also helps to pull in the punters, many of whom are a little older than the average Soho pubgoer. They've been using this establishment for years. The Saturday lunchtime session is particularly popular with West End shoppers, so get there early.

Blue Posts

Open: 11.00–15.00, 17.30–23.00 Mon–Sat. Closed Sun.
Brewery: Whitbread.
Beer: Trophy, Tankard.
Food: Available lunchtime and evening.

Carlisle Arms

2 Bateman St W1. No phone. **N 5**

The Carlisle Arms has been here since 1752 and is presumed to be named after the 2nd Earl of Carlisle who occupied Carlisle House in Soho Square at the beginning of the 18th century.

A cosy, snug little pub, the Carlisle has an unusual semi-circular bar which is usually embellished with a vaseful of fresh flowers. Very popular with film-makers and those in advertising, the pub is usually packed solid at lunchtime but empty in the evenings. The sandwiches are very acceptable but there aren't enough bar stools.

> *Carlisle Arms*
>
> *Open:* 11.00–15.00, 17.30–23.00 Mon–Sat; 12.00–14.00, 19.00–22.30 Sun.
> *Brewery:* Charrington.
> *Beer:* Bass, IPA.
> *Food:* Snacks available lunchtime and evening.

The Clachan

34 Kingly St W1. 01-734 2659. **C 5**

A splendid Victorian wooden bar dominates this otherwise boring pub, recently given a revamp by Nicholson's, owners of the Argyll Arms. Now even more of an eyesore than it once was; three different types of floral wallpaper combine with a heavily-patterned carpet to produce an almost painful overall effect. Apart from the bar itself and an electronic trivia game in one corner, The Clachan has little to recommend it.

> *The Clachan*
>
> *Open:* 11.00–15.00, 17.30–23.00 Mon–Sat; 12.00–14.00, 19.00–22.30 Sun.
> *Brewery:* Free House (Nicholson's).
> *Beer:* Taylor Walker, Burton, Tetley, Adnam's, Friary Meux, Marston's Pedigree, Boddington's.
> *Food:* Meals and snacks lunchtime and evening.

Coach & Horses

1 Great Marlborough St W1. 01-437 3282. **D 4**

Overshadowed by Norman Balon's 'mediapub', this Coach & Horses is nonetheless of historical interest. Built in 1739, it was originally a vintner's shop before being converted into a pub in 1750. In 1768 the pub was rebuilt and many of the external features still survive. The four-storeyed frontage is considered to be of particular architectural merit. Until the early part of the 19th century it was also used as an improvised courthouse, trying those accused of committing petty crimes.

The Coach & Horses is now typical of many pubs in and around the north-west corner of Soho, with a small bar and two sections of seating. On weeknights it usually reverberates with post-office bonhomie, but is dead at weekends. The upstairs 'wine bar' is available for private parties and darts matches. Very handy for Marks & Spencer; the food is as good as the beer.

Coach & Horses

Open: 11.00–15.00, 17.30–23.00 Mon–Sat. Closed Sun.
Brewery: Whitbread.
Beer: Wethered, Flower's, Castle Eden, Abbot Ale.
Food: Meals and snacks available lunchtimes only.

Coach & Horses

29 Greek St W1. 01-437 5920. **O 7**

A celebrated Soho institution, noted not least for the extraordinary behaviour of its landlord, Norman Balon. Balon, a tall, gaunt Walter Matthau-look-alike, has presided over the Coach for more than 20 years. His tyrannical rule over staff and customers has earned him a reputation as London's rudest landlord. For sevenpence, he will sell you a box of matches bearing just that description.

It is not advisable to ask Norman for a drink, change for cigarettes or even the loan of a telephone book. With Norman, everything is too much bother. Even some of the regulars would sooner shuffle around the bar without a drink than catch the Great Man's eye.

In spite of Norman's manners, the Coach is extremely popular and over the years has built up a reputation as the

literati's local. The offices of *Private Eye* used to be on Greek Street (though they have since moved to Carlisle Street) and for some time the '*Private Eye* lunch' has been held fortnightly in Norman's upstairs restaurant. In publishing circles, an invitation to this event is probably more prized than a lifetime's membership of the Groucho Club. Women are rarely invited (gorgeous, pouting Tina Brown, then of *The Tatler*, was a notable exception) and the atmosphere is redolent of the common room of a boys' public school. The more interesting politicians of the day are frequent invitees and occasionally the bonhomie causes them to commit the odd indiscretion. It was at a *Private Eye* lunch that Richard Crossman, a former Labour cabinet minister, confirmed to Auberon Waugh that he and Hugh Gaitskell had committed perjury in a celebrated 1950s libel case.

The Coach has a coterie of well-known regulars, including veteran Soho habitué Jeffery Bernard who often writes about the pub in his weekly *Spectator* column. Bernard, who was convicted of running an illegal book from the Coach & Horses in 1986, still drinks here and always features, albeit only by name, in Michael Heath's *Private Eye* strip cartoon 'The Regulars'.

Coach & Horses

Open: 11.00–15.00, 17.30–23.00 Mon–Sat; 12.00–14.00, 19.00–22.30 Sun.
Brewery: Taylor Walker.
Beer: Taylor Walker, Burton.
Food: Meals and snacks available lunchtime only.

Comptons

52–53 Old Compton St W1. 01-437 4445. **L 7**

Formerly known as the Swiss Tavern and, until it was tarted up by the brewery in 1986 at a cost of £80,000, had a clientele largely made up of local lowlifes. When the pub reopened as Comptons, two bouncers were on the door to ensure that the rougher elements took their custom elsewhere.

Inevitably, the atmosphere has changed. It lacks the scruffiness which made the Swiss so appealing. But the bar staff are friendly, and new manager Jack Fuller, formerly guv'nor at the Golden Lion, has brought some of the Lion's regulars with him. Comptons is almost a gay pub but not quite; straights should not feel intimidated.

The building is Georgian and was originally a hotel, which Richard Wagner used when he began work on *The Flying Dutchman*. Nobody knows which room he stayed in, but if it was on the third floor it would have been destroyed by the composer's compatriots during the Blitz.

> *Comptons*
>
> *Open:* 11.00–15.00, 17.30–23.00 Mon–Sat; 12.00–14.00, 19.00–22.30 Sun.
> *Brewery:* Charrington.
> *Beer:* Bass, IPA.
> *Food:* Meals at lunchtime, snacks in the evening.

The Crown

64 Brewer St W1. 01-734 0466. **G 10**

Noisy, crowded pub popular with locals and more discerning admen. The Crown has a scruffy, authentic charm and its large ground floor bar with food counter at the back serves as a useful haven after a Brewer Street shopping spree or before a visit to the theatre. Food is home-cooked, imaginative and represents excellent value for money. A vast collection of wartime memorabilia and old newspapers decorate the walls and offers the solo drinker a welcome diversion. It is possible to play darts here, but the board, like many in Soho, is regarded as the preserve of the regulars.

> *The Crown*
>
> *Open:* 11.00–15.00, 17.30–23.00 Mon–Sat; 19.00–22.30 Sun.
> *Brewery:* Charrington.
> *Beer:* Bass, IPA.
> *Food:* Snacks and meals available every lunchtime and some evenings.

Crown & Two Chairmen

32 Dean St W1. 01-437 8192. **M 5**

This pub owes its unusual name to the fact that it stands opposite the site of a studio in which Sir James Thornhill (father-in-law of William Hogarth) painted Queen Anne. She was brought to Soho by sedan chair and her two bearers would repair to this pub for refreshment. Let us hope that the hostelry offered them a little more atmosphere then than it does now. Owned by Clifton Inns, it has suffered as a result of corporate bad taste; decor is wildly over the top and ghastly piped music blares out continually. However, food is reasonably priced and home cooked by the manager's wife. It is perhaps surprising that Clifton Inns have not replaced her with a bank of vending machines.

Crown & Two Chairmen

Open: 11.00–15.00, 17.30–23.00 Mon–Sat; 12.00–14.00, 19.00–22.30 Sun.
Brewery: Free House (Clifton Inns).
Beer: Taylor Walker, Friary Meux, Burton.
Food: Meals and snacks lunchtime and evening.

De Hems

11 Macclesfield St W1. 01-437 2494. **M 9**

During the Second World War, this pub served as a refuge for members of the Dutch Resistance staying in London. They slept in rooms on the first floor which have since become a venue for parties and other functions. Formerly the Macclesfield Tavern, the pub took its present name from the Dutchman who ran it until the 1960s. Under Mr De Hems, it enjoyed a reputation for good seafood; oysters used to be served at the food bar on the ground floor.

In the 70s, however, De Hems degenerated and became extremely seedy. At lunchtime, the large red banquettes would be strewn with semi-comatose gentlemen of the road. In the evenings, loutish Glaswegians would dominate the proceedings, much to the bewilderment of the small groups of middle-aged Dutch businessmen who occasionally returned to the pub for old times' sake.

Eventually, the brewery took action. In 1986, the pub was gutted in a renovation which took six months and cost a quarter of a million. The idea was to reproduce the atmosphere of a traditional, tobacco-stained Dutch bar. Perhaps the designers have gone a little far with the prints (a cheap reproduction of virtually every well-known Dutch old master can be found on the walls) but full marks for effort. De Hems is the only pub in Britain which offers genuine imported Oranjeboom lager (everyone else sells the inferior, British-brewed version) and it must be one of the few places in London serving Dutch snacks such as hareng (rollmops) and smoked eels.

De Hems

Open: 11.00–15.00, 17.30–23.00 Mon–Sat; 12.00–14.00, 19.00–22.30 Sun.
Brewery: Ind Coope.
Beer: Taylor Walker, Tetley's, Burton.
Food: Snacks and meals until 22.30 each day.

Devonshire Arms

17 Denman St W1. 01-437 2445. **H 10**

Another Clifton Inn, designed to satisfy a passing tourist's perception of what a traditional London pub should look like. There is sawdust on the floor, real ale in the pump and enough olde worlde brasswork to dazzle the patrons at 20 yards.

However, this is a well-run house, with an exceptionally affable landlord, who takes a keen interest in the running of his pub. Lavatories, for instance, are squeaky clean and the food, if predictable, is very acceptable for the price. In winter, drinkers are encouraged to sample the hot toddy, a traditional, authentic British cold-weather drink made from whisky and spices which can only be found in pubs catering for tourists.

> ### *Devonshire Arms*
>
> *Open:* 11.30–15.00, 17.30–23.00 Mon–Sat. Closed Sun.
> *Brewery:* Free House (Clifton Inns).
> *Beer:* Shepherd Neame, Royal Oak, Huntsman plus one 'guest beer' which changes every month.
> *Food:* Available lunchtime and evening.

Dog & Duck

18 Bateman St W1. 01-437 3478. **M 5**

The Dog & Duck has a beautifully preserved exterior and the Victorian mirrored fittings inside are equally impressive. It is easily one of Soho's best pubs, even though it can become very crowded. In summer months an overspill of patrons (largely G and T-supping adpersons) always ends up on the pavement, much to the chagrin of the local police.

Unfortunately, this agreeable atmosphere tends to inspire excess and after an evening here, many a Soho film editor, copywriter or plain layabout has been forced to take advantage of the relatively secluded Bateman Street gutter. Not a pretty sight. Even George Orwell, a man known to detest bohemianism and debauchery succumbed to the pub's pleasures when he came here with a friend to celebrate the selection of *Animal Farm* by the American Book of the Month Club.

The pub has been established here since the early 17th century and it is thought that its name harks back to the days when Soho was a hunting ground.

> ### *Dog & Duck*
>
> *Open:* 11.30–15.00, 17.30–23.00 Mon–Sat; 12.00–14.00 Sun.
> *Brewery:* Taylor Walker.
> *Beer:* Burton, Taylor Walker.
> *Food:* Bar snacks at lunchtime only.

Dog & Trumpet

38 Great Marlborough St W1. 01-437 5559. **D 5**

The name is a reference to the recording industry which flourished in these parts in the 1960s. The Dog & Trumpet is at the north end of Carnaby Street, the epicentre of 60s Soho. Now the street is an embarrassing anachronism, but the pub (which used to be called the Marlborough Head) goes from strength to strength. Recently revamped, the Dog is reminiscent of a provincial disco – among the regulars you'll always find lots of office boys and girls togged out in designer labels anxious for an eventful Saturday night. The vast, pretentious ground floor, complete with Victorian skylight, is not the main attraction. The basement offers the best venue for pool in Soho. Smoky, sleazy and seedy, this part of the pub is a dream for anyone wishing to emulate Fast Eddie Felson.

Dog & Trumpet

Open: 11.00–15.00, 17.30–23.00 Mon–Sat; 12.00–14.00, 19.00–22.30 Sun.
Brewery: Taylor Walker.
Beer: Taylor Walker, Tetley's, Burton, Friary Meux.
Food: Snacks and full meals at lunchtime; snacks only evening.

Duke of Argyll

37 Brewer St W1. 01-437 6819. **J 8**

Large Clifton Inns house, more tastefully decorated than some of their Soho hostelries, with splendid mock Victorian jardinières hanging outside. Good value food is geared to tourist tastes: traditional lunch of roast beef with three veg is served every Sunday and other pub staples are available at other times. This is one of the handful of Soho pubs which offers live entertainment, trad jazz – for which there is no extra charge – is performed by a resident band every night from about 8pm. The wide selection of real ales is obviously an attempt to give the pub an authentic English flavour. It is a shame that it has so few genuine regulars.

Duke of Argyll

Open: 11.00–15.00, 19.30–23.00 Mon–Sat; 12.00–14.00, 19.00–22.30 Sun.
Brewery: Free House (Clifton Inns).
Beer: Combes, Tiger, Ruddle's, Eagle IPA, Charles Wells, Bombardier.
Food: Available lunchtime and evening.

Duke of Wellington

77 Wardour St W1. No phone. **L 8**

Having barred a number of known troublemakers, the Wellington has established a new group of regulars, most of whom work in films or advertising and consume vast quantities of draught Beck's lager. It's difficult to believe that this was once known as one of Soho's rougher hostelries. The atmosphere is now very restrained and the seating very comfortable. The pub has been furnished with large floral sofas and neat coffee-type tables on which you can plonk your plonk. Not everyone's idea of a typical hostelry, but very handy for a pre-theatre drink, particularly if you've got tickets for The Globe or Queens on Shaftesbury Avenue.

Food at present is very limited, but the big plus of the Wellington is live jazz on a Sunday night. This came about because the two women who used to run the pub, Jan Miller and Ann Dempster, helped to publicise the 1986 Soho Jazz Festival. Now a resident combo comprising sax, keyboards and cello, belts out a few numbers every week, mainly for locals who live in the area. Admission is free, but it might be an idea to buy a drink.

Duke of Wellington

Open: 11.00–15.00, 17.30–23.00 Mon–Fri; 11.00–15.00, 18.30–23.00 Sat; 12.00–14.00, 19.00–22.30 Sun.
Brewery: William Younger.
Beer: Younger's IPA, Scotch.
Food: Bar snacks at lunchtime only.

The Falcon

20 Wardour St W1. No phone. **M 10**

Sleazy little hostelry, useful to quench the thirst after a visit to the Wong Kei virtually opposite. Downstairs bar (very dark) could do with a lick of paint, but at least the customers are genuine local low-lifes. No media trendies here. The upstairs bar is more comfortable, and it is possible to get a seat (Habitat-style wooden dining chairs) early in the evening. Food is basic pub fare – chilli, shepherd's pie, ploughman's etc – but reasonably priced.

The Falcon

Open: 11.00–15.00, 17.30–23.00 Mon–Sat; 19.00–22.30 Sun.
Brewery: Watney Combe Reid Truman.
Beer: Webster's Yorkshire, Combes.
Food: Available lunchtime only.

The French House

49 Dean St W1. 01-437 2799. **M 7**

A quintessential Soho pub, catering primarily for the local demi-monde, who usually swan in at about noon and stagger out three hours later. Who can blame them? The French offers an excellent selection of French wines, aperitifs and digestifs and landlord Gaston Berlemont is probably one of Soho's most engaging and idiosyncratic hosts. Gaston, who was born above the pub in 1914 and took it over from his father at the end of the Second World War, can be seen most evenings behind the bar, sporting a handlebar moustache and quaffing Mumm with the regulars. The French, which used to be called the York Minster, is one of only a handful of Soho pubs which retain a genuine bohemian charm. The landlord's determination to preserve its atmosphere has obviously paid dividends; the pub is usually jam-packed by 8pm each evening.

Gaston boasts an impressive list of former clients. The walls of the small wooden bar are covered with signed photographs of the vaudeville stars and famous sportsmen who imbibed here in the past. When Gaston's father ran the French, Maurice Chevalier used to drop in frequently for one of M. Berlemont's sixpenny glasses of wine. During the Second World War, the pub became a refuge for those members of the French armed forces who hadn't succumbed to the corruption of Vichy and managed to escape the Nazi jackboot. De Gaulle drank here.

After the conflict, well-known drinkers such as Brendan Behan and Dylan Thomas were regulars. In the 50s, both gentlemen had their farewell parties at the French before heading for America.

You don't come here for the beer. Two varieties of unremarkable keg bitter are available, but Gaston will not serve pints. The cognoscenti say this is because he does not want to encourage the football crowds. Goodness knows what the lads from Arsenal's North Bank or Chelsea's Shed End would make of the Gitane-puffing habitués anyway. Gaston claims never to have heard of Coca-Cola and he won't sell peanuts or crisps. Woe betide anyone who asks for a Malibu.

The French House

Open: 11.30–15.00, 17.30–23.00 Mon–Sat (occasionally closed on Sat eve); 12.00–14.00 Sun.
Brewery: Watney Combe Reid Truman.
Food: Not available.

The Glassblower

42 Glasshouse St W1. 01-734 8547. **F 10**

Formerly the Kilt & Celt, this pub must be one of the largest in Soho. Two enormous floors serve a hard-core of regulars. The downstairs bar is the noisiest; here large groups of cheaply-suited men will eye up the equally large groups of Top Shop girls. Occasionally the din from the juke-box will subside and they are able to talk to each other. Upstairs is a trifle more refined; Clifton Inns, the owners, have installed large sofas and soft lighting. This is their idea of sophistication.

The food, however, is surprisingly good, far superior to what you might find in similar 'chain pubs'. There is an excellent selection of cheeses and home-made pies (fidget, pigeon and mushroom) which offer a tasty alternative to the ubiquitous quiche. Roast beef is served fresh every lunchtime, microwaved every evening.

The Glassblower

Open: 11.00–15.00, 17.30–23.00 Mon–Sat; 12.00–14.00, 19.00–22.30 Sun.
Brewery: Free House (Clifton Inns).
Beer: Brakspear's, Greene King Abbot Ale, Webster's Yorkshire, Courage Directors.
Food: Available lunchtime and evening.

The Glasshouse

55 Brewer St W1. 01-734 4771. **H 9**

Small, cosy pub much frequented by the post-office crowd and a handful of locals. Worth a visit for a squint at the Victorian glass frontage and cheap bar snacks: toasted sandwiches made while you wait. The upstairs bar used to be a pool room but has since been converted into a wine bar in which full meals are available together with a limited selection of wines.

The Glasshouse

Open: 11.00–15.00, 19.30–23.00 Mon–Fri; 18.30–23.00 Sat; 19.00–22.30 Sun.
Brewery: Taylor Walker.
Beer: Taylor Walker, Tetley's, Burton.
Food: Full meals and snacks lunchtime and evening.

Golden Lion

51 Dean St W1. 01-437 1896. **M 8**

One of only three gay pubs in Soho, and the longest established; it's been a haunt of homosexuals, particularly theatricals, since the 1920s. Even Noël Coward forsook more stylish establishments for this cosy little meeting place.

For decades the bar at the front of the pub has been patronised by lone homosexual men who find its atmosphere relaxing. Others may find it slightly sleazy, even though the brewery have recently redecorated and put down a carpet. In the early 1980s, a civil servant, Dennis Nilsen, picked up two young drifters in the downstairs bar, took them home and strangled them before concealing their remains in a drain. He is now serving a life sentence.

Women will probably find the atmosphere of the smarter upstairs bar more welcoming, although the service in both bars is friendly and efficient.

Golden Lion

Open: 11.00–15.00, 17.30–23.00 Mon–Sat; 12.00–14.00, 19.00–22.30 Sun.
Brewery: William Younger.
Beer: Younger's No 3, Younger's IPA.
Food: Available lunchtime and evening.

Green Man

57 Berwick St W1. 01-437 1755. **G 2**

Friendly Victorian pub at the junk jewellery end of Berwick Street. The circular bar attracts all manner of Sohoites: media men, office workers and those who work in the rag trade, north of Oxford Street. The beer is not brilliant, but the staff are obliging and the food excellent. The tweely-named 'Berwick Pantry' serves up some of the best pub food in the area, cooked by the licensee's wife.

Green Man

Open: 11.00–15.00, 17.30–23.00 Mon–Sat. Closed Sun.
Brewery: Charrington.
Beer: Bass, IPA.
Food: Snacks and meals available lunchtime only.

Intrepid Fox

99 Wardour St W1. 01-437 5025. **K 7**

Despite Soho's links with fox-hunting, the name of this pub has nothing to do with the sport. It comes from the Whig statesman Charles James Fox who used to visit the pub and befriended the landlord, one Samuel House. House was so touched by Fox's warmth that in 1784 he decided to rename the pub in his honour. And during the election of that year, House served free beer to anyone who promised to vote for his mentor.

The Fox is now used mainly by film executives who work in the offices of the giant corporations along Wardour Street. Previously, it attracted a somewhat shady clientele, particularly in the evenings, who used to make the atmosphere a little strained. But although the pub still brings in a few ne'er-do-wells, they are not the violent kind. The headcases have moved on, and the glasses don't have to be replaced quite so frequently.

Intrepid Fox

Open: 11.00–15.00, 17.30–23.00 Mon–Sat; 12.00–14.00, 19.30–22.30 Sun.
Brewery: Taylor Walker.
Beer: Taylor Walker, Benskins, Burton, Tetley's.
Food: Available lunchtime only.

John Snow

39 Broadwick St W1. 01-437 1344. **G 6**

In 1854 a cholera epidemic swept Soho resulting in 200 fatalities. A young doctor, John Snow, traced its cause to the water pump which stood on Broadwick Street outside the pub, then known as the Newcastle-upon-Tyne. Within a few days, the parish council had removed the pump, stemming the outbreak, and young Snow had earned his place in the annals of medicine. This pub took his name in the 1950s, when the previous John Snow, opposite, was demolished.

In the last few years, the atmosphere of the Snow has changed dramatically. It used to be an honest-to-goodness drinkers' pub and boasted a bohemian clientele; pop and jazz musicians in particular, were regulars, and Pete Townshend frequently dropped in while on visits to his music publishers further down the road. In 1984, however, the tenant retired and the brewery moved quickly. The pub was gutted, redecorated and a different breed of Soho habitué, the mediaman, took over. Only the magnificent art deco lamps which stand on the bar, and the signs describing John Snow's achievement remain.

That said, the pub is remarkably well run. Steve, the present manager, is a convivial host who has built up a large crew of regulars, not just from advertising. One symptom of the pub's regeneration is the occasional patronage of Barbour-wearing Sloanes who work for *Harpers & Queen*, based across the road. Pimms is now available in the summer.

The upstairs bar, available for hire, is more macho than the one below. Beefy regulars dominate the two pool tables, which are a considerable draw in an area which has a shortage of such entertainment. If you want a game, chalk your name up on the blackboard and have your 50p piece ready. Winner stays on.

John Snow

Open: 11.00–15.00, 17.30–23.00 Mon–Sat; 12.00–14.30, 19.00–22.30 Sun.
Brewery: Watney Combe Reid Truman.
Beer: Ruddle's, Combes, Webster's.
Food: Bar snacks and meals weekday lunchtimes.

King of Corsica

90 Berwick St W1. 01-437 3014. **J 6**

Theodore, who was proclaimed King of Corsica in 1736, died in exile in London in 1756. He was buried in the graveyard of St Anne's church, having spent the last years of his life in utter penury. A print depicting the king in his heyday hangs on the wall of the bar.

A tavern has stood on this site since the 17th century. Originally the Hampshire Hog and subsequently the City of London, the pub was given its present name in the 1950s when it was rebuilt, having been devastated during the Blitz. The present pub attracts a very macho clientele, mainly traders from the market who sit down to play cards after a day's work. Coffee is available at the bar to warm them up in the winter.

> *King of Corsica*
>
> *Open:* 11.00–15.00, 17.30–23.00 Mon–Sat; 12.00–14.00, 19.00–22.30 Sun.
> *Brewery:* Charrington.
> *Beer:* IPA.
> *Food:* Meals and snacks lunchtime and evening.

King's Arms

23 Poland St W1. 01-734 5907. **G 3**

The King's Arms is one of the three pubs in Soho which can properly be described as gay. Since 1983 this 17th-century hostelry, named in honour of James II, has catered almost exclusively for homosexuals.

Not a pub for a quiet drink. Pop music blares out constantly from the enormous hi-fi behind the bar and evenings attract a noisy clone crew wearing tight jeans, denim jackets and uniformly small moustaches. At lunchtime, the regulars are more restrained; mainly, it seems, shop assistants from Regent Street. Food is basic pub fare such as shepherd's pie and lasagne.

> *King's Arms*
>
> *Open:* 11.00–15.00, 17.30–23.00 Mon–Sat. Closed Sun.
> *Brewery:* Courage.
> *Beer:* Courage Best, Directors.
> *Food:* Meals and snacks lunchtime only.

King's Head

48 Gerrard St W1. No phone. **O 8**

The *trompe l'oeil* 'windows' painted above this pub give no indication of just how scruffy and seedy a dive it really is. Much-frequented by the local Chinese, the King's Head is one of the old-style Soho pubs.

The ground floor bar is actually quite refined in comparison with the one downstairs; a sign above the stairs proclaims that this is the 'oldest dive bar' in London. Certainly it is one of the tawdriest drinking venues in Soho. However, it manages to retain a louche charm. The downstairs bar is usually full on Friday and Saturday evenings, while upstairs also attracts a regular coterie of disgruntled deadbeats. Those who enjoy traditional English pub food will appreciate the delightful fare available here, this is one of the last bastions of plastic-wrapped pork-pies and factory-made pasties.

King's Head

Open: 11.00–15.00, 17.30–23.00 Mon–Sat; 12.00–14.00, 19.00–22.30 Sun.
Brewery: Courage.
Beer: Courage keg bitters.
Food: Snacks available lunchtime and evening.

Leicester Arms

44 Glasshouse St W1. 01-734 7641. **F 11**

Another aberration that is the work of Clifton Inns, the Leicester Arms is intended to tap the tourist trade with spirits and aperitifs dispensed from mock oak barrels and a selection of real ales. Decor is typically corporate; a stack of secondhand books in the corner is supposed to evoke the atmosphere of an old-fashioned study.

An ordinary pub for a very ordinary clientele; if it weren't for the prices, you could be anywhere in England. The most exciting aspect of the Leicester Arms, in fact, is the questionnaire about the licensing laws that you're encouraged to fill in. Don't forget to take a pen.

Leicester Arms

Open: 11.00–15.00, 17.30–23.00 Mon–Sat; 12.00–14.00, 19.00–22.30 Sun.
Brewery: Free House (Clifton Inns).
Beer: Royal Oak, Palmers, Charles Wells, Shepherd Neame.
Food: Meals and snacks available lunchtime, and evenings until 22.00.

Lyric Tavern

37 Great Windmill St W1. 01-437 3983. **J 9**

Easily the cosiest of Soho's Chef & Brewer establishments, the Lyric has a firm following among theatricals and media types and does not attract many tourists. The small bar is well run by a manager and barmen, dressed somewhat formally in white shirts and black ties. Given the inebriated state of many of the drinkers here, such decorum seems unnecessary. But this is not a dive and the impressive collection of Victoriana on the walls is well worth a look. The place has been refurbished with care and the Victorian tiling in the lobby is authentic. However, the hi-fi system should put paid to any notion that this might be a pub in which you can enjoy a quiet drink.

The food is acceptable, if a little predictable. Burgers and toasted sandwiches are cooked to order, the rest comes via the microwave.

Lyric Tavern

Open: 11.00–15.00, 17.30–23.00 Mon–Sat; 19.00–22.30 Sun.
Brewery: Watney Combe Reid Truman.
Beer: Webster's, Combes.
Food: Snacks and meals lunchtime and evening.

Nellie Dean

89 Dean St W1. 01-437 7196. **L 3**

A cosy local, the Nellie Dean has recently been revamped. The management are keen to keep out the hoi polloi; a sign on the door warns those wearing overalls that they will not be admitted. Not to worry, this is not one of the area's most interesting pubs. The walls are covered with hastily cobbled-together Victoriana which includes music hall librettos and cheap prints. Drinkers are mainly locals, since the pub would hardly be noticed by the casual passer-by.

Nellie Dean

Open: 11.00–15.00, 19.30–23.00 Mon–Sat; 12.00–14.00, 19.00–22.30 Sun.
Brewery: Courage.
Beer: Courage Best, Directors.
Food: Snacks available lunchtime and evening.

Old Coffee House

49 Beak St W1. 01-437 2197. **F 7**

As its name suggests, this pub started out as an 18th-century coffee house, but the present building is Victorian. The Soho Society's 1986 Pub of The Year is a cosy, jolly establishment, patronised by local residents in the evenings and at weekends and by businessmen at lunchtime in the week. The food, cooked on the premises by Diane Waumsley, wife of manager Les, is of a high standard.

The upstairs room, used at lunchtimes as a dining area, is one of the best party venues in Soho. What it lacks in class it makes up for in atmosphere and it's ideal for hastily-arranged office parties. The room is available free of charge, providing you pay for a buffet (sausage rolls, vol-au-vents etc) and don't turn up with flagons of home-brew. The small bar upstairs has a full range of drinks; inebriated partygoers are thus spared the long, potentially dangerous journey to the bar downstairs.

Old Coffee House

Open: 11.00–15.00, 17.30–23.00 Mon–Sat; 12.00–14.00, 19.00–22.30 Sun.
Brewery: Watney Combe Reid Truman.
Beer: Ruddle's County, Webster's Yorkshire, Combes.
Food: Snacks and meals always available.

Pillars of Hercules

7 Greek St W1. 01-437 1179. **N 4**

Pokey mock-Tudor hostelry which stands on the site of earlier pubs of the same name. Apparently the English poet Francis Thompson (then starving and addicted to opium) was gathered up in the doorway by a benefactor, Wilfrid Meynell, who subsequently saw to it that some of Thompson's work reached the printed page. Present-day regulars could also be considered degenerate, although they are more likely to be addicted to McEwan's Export. Useful pub for those who seek anonymity; the bar is very dark.

Pillars of Hercules

Open: 12.00–15.00, 17.30–23.00 Mon–Sat. Closed Sun.
Brewery: William Younger.
Beer: Scotch Keg, Tartan, McEwan's Export.
Food: Available lunchtime only.

Queen's Head

15 Denman St W1. 01-437 1540. **J 10**

A sign marked 'What's On' on one of the walls announces that a cribbage set is available from behind the bar. This is probably the most action you'll get at this small, cosy pub close to Piccadilly Circus. Unfortunately, the pub's proximity to the Circus has persuaded the owners, Chef & Brewer, to attempt to pull in the tourists. They've decorated the bar with a mish-mash of modern and Victorian tat which is far from easy on the eye. However, the parties of European visitors who pack out the pub before and after the show, don't seem to mind. They even tolerate the ghastly food served here: by about 8pm, the pasties and beans left over from lunchtime look distinctly lifeless.

Queen's Head

Open: 11.00–15.00, 17.30–23.00 Mon–Sat; 12.00–14.00, 19.00–22.30 Sun.
Brewery: Taylor Walker.
Beer: Taylor Walker, Friary Meux.
Food: Snacks and meals lunchtime and evening.

Red Lion

20 Great Windmill St W1. 01-437 4635. **J 9**

Redecoration is long overdue at this scruffy, unremarkable pub near Piccadilly Circus. The interior is beginning to resemble De Hems in its Skid Row days. But when the brewery do get round to a revamp, let us hope that they won't remove the black and white photographs which adorn the walls, recalling the days when it was used by artistes from the Windmill and Globe theatres. Musicians would also pop in for a pint en route to the unofficial Musicians' Labour Exchange at the Musicians' Union offices on Archer Street. The staff are definitely the pub's saving grace. Friendly and patient, they deserve an award for bravely coping with some of the most deadbeat regulars in Soho.

Red Lion

Open: 11.30–15.00, 17.30–23.00 Mon–Sat; 12.00–14.00, 19.00–22.30 Sun.
Brewery: Charrington.
Beer: Bass, IPA.
Food: Snacks and meals lunchtime and evening.

Red Lion

14 Kingly St W1. 01-734 4985. **D 6**

Clean, cosy local which should satisfy the most pernickety beer bore. This is the only pub in Soho which serves the legendary ale brewed in Tadcaster, Yorks by the Samuel Smith company. Unlike most other real ales, which are kept in wood and then transferred to metal kegs for ease of delivery, Sam Smith's is pumped to the bar direct from oak barrels. Apparently this enhances the flavour.

The Red Lion has recently been extended, so you should have no problem finding a seat, either upstairs or downstairs. The decor is acceptable, there are no garish lapses of taste and the regulars are in general a subdued, civilised lot.

Red Lion

Open: 11.00–15.00, 17.30–23.00 Mon–Sat; 12.00–14.00, 19.00–22.30 Sun.
Brewery: Sam Smith's.
Beer: Old Brewery Bitter, Museum Bitter.
Food: Cooked to order and available at all times.

Shakespeare's Head

29 Carnaby St W1. 01-734 2911. **D 5**

Established in 1735 by Thomas and John Shakespeare (distant relatives of the Bard), the Shakespeare's Head is a classic Soho tourist pub, embracing all the Olde English clichés in the book. The 'fare' is 'traditional', the ales are 'real' and cute little pots and pans hang down from phoney beams. Americans and Europeans alike flock here. The pub's most interesting characteristic is the life-size bust of Shakespeare which surveys Carnaby Street from a mock window above. The observant will notice that he has only one arm, the other having been blown off in the Blitz.

This is one of a handful of pubs in Soho which have taken to serving tea in the afternoons. In summer, grab one of the seats outside and watch the mods walk by.

Shakespeare's Head

Open: 11.00–15.00, 17.30–23.00 Mon–Sat; 12.00–14.00, 19.00–22.30 Sun. (Tea served 15.30–17.30 Mon–Sat.)
Brewery: Watney Combe Reid Truman.
Beer: IPA, Everard's Old Original, Everard's Tiger.
Food: Meals and snacks lunchtime and evening.

The Ship

116 Wardour St W1. No phone. **K 5**

At first sight it seems that The Ship, like many of the best Soho pubs, has precious little to recommend it. The beer is unremarkable, the decor is tatty and the staff often bad tempered. Yet this small pub attracts an extraordinarily loyal clientele, mainly musicians wanting to unwind before a performance at the Marquee Club a few doors down the road. In the 60s, The Who, The Rolling Stones and The Kinks all drank here and the pub has since become an unofficial employment agency for out of work keyboard-players, sound engineers and backing singers. They wait around the bar early in the evening sipping a half pint in the hope that one of the bands booked to appear at the Marquee will be a man short.

The Ship

Open: 11.00–15.00, 17.30–23.00 Mon–Sat; 12.00–14.00, 19.00–22.30 Sun.
Brewery: Fuller's.
Beer: London Pride, ESB.
Food: Bar snacks available at all times.

Spice of Life

6 Moor St W1. 01-437 7013. **O 6**

Large, loud pub off Cambridge Circus, which, as its name implies, attracts a wide range of regulars – at lunchtime struggling businessmen, in the evenings recherché punks, off-duty prostitutes and student poseurs from St Martin's School of Art. This colourful clientele makes the pub well worth a visit, particularly on a Saturday night when it seems that half of Soho has managed to cram itself through the doors.

Plans are afoot to extend the pub further up Romilly and Moor Streets and Brian McEvoy, manager of the Spice, boasts that one day he'll swallow up Norman Balon's Coach & Horses.

Spice of Life

Open: 11.00–15.00, 17.30–23.00 Mon–Sat; 12.00–14.00, 19.00–22.30 Sun.
Brewery: McMullens.
Beer: Country Bitter, AK Mild, Yorkshire.
Food: Meals and snacks available lunchtime only.

Star & Garter

62 Poland St W1. 01-439 2787. **G 5**

There has been a pub here since at least 1825 and it's possible that Shelley might have popped in for the odd drink; after being sent down from Oxford, he took lodgings on Poland Street. Following a revamp, the pub now appears in the *Good Beer Guide* and in 1985 was voted the Soho Society's Pub of the Year. It has also received a number of awards from the brewery, most notably for being the cleanest Courage pub in London.

The redecoration drove out many of the pub's more unsavoury regulars and the house is now efficiently run by Kelvin and Angela Barrow. Angela does all the cooking. The clientele is made up largely of advertising types; occasionally the odd punk or mod will stray in from Carnaby Street but they are always well behaved.

Star & Garter

Open: 11.00–15.00, 17.30–23.00 Mon–Sat. Closed Sun.
Brewery: Courage.
Beer: Directors, Courage Best.
Food: Meals at lunchtime, snacks in the evening.

The Store

15 Beak St W1. 01-734 5870. **E 8**

This pub has almost as many pretensions as the people who drink here. Its owners, the London Hosts Group, have set out to create an American-style bar where you can order a Jack Daniels or Budweiser and fantasise that you're the kind of dude who might appear in a blue jeans commercial. Most of the regulars are from the advertising industry; if you arrive just before closing time in the afternoon, the chances are you'll witness the ritual round of firm handshakes as the lads disperse. The bar has a magnificent collection of business cards mounted on one wall!

If you manage to fight your way through to the bar (it gets very crowded at lunchtimes and early evenings), you'll find a comprehensive selection of drinks. The bitter isn't up to much, but you can choose from six different imported lagers or opt for wine, which is available by the glass, half-bottle, bottle or litre.

Although The Store seems to be very much a product of the 1970s, its origins go back to the 17th century, when a coffee house stood on this site. For at least 150 years, the establishment was known as the Cumberland Stores and in the 70s it became very popular with those members of the rugby fraternity who liked to head Up West for a few jars on a Saturday night. The owners abridged the name about five years ago when the pub was revamped in an attempt to win over a new, less boisterous clientele. Like the Duke of Wellington on Wardour Street, this was another Soho pub run by two women. But Jocelyn and Sue left some time ago and The Store is now run by Gordon Inglis.

The Store

Open: 11.00–15.00, 17.30–23.00 Mon–Fri; 11.00–15.00 Sat. Closed Sun.
Brewery: Free House.
Beer: Webster's Yorkshire.
Food: Meals at lunchtime, snacks in the evening.

Sun & Thirteen Cantons

21 Great Pultney St W1. 01-437 4426. **G 7**

This pub owes its unusual name to the Swiss woollen merchants who had premises in Golden Square in the 19th century. It was originally known as The Sun, but the merchants persuaded the innkeeper that their custom deserved recognition; at the time Switzerland was made up of 13 cantons. For decades, the pub was well known as a centre for Swiss exiles living in Soho, but now that the Swiss community has dwindled in number, it has become an ordinary Soho local.

This is one of the few pubs in Soho which the breweries have left alone. The interior is not flashy, there's no music, prices are reasonable and it is impossible to buy a Tequila Sunrise. Most of the regulars are local residents – many of them defected from the John Snow on Broadwick Street when the brewery turned it into a pseudo-cocktail bar. Also, the Sun is probably the only pub in Soho which offers seating outside. In summer, park yourself on one of the benches, sip a Pernod and inhale the motorcycle fumes. You could be in Paris.

Sun & Thirteen Cantons

Open: 11.00–15.00, 17.30–23.00 Mon–Fri; 11.00–15.00, 19.30–23.00 Sat; 19.00–22.30 Sun.
Brewery: Watney Combe Reid Truman.
Beer: Ruddle's County, Webster's Yorkshire, Combes.
Food: Meals and snacks available lunchtime only.

Three Greyhounds

25 Greek St W1. 01-437 6680. **O 6**

This pub's mock-Tudor exterior is probably its most interesting characteristic, although the mural behind the bar is also worth a look. The name, like that of the Dog & Duck on Bateman Street, is a throwback to Soho's hunting age. Patrons are now quite a rough crowd and after about 10pm this small, dark pub becomes very sleazy and smoky. Off-duty hostesses from the near-beer bars have been known to come here for a real drink.

Three Greyhounds

Open: 11.00–15.00, 17.30–23.00 Mon–Sat; 12.00–14.00, 19.00–22.30 Sun.
Brewery: Taylor Walker.
Beer: Taylor Walker, Burton.
Food: Meals and snacks available lunchtime only.

West One

1–3 Warwick St W1. No phone. **F 10**

An extraordinary establishment, and living proof that there is one corner of Soho that is forever Croydon. West One is a Debbie's Delight, an haute-naff video pub behind Regent Street which attracts young dollies by the Cortinaload. They come here for the steamy atmosphere, the music and of course the guys; bedenimed hunks with designer stubble who throw them a smouldering look and buy them a Bacardi.

West One is actually more of a disco than a pub, not dissimilar to the ropey little nightspots which can be found in the High Streets of provincial towns. From opening through until closing time, the video juke box is pumped with pound coins and three screens dominate the dark, uncomfortable bar.

However, not all of West One's customers come from the suburbs. It's also very popular with tourists intent on having a good time. A night out at West One seldom disappoints, but hurry on down there, rumour has it that this Soho pub is earmarked for a change of image in 1988.

West One

Open: 11.00–15.00, 17.30–23.00 Mon–Sat. Closed Sun.
Brewery: Charrington.
Beer: Stones.
Food: Not available.

White Horse

16 Newburgh St W1. 01-437 2799. **E 5**

Tucked away in the north-west corner of Soho close to Carnaby Street, the White Horse is not easy to find. If you succeed, though, your efforts will be well rewarded. The food is exceptional. Everything is freshly cooked to order and the menu changes daily. Staples such as ham, egg and chips are available along with more adventurous fare such as meatballs with pasta verde (the pasta comes from Lina Stores in Brewer Street). Prices are very modest, but get there early (or late) if you want a seat.

The present landlord, Perry Hood, took over in 1983 when the previous tenant, a former policeman, retired. For years it had been known as the Factory Pub. The right-hand bar was always packed with detectives from West End Central police station and Great Marlborough Street Magistrates Court; the left-hand bar attracted a very different clientele, but they have always shared the same set of lavatories.

Now most of the punters at the White Horse are either in the media or pretend to be. Continental lagers are consumed in large quantities and the upstairs restaurant (bookable for private parties) is the venue of many an expense-account lunch. A sign on the door proclaims that persons wearing overalls or dirty clothing will not be served.

White Horse

Open: 11.00–15.00, 17.30–23.00 Mon–Fri; 11.00–15.00 Sat. Closed Sun.
Brewery: Charrington.
Beer: Bass, IPA.
Food: Wide selection at lunchtime only.

White Horse

45 Rupert St W1. 01-437 5745. **K 8**

Tourist pub, very popular during the war when the Windmill Theatre was in its heyday, in a good position for attracting the pre- and post-theatre crowd. Helpful, friendly bar staff are willing to offer directions or fathom out the London Transport bus map. Groups of squaddies have adopted the pub, largely as a result of its extensive display of military memorabilia, and veteran GIs on holiday are also to be found peering at the framed photographs. Food is served upstairs in a slightly more formal setting than most pubs, with waitress service.

White Horse

Open: 11.00–15.00 Mon–Sat; 12.00–14.00, 19.00–22.30 Sun.
Brewery: Taylor Walker.
Beer: Taylor Walker, Burton, Friary Meux.
Food: Snacks and meals lunchtime and evening.

WINE BARS

Andrew Edmunds

46 Lexington St W1. 01-437 5708. **G 6**

Wine bar named after the patrician owner of the print gallery next door, who took over these premises in 1986, having seen a number of similar establishments rise and fall. Although he has still not got round to engaging a signwriter to put his name above the door, Edmunds has established what is easily one of the best wine bars in Soho, with imaginative food and an excellent selection of wines including vintage ports and six champagnes.

The food is probably as good as might be served in a brasserie or nouvelle-style French restaurant and considerably cheaper. In fact since Edmunds first took over, the wine bar has become much more of a restaurant, but you can still come here just for a glass of wine. Daily specials are available together with snacks such as brie in a hot baguette.

Space is limited. The tables are placed too close together and the wine bar should therefore be written off as a venue for an intimate lunch à deux or business meeting. A major plus, however, is the total lack of background music; Andrew

Edmunds relies on lively conversation to generate its atmosphere. There are two tables outside which serve as a useful venue for a summer lunch; Lexington Street, however, is not one of Soho's most inspiring streets. Booking is essential, particularly at lunchtime, and be sure to request an upstairs table; atmosphere downstairs is sadly lacking.

Andrew Edmunds

Open: 12.00–15.00, 17.30–23.00 Mon–Fri. Closed Sat & Sun.
Booking: Essential at lunchtime.
House wine: £6.00.
Credit cards: Access, Visa.

Clowns

63 Frith St W1. 01-734 3312. **M 4**

Cosy, unpretentious little place hidden in a subterranean room beneath an Italian sandwich bar. Italian wines are a speciality and you'd be mad not to sample Clowns' pasta dishes which are made on the premises and very filling. The pasta comes from Camisa's. Other dishes include omelettes, home-made soups and salads. Most are excellent value.

Clowns is closed in the evening, but can be hired for private functions. In fact Clowns is the perfect venue for any young art student who might want to hold a party. Bring your own jazz tapes and don't forget to wear a scowl. They serve espresso.

Clowns

Open: 12.00–15.00 Mon–Fri. Closed Sat & Sun.
House wine: £4.95.
Credit cards: Amex.

Dean's

26–29 Dean St W1. 01-437 4809. **M 5**

Formerly Pauline's, this wine bar is managed by, and adjacent to, the Quo Vadis restaurant. Its garish exterior clashes somewhat with the light green façade of the main restaurant, one of the most impressive buildings in Soho. Although both establishments share the same kitchen, the menus are very different. Here the fare is simpler and plainer, and is not based on traditional Italian cooking. One or two pasta dishes are usually available each day, but you are just as likely to find moussaka, goulash or even steak and kidney pie on offer. Also a wide range of unusual salads. The wine list is international, but predominantly Italian, and the house wine is usually a good bet. Service is particularly friendly.

While Dean's does not have the sumptuous, glamorous ambience of its parent, a meal here offers remarkable value. Booking is essential at lunchtimes, since the 70s-style tables and wicker chairs are usually crowded out with film company staff on the lower rungs of the career ladder, attracted by the reasonable prices and kitsch movie posters. Their bosses are usually to be found next door.

Dean's

Open: 12.00–15.00, 17.30–22.30 Mon–Fri. Closed Sat & Sun.
Booking: Advisable at lunchtime.
House wine: £4.95.
Credit cards: Access, Amex, Diners, Visa.

Kettners Champagne Bar

29 Romilly St W1. 01-437 6437. **O 7**

Snazzy champagne bar which is part of the enormous Kettners pizza restaurant. The bar itself is much more upmarket than the restaurant, attracting a regular clientele of high-earning City yuppies who wouldn't dream of dining on pizza.

In the early evenings Kettners is prone to overcrowding. There must be more comfortable places to quaff champagne in Soho. None, however, are as trendy as this.

Although the decor is in need of a rethink (those wicker chairs and cheap prints have got to go) the champagne list is impressive and probably the most comprehensive in the area. Sixty or seventy varieties are available, by the glass, half

bottle, bottle, magnum, Jeroboam, Methuselah and Balthazar. Dom Perignon 1980 is the most expensive champagne Kettners serve, the cheapest their own 'house' bubbly. Those who don't like champagne can drink Peroni beer or over-priced orange juice. Food is limited to morsels of pizza (cheap) or sandwiches (expensive).

> ### Kettners Champagne Bar
>
> *Open:* 12.00–15.00, 17.30–24.00 Mon–Sat. Closed Sun.
> *House champagne:* £15.25.
> *Credit cards:* Access, Amex, Diners, Visa.

Last Resort

2 St Anne's Court W1. 01-734 0174. **K 4**

Highly successful wine bar which opened in 1987 in premises adjacent to the unremarkable Ashley's restaurant. Since wine bar and restaurant share the same kitchen, the Last Resort can offer a much wider range of food than most and the adventurous menu would outclass many of Soho's eating houses. A selection of hot dishes, which changes regularly, is always available. The salads, too, are interesting and anyone who isn't very hungry can always opt for a sandwich: those served here are of the superior, designer sort.

The ambience, however, leaves a lot to be desired. Decor is passé hi-tech and two screens belt out pop videos throughout the lunchtime and evening sessions. The business-suits and hairlines suggest that many of the regulars would be more at home watching films featuring the likes of the Eagles and Fleetwood Mac than the contemporary bands shown here. However, videos or not, the wine bar is usually packed out, particularly at lunchtime.

Last Resort

Open: 11.30–15.00, 17.30–23.00 Mon–Fri; 18.00–23.00 Sat. Closed Sun.
Booking: Essential at lunchtime.
House wine: £4.45.
Credit cards: Access, Amex, Diners, Visa.

Morgan's

4–6 Ganton St W1. 01-734 7581. **E 5**

Pleasant little wine bar, somewhat overshadowed by the unattractive red-brown structures of Blake House and the National Magazine Company nearby, but well patronised by the female journalists and advertising staff of the latter. Food is reasonably priced, but the menu – largely wine bar staples such as pâté, quiche, ratatouille and chilli-con-carne – would not win any prizes for invention. The daily specials, however, can be more interesting and meat-lovers will welcome the selection of steaks.

The wine list is mainly French but includes a handful of Californian, Italian, German, Portuguese and one English wine, Lamberhurst Muller Thurgau, which is produced in Kent. The sometimes noisy upstairs bar leads down to a more intimate subterranean drinking area, and if you feel you can brave the English weather, carbon monoxide fumes and staring passers-by there are tables outside.

> *Morgan's*
>
> *Open:* 11.00–15.00, 17.30–23.00 Mon–Fri; 12.00–15.00 Sat. Closed Sun.
> *Booking:* Advisable at lunchtime.
> *House wine:* £5.20.
> *Credit cards:* Access, Amex, Diners, Visa.

Shampers

14 Kingly St W1. 01-437 1692. **E 7**

Shampers is one of Soho's, if not London's, best-known wine bars. In the 10 years in which it has been open, it has developed a reputation for excellent, imaginative food. However, Shampers' has its drawbacks; food is not cheap, and it seems to attract a loud, boisterous clientele. This is the kind of wine bar which is more likely to appeal to the besuited businessman than the super-trendy Sohoite. Here he can relax over lunch with his cronies without having to go to the expense of paying for a proper restaurant, and can usually be found standing alongside the bar at the back chatting with the proprietor.

The food is of an exceptionally high standard. It is prepared on the premises from fresh ingredients every day – even the mayonnaise is home-made. Shampers' ham and cheese pie and gourmet salad are favourites, also barbecue pork served with pasta. There is usually a choice of three or four hot dishes each day, along with a wide range of salads. A lot of champagne is drunk here: 15 varieties are available, all of which go marvellously with the Loch Fyne oysters which they serve when there is an 'r' in the month. The house wine is always acceptable, if a little expensive.

While most people will continue to think of Shampers as a wine bar, it is worth noting that the basement has been converted into 'The Brasserie'. A rather cold looking room in green and white, it offers a fixed price international menu: two courses plus coffee for £10.50, in an area of Soho otherwise devoid of this sort of establishment.

Shampers

Open: 11.00–15.00, 17.30–23.00 Mon–Fri; 11.00–15.00 Sat. Closed Sun.
Booking: Advisable at lunchtime.
House wine: £5.75.
Credit cards: Access, Amex, Diners, Visa.

Tracks

17a Soho Square W1. 01-439 2318. **M 2**

Soho Square is not exactly chock-a-block with decent places to eat and drink and Tracks, therefore, serves a very important function. This comfortable wine bar is virtually next door to the offices of the CBS record company; many a frazzled A & R man has sought solace here during the 10 years Tracks has been open. Most of the regulars work in the music industry (Paul McCartney's office is just across the square) or in advertising. The food is basic wine bar fare – salads, chillis, curries etc – but there is a good selection of wines from several different countries, including France, Greece, Austria and England. In the summer Sangria and Buck's Fizz are sold by the jug and drunk at the tables outside.

The decor is very 1970s and the kitchen staff wear aprons which match the upholstery. These excesses aside, Tracks, which also serves morning coffee and afternoon tea, is a useful place for a quiet drink and a read of the papers. *The Times, The Guardian* and *The Independent* are available for the use of patrons.

Tracks

Open: 10.00–23.00 Mon–Fri. Closed Sat & Sun.
Booking: Advisable.
House wine: £4.45.
Credit cards: Access, Amex, Diners, Visa.

DRINKING CLUBS

Soho's afternoon drinking clubs have taken a pasting from the authorities in recent years, and the new licensing laws seem set to finish them off, but some still thrive in spite of the pressures. They can often be found in most unexpected places, in basements below perfectly respectable offices and above shops. Their hours are as erratic as their membership fees are variable, but most are open during weekday afternoons. If the proprietor likes the look of you, the chances are you'll get in free. Otherwise, unless you know someone who already belongs to the club, and are prepared to pay a large joining fee, you may find it difficult to become a member.

Colony Room **M 6**

41 Dean St W1. 01-437 9179. A famous Soho drinking haunt and one which has attracted dozens of writers, painters and actors in the 30 or so years it has been open. The club was set up by the legendary Muriel Belcher who, in her heyday, catered for left-wing politicians and the cream of Soho's bohemians including Colin MacInnes and Dylan Thomas. The club has now become the preserve of a tiny minority of Sohoites who regard the square mile as consisting only of this club, the French pub, the Coach and Horses and, at a pinch, Kettners Champagne Bar. Current alumni include Peter Boizot, Francis Bacon and the redoubtable Jeffery Bernard whose genuinely witty 'Low Life' column in *The Spectator* often refers to the antics of those who frequent this tacky little upstairs room, with its small piano and colonial souvenirs.

Since Muriel's death in the 70s, the Colony is now run by the cantankerous Ian Board who served Muriel for many years as head barman. Mr Board is a typical rum Soho character, prone to barking rudely down the phone to strangers and generally inflicting his colourful personality upon the club's members. Membership is sometimes available, but this really depends upon Mr Board's frame of mind. Best to approach him before lunch.

Gerry's

M 8

52 Dean St W1. 01-437 4160. One of the most respectable and well-established drinking clubs in Soho, Gerry's is run for what the proprietor describes as 'members of the theatrical profession'. The club, which was set up in the 50s in Shaftesbury Avenue, is now located behind an imposing wooden front door in Frith Street. You have to use the entryphone to get in, but even then there is no guarantee that you will be invited down.

The club itself is confined within a small basement room. The walls are decorated with playbills and dozens of framed black and white photographs of famous hoofers and actors. If you're a member, Gerry's has a homely, welcoming atmosphere; if you're not, it may seem very chilly. Although membership is by no means exclusive – the roll is currently 2000-strong – it is impossible to join unless you are introduced by an established member.

New Rupert Executive Club

M 11

5 Wardour St W1. 01-437 9639. The New Rupert is typical of countless drinking clubs in Soho. Several flights of stairs lead you to a shabby single room on the 2nd floor dominated by a bar which runs across one wall. This is very much an afternoon drinkers' club, opening after the pubs shut and closing when the last of the sozzled regulars makes the hazardous journey down the stairs. Not one of Soho's more sophisticated watering holes, the New Rupert appeals primarily to seedy business-types. No food available.

5 Shopping

Shopping in Soho can be a rewarding, yet expensive experience. The district's narrow streets and alleys are densely packed with all manner of emporia, some of which have been here for more than a hundred years. The square mile also has its share of chain-stores run in a pre-ordained fashion by bosses based elsewhere, but these are worthy of only scant attention. Much more interesting are the small, family-run establishments which have helped, over generations, to form Soho's unique character.

Historically, this is an area which has always attracted émigrés: Huguenots, Greeks, Germans, Italians, Swiss and, more recently, Chinese. All have made their mark on the retail outlets which play such an important part in the social and economic life of Soho. Its cosmopolitan character is best illustrated by the astonishing range of food shops – Italian delicatessens, French charcuteries and patisseries and Continental coffee stores. Many were set up in the last century to sell familiar foods to those exiles who had settled here, and the shopkeepers were assured of a ready market.

Meanwhile the artisans were also enjoying a boom in business. The Huguenots had been the first to establish their small studios and workshops in Soho at the end of the 17th century trading as gold and silversmiths, jewellers, engravers, weavers, clock and watchmakers. Gradually other groups began to realise the potential of the area. Attracted by the low rents and the proximity of their potential customers in the smarter districts of Mayfair and St James's, gunsmiths, furniture-makers, musical instrument-makers and even painters set up shop in Soho in the late 18th and early 19th centuries.

However, with the advent of mass-production, a lot of the traditional craft industries were doomed. By the end of the

Second World War, many of the food shops which had been catering for the craftsmen also closed. Much-loved delis and pasta purveyors were wiped off the Soho map by the pornographers and the property speculators. The high rates and rents demanded by the local authority and the landlords who held the freeholds forced many once-famous Soho names to call it a day. Among them were A Gomez Ortega (a Spanish food shop), four Italian delicatessens: Gemmani, King Bomba, Cherico, Parmigiani Figlio and, most recently, Joelson's Jewish grocers.

Some specialist food shops, however, have succeeded in staying afloat. Many are still family businesses handed down through the generations or bought up by like-minded shopkeepers with a healthy disrespect for the expansionist ambitions of the office developers. In the last 10 years, the Soho Society has played a key role in opposing (and in many cases thwarting) planning applications which would cause a further decline in the number of retail outlets in Soho. The Society is convinced that local people, living and working in the area, are entitled to decent shopping facilities.

The recent closure of many of Soho's seedier strip clubs and peep shows has led to an upsurge in retail development in the area. Fashion designers in particular, are opening up shops here and revitalising sections of Soho previously the preserve of the pornographers. At present, the locals are offering a guarded welcome to these new entrepreneurs, and there is some concern that Soho might go the same way as Covent Garden, becoming a dinky little toy village functioning only for the amusement of trendies and tourists. It remains to be seen whether the fears of the locals are justified. With luck the old and the new will be able to co-exist, ancient tobacconists such as Inderwick's rubbing shoulders with *Blitz*-reading fashion designers.

The sheer variety of shops in the area makes Soho one of London's most convenient shopping districts. Where else, in one street, can you buy a pound of fresh pasta, an avant-garde designer suit, wine, a pair of lobster crackers, freshly ground coffee and endless foreign magazines?

All shops are closed on Sunday unless otherwise stated.

DESIGNER CLOTHES AND ACCESSORIES

Academy **E 5**

15 Newburgh St W1. 01-439 3225. Showcase for young design talent, mainly from the UK. Students leaving college frequently turn up here with their offerings and not all are sent away. As the students do not demand such high rates of commission as established designers, retail prices are relatively low. Clothes have no overall theme, the frequently changing range is influenced by the eclectic taste of the owners. Decor is changed every six months. *Open 10.00–18.00 Mon–Sat.* Access, Amex, Diners, Visa.

American Retro **N 6**

35 Old Compton St W1. 01-734 3477. Newish fashion clothing and accessories shop where you'll surely find that present for the ennuied yuppie who already owns an ostrich-skin Filofax. How about a matt black hand-held photocopier? More cumbersome than a notebook and pencil perhaps, but oh, so stylish . . . American Retro is *the* place for yupphemera in Soho. Like Paul Smith and Oggetti, AR's owner Sue Tahran, has put together a selection of accessories which are essential if you want to be taken seriously in the fickle, fashionable world of the Soho Media Set. Classic designs like Zippo lighters and Braun alarm clocks are consistently popular here, along with well-made, well-priced shirts and jeans. *Open 10.00–19.00 Mon–Sat.* Access, Amex, Visa.

Benedetto **H 6**

8 Silver Pl W1. 01-734 0089. Precious little fashion shop, owned and run by a precious little New Yorker called Ben De Lisi. His designs for women (mainly in linens and cottons) are in the middle to upper price range. Formal wear is a speciality, and this is definitely the place to come for that ravishingly

different bridal gown. Customers are flattered by a coterie of dressers, all of whom are, of course highly trained salespersons. If you're lucky, you may have the opportunity to be fitted by Ben himself. *Open 10.00–18.00 Mon–Sat (to 19.00 Thur), 10.00–18.30 Sat.* Access, Amex, Diners, Visa.

Beau Monde **G 6**

43 Lexington St W1. 01-734 6573. Another new outlet for young, unknown designers which specialises in tailored suits for fashionable women. Interesting range of accessories, particularly strong on hats. The policy is not to have 'seasons'; stock changes frequently. *Open 10.00–18.30 Mon–Sat.* Access, Visa.

Blackout **J 9**

33 Great Windmill St W1. 01-439 1998. Friendly, well-run shop specialising in original American clothing from the 40s, 50s and 60s. Most of the stock is available for hire, including accessories such as hats, ties and cummerbunds. A huge range of cocktail dresses can ensure that you need never be seen in the same outfit twice. And if you really fall in love with something, Blackout will also make up copies of the originals they hold in stock. *Open 12.00–19.00 Mon–Fri (to 20.00 Thur), 11.00–18.00 Sat.* Access.

Boy Soho **O 6**

10–11 Moor St W1. 01-439 0592. Hot-spot for post-punk casual wear, BOY exploded on the London scene in 1977 and is still going strong. Colours are aggressively primary, there is the occasional throwback to bondage wear and a good portion of stock is bedecked with the BOY Eagle logo, with its Nazi overtones. Prices are as ludicrously high as they always were, but the customers, including Boy George, who opened this branch in 1987, are obviously prepared to pay them. *Open 11.00–19.00 Mon–Sat.* Access, Amex, Diners, Visa.

The Cavern

D 5

22 Fouberts Pl W1. 01-437 0254. Formerly the Carnaby Cavern, this is one of the last remaining outposts of the mod era, still retailing target sweatshirts, chequered cardigans and boating blazers. Most customers are now the junior mod revivalists who pack out the street on summer Saturdays, but over its 25-year history, the shop (which has moved twice in that time) has enjoyed the patronage of some of the world's leading groovers, including The Beatles, The Who, The Small Faces, The Kinks and Tina Turner. Styles have not changed since then, and although prices have inevitably gone up, the Cavern's clothes are still within reach of impecunious schoolboys in search of an identity.

All the stock (with the exception of classic Fred Perry's) is made on the premises and the Cavern also offers a made-to-measure suit service. Finished garments are usually ready to wear within a day. Much to the chagrin of the mods, the Cavern also caters for skinheads (Tonik jackets for the lads, micro skirts for the girls). *Open 09.00–18.00 Mon–Sat.* Access, Amex, Visa.

Christopher New

N 7

52 Dean St W1. 01-734 5363. Christopher New was one of the very first designers to set up shop in Soho. Although he has spawned countless imitators, New is still one of the most highly regarded. His eclectic range of casual wear is aimed at the free-spending trendy who is after a designer pair of boxer shorts (available in silk or cotton), a loud yet smart jacket or an upmarket T-shirt. Unusual range of accessories, including Mulberry personal organisers: more exclusive and stylish than the ubiquitous Filofax but compatible with the latter's inserts. *Open 10.00–18.00 Mon–Sat.* Access, Amex, Diners, Visa.

Dress to Kill

E 5

13 Newburgh St W1. 01-434 0168. A sign in the window announces that Dress to Kill offers cocktail dresses for hire.

Evidently there is a demand for such fripperies, recession or no recession. Garments in general are stunning, ideal for film premières or charity balls. Clientele is mainly showbiz set: aspiring pop starlets, bit-part actresses, television companies etc. The collection is not suitable for men unless they frequent Madame Jo-Jos! Hefty deposit required on most dresses. *Open 11.00–18.00 Mon–Fri (Mon–Sat in summer).* Access, Amex, Diners, Visa.

Eye-Tech **H 9**

44 Brewer St W1. 01-734 1415. Very trendy mid-price optician, specialising in extravagant eyewear and designer labels. Enormous collection of Ray-Bans (glasses and shades), bi-focals for the Young Fogey and frames in real tortoiseshell. Tinted contact lenses for those tired of their natural eye colour are also available. Eye-Tech promises an emergency service which provides replacement lenses and specs within a day. Appointments for NHS eye-tests not normally necessary. *Open 10.00–18.00 Mon–Sat.* Access, Visa.

Fans **N 6**

24 Frith St W1. 01-439 1294. Vast emporium of tat sited in what used to be Bifulco Stores, one of Soho's finest Continental butchers. (Bifulco moved north to St John's Wood when their lease expired.) Fans offers an enormous selection of tasteless badges, T-shirts, posters and greetings cards. One popular 3D T-shirt depicts the scene in *Alien* when the monster emerges from John Hurt's midriff, complete with plastic blood and torn stomach lining.

The greetings cards include plenty carrying images of full-frontal nudes but the police don't seem to object. One of the best-selling lines, however, is the Lenin badges (imported from the Soviet Union) which go down a storm with teenage American tourists. Apparently wearing one of these back home in Iowa, Michigan or Minnesota is tantamount to shooting the President. *Open 10.00–22.30 Mon–Sat, 12.00–20.00 Sun.* Access, Amex, Visa.

F.FWD (Fast Forward)

E 5

14a Newburgh St W1. 01-439 0091. Consummate yuppie gadget shop which wholesales to other shops in the area such as American Retro on Old Compton Street. Cool, cool staff ooze trendiness. Usual range of gadgets includes credit card-sized needlework kits (but are those who buy this kind of gear the type who sew their own buttons on?), cappuccino machines and Braun lighters. Also attractive but expensive collection of fountain pens from the 30s and 40s. *Open 10.00–19.00 Mon–Sat.* Access, Amex, Diners, Visa.

Just Facts

G 6

43 Broadwick Street W1. 01-734 5034. The only shop in the world which stocks the entire Filofax range. It had to be in Soho; no self-respecting media trendy would buy his inserts anywhere else. Choose from a range which includes maps of Rome and Milan, Eurocheque holders and expenses forms with built-in envelopes for lunch receipts. Binders start at cheap plastic and finish at ostrich skin, currently top of the range but somewhat ostentatious. *Open 09.30–18.00 Mon–Fri, 10.00–16.00 Sat.* Access, Amex, Visa.

Maison du Pantalon

D 5

12a Foubert's Pl W1. 01-434 0627. Typical of the new wave of Soho designer shops which have replaced many of the tat merchants who used to have premises in the Carnaby Street area. Maison du Pantalon's relaxed, own-label casual togs are designed and made in Sweden. So far this is the company's first British outlet. Also a limited range of men's clothes which carry the Clochard label, and accessories including leather belts and hats. *Open 10.00–18.00 Mon–Sat (to 19.00 Thur).* Access, Amex, Diners, Visa.

Marvelette

L 10

4 Rupert Court W1. 01-434 9656. New and secondhand classic period clothes, mainly from the 40s and 50s. Here you'll find an

authentic zoot suit or box jacket, direct from the US, dating back to the golden age of swing. Most merchandise is in very good nick, so prices are about the same as you'd pay for inferior contemporary copies. *Open 11.00–19.00 Mon–Sat.* Access, Visa.

Peter Hoggard **L 10**

8 Rupert Court W1. 01-734 4484. Opened in 1987 by Peter Leathers and Michelle Hoggard, two designers who had been working in the rag trade together for four years. They concentrate on upmarket women's wear based on classic silhouettes such as tailored suits in Irish linen. Small range of menswear plus designer jewellery and accessories which include belts and braces. *Open 11.00–19.00 Mon–Sat.* Access, Amex, Diners, Visa.

Pure Fabrication **L 10**

5 Rupert Court W1. 01-437 1001. Small Soho-based designers and producers of heavy metallic jewellery. Owners also have a penchant for oddities such as brooches featuring plaster ducks on a background of suburban chintz. Not for the self-conscious. Also, belts and bags in rag leathers. *Open 11.00–19.30 Mon–Sat.* Access, Amex, Visa.

Richmond Cornejo **E 5**

2 Newburgh St W1. 01-734 5782. One of the handful of high-fashion shops which have recently revitalised this far-flung corner of Soho. The shop was opened in 1987 by two designers, John Richmond and Maria Cornejo. Stock is expensive but unusual; which accounts for the interest shown by magazines such as *Blitz* and *I-D* when RC was launched. More expensive items are one-offs and only available here, cheaper range goes out to other fashion stores such as Joseph. *Open 11.00–18.30 Mon–Fri, 10.30–18.00 Sat.* Access, Amex, Visa.

Swank

L 7

72 Old Compton St W1. 01-437 3155. Mid-price Italian and French designer casual wear for men, aimed at the younger end of the market. Excellent collection of shirts in pure cotton, including the Replay range, and patterned sweaters imported from the Continent. The latter are expensive, so it's probably worth waiting until sales time when Swank offer generous reductions. *Open 09.30–18.30 Mon–Sat.* Access, Amex, Visa.

This Address

G 6

51 Lexington St W1. 01-734 2793. Two young designers, Angie Collins and Tina Stevens, set up this fashion shop in 1987. The aim is to please the young trendy-about-town without making excessive demands on her bank balance. Fun wear is the theme, plus the occasional oddball 'accessory' such as a Bakelite telephone. In summer, genuine 50s sunglasses raked up from a warehouse in Italy. *Open 10.00–18.00 Mon–Sat.* Access, Amex, Diners, Visa.

Woolf/Soho

J 8

21 Brewer St W1. 01-439 1107. Off-the-peg designer clothes at reasonable prices. Selection of Williwear shirts, and linen suits a little too avant-garde for office wear. Serious fashion fiends would probably wish to spend more, but Woolf's classy leather bags are a must. Jewellery too. *Open 10.00–19.00 Mon–Sat.* Access, Amex, Visa.

Workers for Freedom

F 10

4/4a Lower John St W1. 01-734 3767. Set up in 1985, Workers for Freedom has enjoyed massive media hype and the patronage of many a pop star. The designers who initiated WFF consider themselves in the forefront of the Soho revival. Fabrics are natural and designs baggy, sometimes with a Latin American influence. Summer collections usually stunning; WFF have a knack of using linen to its best advantage, with details all hand-sewn. Prices quite reasonable for designer clothing. Unlike some designer shops (and one or two of the upmarket chains) the atmosphere is not at all intimidating despite the ever-changing decor. *Open 10.30–18.00 Mon–Sat.* Access, Amex, Visa.

Zeitgeist **K 7**

4a Peter St W1. 01-734 8343. Zeitgeist bill themselves as 'the West End's one and only' rubber and leather boutique. The stock upstairs is relatively unremarkable: rubber skirts and dresses, T-shirts etc, which can be rolled on with the aid of talcum powder. Skip the underwear. The fetishist department, downstairs, however, is much more interesting: plenty of bizarre garments in rubber and leather, plus useful accoutrements such as rubber dildos and bondage straps. Not the place for a quiet suit for the office. *Open 10.00–19.00 Mon–Sat.* Access, Visa.

FOOD AND DRINK

BUTCHERS

J. & J. Dalli **F 10**

78 Brewer St W1. 01-437 8870. Continental butcher who sells a number of ready-prepared specialities, including kebabs, spare ribs in barbecue sauce and stuffed peppers. Two grades of mince available, one good enough for steak tartare. A sign outside in English and Japanese proclaims that Dalli sells beef for teriyaki. Game available when in season, and there's genuine sawdust on the floor. *Open 07.30–18.00 Mon–Fri, 07.30–16.00 Sat.* No credit cards.

Slater & Cooke Bisney & Jones **H 9**

65–67 Brewer St W1. 01-437 2026. Owned by a Dutchman and managed by an Italian this pukka-sounding butcher is one of

Soho's best, providing English as well as Continental cuts. Trade clients include the Dorchester and Trader Vic's at the Hilton. Can be pricey, but quality, service and range is always first class. If you're after something obscure they'll do their best to have it in the shop within 24 hours. Excellent source of barbecue ingredients: a range of sausages is available along with ready-made kebabs and chunky spare ribs. Larger orders will be delivered (CoD). Spotless, tiled interior which is reminiscent of some of the great food halls in Paris. For hygiene's sake, cash is taken by a lady serving behind a separate till and not by anyone involved in chopping up the meat. *Open 07.00–17.00 Mon–Thur, 07.00–17.30 Fri, 07.00–15.00 Sat.* No credit cards.

COFFEE

Algerian Coffee Stores **M 7**

52 Old Compton St W1. 01-437 2480. Well-preserved coffee shop, established in 1887 by a Belgian Arab, Mr Hassan. Many of the original fittings remain, although the shop is now owned by the Crocetta family, stalwarts of the Soho Society. The aroma alone is enough to see off the hangover of even the most committed Soho inebriate, but cups of espresso to drink on the premises or take away are also available. The coffee is roasted by a friend of the family in Wimbledon. Over 25 different types of coffee to choose from, the most expensive being the original Jamaican Blue Mountain. Blends include Lebanese (with cardamom), Viennese (with figs and cardamom) and French (with chicory). Eighty-five different leaf, flavoured and herb teas are also available, along with some of the most reasonably-priced cappuccino machines in Soho. Mail order too. *Open 09.00–17.30 Mon–Sat.* Access, Amex, Diners, Visa.

A. Angelucci **N 6**

23b Frith St W1. 01-437 5889. One of only three specialist coffee merchants remaining in Soho, the present generation Angeluccis, Andy and sister Alma, have run this tiny establishment since 1958. The shop was opened in 1931 by Mr Angelucci, primarily to sell coffee to the Italians. Gradually, he expanded and began selling pasta and serving cocktails and a small bar was set up at the front of the shop. It has now disappeared and Alma and Andy are winding down their pasta operation to make more room for coffee. They sell 31 varieties, including top-quality Jamaican Blue Mountain and Nicaraguan, very popular with left-wingers who buy it in support of that country's revolution. *Open 09.00–17.00 Mon–Sat, 09.00–13.00 Sun.* No credit cards.

Carwardines **L 7**

70 Old Compton St W1. 01-437 4177. Twenty different blends of coffee are sold here, along with all the paraphernalia necessary to make an authentic cappuccino or espresso. Although a coffee shop has been established here since before the war, Carwardines only took over about 20 years ago. Since they have diversified into health foods, the shop has lost some of its charm, but service is still impeccable. *Open 09.30–17.30 Mon–Fri, 09.00–16.00 Sat.* Access, Diners, Visa.

DELICATESSENS

Fratelli Camisa **K 6**

1a Berwick St W1. 01-437 7120. Ennio Camisa opened his delicatessen on this site in 1944. Now, Fratelli Camisa, run by his sons Alberto and Francesco, is probably the largest supplier of fresh pasta in the area – they sell several hundredweight of the stuff a week. Plain pasta, wholemeal pasta and pasta flavoured with tomato, spinach and basil is made above the shop in a room beneath the one in which Alberto was born. You can also buy a wide range of ingredients for making authentic sauces: fresh basil, garlic, pine kernels, capers, olive oil. And the sausages, made by a charcutier friend of Alberto's, from pure belly pork (without preservatives) are superb.

Although Camisa's stock a wide variety of foods – salamis,

mortadella, chorizo, Parma ham and bacchala (dried Italian cod) – Alberto has a special interest in cheese. The family comes from Parma in Emilia Romagna and he sells 15 varieties of Parmesan, the local cheese. The whole cheeses, imported direct from Italy, can be seen maturing on racks at the rear of the shop. There's also a wide selection of British and Continental cheeses. If you're after something particularly unusual with which to impress your guests at your next dinner party, Alberto will endeavour to obtain it within 48 hours.

Prices are on the whole very reasonable. Camisa's offer a delivery service (no extra charge for central London) and also cater for functions and parties. *Open 09.00–18.00 Mon–Sat (Thur to 14.00).* Access, Amex, Visa.

I Camisa & Son L 8

61 Old Compton St W1. 01-437 7610. Perhaps overshadowed by the Camisa's in Berwick Street, this shop nonetheless offers the bon viveur a similar selection of Continental goodies. (Differences within the family caused the businesses to be split and they are now under separate management.)

Fresh pasta is of course a speciality, along with a wide range of salamis and hams. Gaby, who manages the shop, has thoughtfully provided the customers with a chart describing the different varieties of charcuterie. Newcomers to fresh pasta can also take away a useful handout which gives precise cooking instructions, together with a few ideas for sauces. Tortelloni (pasta stuffed with ricotta and spinach) is the top seller here. Be warned: its delicate flavour can be spoiled by a heavy sauce. Save the fresh pesto (also made on the premises) for the taglierini. Other Italian treats include truffles from Piedmont (when in season), I Camisa's own-label olive oil, panettone (traditional Italian Christmas/Easter cake) and jars of seafood salad for antipasto. *Open 08.30–18.00 Mon–Sat.* No credit cards.

Lina Stores J 8

18 Brewer St W1. 01-437 6482. Lina's fresh pasta, all varieties made on the premises, is a Soho legend. Home-made tomato and pesto sauces are also available, along with the countless other ingredients which make good Italian, home-cooked food such a rewarding experience. Spices are sold by the half-ounce from enormous jars along the wall and pulses and rice from huge sacks on the floor. Fresh bread is piled up daily in the window and sells out very quickly.

Prices are very reasonable, unless you go mad and insist on the likes of first-pressing olive oil. Sausages and salamis are probably better at Camisa's but the pasta is easily on a par. You're more likely to find fresh basil here as well. Jolly staff, particularly at midday if the proprietor has been out to get the ritual pints of beer. *Open 08.00–17.45 Mon–Fri (Thur to 13.00), 08.00–17.00 Sat.* No credit cards.

Randall & Aubin

K 8

16 Brewer St W1. 01-437 3507. Charming Continental boucherie, charcuterie and delicatessen, which opened in 1906. It was bought by the Galer family in 1946. Mrs Galer still runs the shop, beadily supervising operations from the cash desk, but occasionally stepping behind the marble counter to carve ham from the bone. The ham is one of the joys of Randall's, along with the sausages. Two home-made varieties are available: English-style 'Boardroom' and Toulouse, which are spiced with garlic and come in one long strip. Excellent fresh bread and game when in season. *Open 08.00–17.00 Mon–Fri (Thur to 13.00), 08.00–16.00 Sat.* No credit cards.

Vinorio

O 6

8 Old Compton St W1. 01-437 1024. Useful if you're desperate for fresh pasta or olive oil early evening or on a Sunday morning, but otherwise unremarkable. Although the pasta itself is not made on the premises and only sold shrink-wrapped in plastic, it still puts the dried stuff to shame. Hams, salamis and cheeses hang from the ceiling but are also displayed below the counter. Small off-licence at the back of the shop, sells a limited range of French and Italian wines including marsala, liqueurs such as Strega and Amaretto, and Peroni beer. *Open 09.00–19.00 Mon–Sat (Wed to 13.30), 11.00–13.30 Sun.* No credit cards.

FISH

Richards

K 8

11 Brewer St W1. 01-437 1358. Richards offers an unbelievable array of fish, almost on a par with that of the Chinatown Fish and Meat Market in Newport Place. The last of the traditional Soho fishmongers (excluding a stall in Berwick Street market), Richards shows no sign of going the same way as Bloom's, Fulberg's or Hamburger Products; at present, it seems, business is booming.

Service is informed and considerate; gumbooted staff will explain how to cook skate knobs, how to crack a lobster and how to open an oyster. Less swish fish (cod, herring, and even coley) are also available at very reasonable prices. In season, most shellfish, including jumbo Atlantic prawns and scallops (which come complete with a free ashtray!) can be obtained here. Also a good selection of frozen seafood. *Open 08.00–17.00 Tue–Thur, 08.00–17.30 Fri, 08.00–15.00 Sat. Closed Sun & Mon.* No credit cards.

OFF-LICENCES

Del Monico's **L 8**

64 Old Compton St W1. 01-437 2738. One of Soho's longest established off-licences, Del Monico's offers a comprehensive range of alcohol including mescal (complete with the worm), a number of varieties of tequila, and Babycham. Of late, though, service has not been what it was and prices have been creeping up. Even so, Del Monico's offers much better value for money than any of the high-street chains and the staff really do know what they are talking about. Those Sohoites who bemoan the passing of quarter-bottles of champagne at The French will be relieved to know that Del Monico's sell quarter-bottles of Moët et Chandon – very handy as a morning pick-me-up. *Open 09.00–18.30 Mon–Fri, 10.00–17.00 Sat, 12.00–14.00 Sun.* No credit cards.

Gerry's **L 8**

74 Old Compton St W1. 01-734 2053. Established in 1985 by Gerry, who used to work at Del Monico's, this off-licence may well pose a serious threat to his old employers just a few doors away. Stock is equally comprehensive and prices on a par, and Gerry's score points on service and on their fine array of Riojas – very trendy and likely to appeal to their many ad agency customers. Passable selection of chilled beers. *Open 09.00–19.00 Mon–Fri, 09.00–17.00 Sat, 12.00–14.00 Sun.* No credit cards.

John Milroy

N 4

3 Greek St W1. 01-437 0893. Milroy's Soho Wine Market probably has the finest selection of malt whiskies in London, and since he opened his first shop in Beak Street in 1965, John Milroy has gained a reputation for being one of the leading experts on malts. However, the shop has never attracted much local custom. Most of those who buy here are visitors from abroad, predominantly the Japanese, who seem to have an unquenchable thirst for the stuff.

If you're a novice malt quaffer, Milroy's recommend two popular brands, Macallan and Glenmorangie to get yourself started. Although Milroy's offers malts at a very good price (including bottles for collectors at £500 apiece) other spirits such as gin and vodka cost a lot more than you'd pay at other Soho offies such as Gerry's or Del Monico's. French and some Australian wines also feature. *Open 09.00–18.00 Mon–Fri, 09.30–17.00 Sat.* Access, Visa.

Oddbins

H 9

47 Brewer St W1. 01-437 6371. More recent addition to Soho's range of off-licences. Competitive prices, but not the huge variety you'd find at Del Monico's or Gerry's. No-frills plonk is usually good value along with brand-name spirits which Oddbins buy in bulk and retail quite cheaply. Free glass hire for parties if you buy your booze here (nominal charge if you don't). *Open 09.00–21.00 Mon–Sat.* Access, Visa.

The Vintage House

M 7

42 Old Compton St W1. 01-437 2592. Scruffiest of the three off-licences on Old Compton Street, but well worth a visit for its excellent selection of 1500 vintage ports and convenient opening times. The shop is very popular with collectors of miniatures, who have about 200 to choose from, and account customers, who make up a substantial proportion of trade. Fine Bordeaux, Burgundies and German wines are also a speciality and the shop has a better choice of beers than most.

Open 09.00–23.00 Mon–Sat, 12.00–14.00 & 19.00–22.00 Sun. No credit cards.

SPECIALISTS

ARTISTS' MATERIALS

Cowling & Wilcox H 5

26–28 Broadwick St W1. 01-734 5781. A carrier bag from this artists' materials shop will enable aspiring poseurs to pretend that they too are members of Soho's burgeoning graphic design community. But before you can join this less than exclusive club you may be expected to invest in a ballpoint pen or a sheet of Letraset (Cowling & Wilcox have a large selection of both). There's also a healthy stock of fine art materials, portfolios and paper. Although the staff are helpful, you have to operate the guillotine yourself and the tiresome system of payment involves gathering receipts from around the shop and then queuing again at the cash desk. *Open 09.00–17.45 Mon–Fri, 10.00–17.00 Sat.* Access, Amex, Diners, Visa.

BOOKS

Charlotte Robinson Second Hand and Rare Books H 8

35 Great Pulteney St W1. 01-437 3683. Consortium of seven booksellers led by Ms Robinson, who has been established in Soho for over 10 years. The shop specialises in first editions, most of which are in remarkably good condition. Each bookseller has a separate set of shelves, so if at first you don't see what you want, burrow deeper into the basement. Most of the sellers will be delighted to put down your name (and areas of interest) and drop you a line if they turn up what you want. It can seem a bit stuffy, but browsing is still encouraged. *Open 11.00–18.00 Mon–Fri.* No credit cards.

Quartet Bookshop

G 4

45 Poland St W1. 01-437 1019. Chaotic general bookshop run by the legendary Naim Attallah, who also owns *Literary Review* and the Quartet imprint. Strong on travel, art and 20thC fiction. Most of the staff are bright young things from Oxbridge, recruited by Attallah himself, and they will endeavour to obtain the book you require. It's almost worth visiting the shop just to meet them. *Open 10.00–18.00 Mon–Fri.* Access, Visa.

William R. Barnes

L 6

6 Meard St W1. 01-434 0738. Upmarket new and secondhand bookseller who set up shop in 1987 in what used to be one of Soho's sleaziest streets. Shop has fogeyish, library-like atmosphere, but it's cleaner and cosier than most of the establishments on Charing Cross Road. Mr Barnes concentrates on books about art, cinema and photography but there is a small general section. Staff have impeccable manners. *Open 10.00–18.00 Mon–Sat.* Access, Amex, Visa.

BUTTONS

Taylor's

H 5

1 Silver Pl W1. 01-437 1016. Sweet little emporium in a Soho alley which will almost certainly become an enclave for the trendies over the next few years. Let's hope that this shop, with its brilliant range of hundreds of thousands of buttons, in all kinds of colours and materials, will remain. Helpful staff. *Open 10.00–16.00 Mon–Fri.* No credit cards.

ELECTRICAL

Direct Electronics

O 9

34 Lisle St WC2. 01-437 2524. Paranoiacs' supermarket. A treasure trove of anti-surveillance equipment for left-wing

political activists who believe they are being bugged. Full-range of de-bugging gear including scramblers and devices which tell you you're being bugged before you make that crucial phone call. Aspiring James Bonds are also well-catered for. Bugged briefcases, telephone recording equipment and 'Weapons Locators' are also available. Most of the items on sale cannot, by law, be used in the UK. The owners issue a disclaimer which insists that products are sold for 'export only'. *Open 10.00–17.30 Mon–Fri.* Access, Visa.

LMV Electrical Services — G 6

77 Beak St W1. 01-437 8482. Useful electrical shop specialising in totally untrendy items such as light bulbs, fuse wire and batteries. Staff extremely affable; they are prepared to give advice even if you're not buying. LMV also repair household appliances such as irons and vacuum cleaners. *Open 09.00–17.30 Mon–Fri.* No credit cards.

Soho Electrics — J 8

22 Brewer St W1. 01-437 3054. Efficient all-purpose electrical shop which sells an enormous variety of lightbulbs. Owner Ray Kaye says he'll do his best to find any bulb you require. Also large range of executive pen knives (perfect for the yuppie psychopath) and sleek designer torches. Most popular is the Mag-Lite, a powerful flashlight made of aluminium and available in a range of 'colourways'. The police love them. *Open 09.00–18.00 Mon–Sat.* Access, Visa.

FABRICS

The Fabric Studio — M 4

10 Frith St W1. 01-434 2897. Easy to miss, but the climb up the stairs to the first floor of this building is worth the effort. Exceptional selection of natural and synthetic fabrics which owner Dennis Davis buys direct from the designers or traders such as Liberty. Fabrics are mainly intended for use as garment

material, but some upholstery cloth is occasionally available. No minimum order restrictions. *Open 10.00–17.30 Mon–Sat.* No credit cards.

FLOWERS

Chivers **F 10**

80 Brewer St W1. 01-734 5653. Soho branch of an established central London chain of upmarket florists. Usual range of cut flowers, bouquets, sprays and pot plants, together with orchids. Delivery service, either by Chivers' own van for London addresses or Interflora elsewhere. *Open 09.00–18.00 Mon–Fri.* Access, Amex, Diners, Visa.

FURNITURE

Soho **G 5**

1–5 Poland St W1. 01-376 5855. Shop and design group specialising in minimalist hi-tech furniture and lighting. Some items are very imaginative, others merely overpriced. Soho was in the forefront of the area's revival and is still considered very, very trendy. The sales staff can be a little intimidating, particularly if you look as though you'd feel more at home in Habitat. *Open 10.00–18.00 Mon–Sat.* Access, Amex, Visa.

GAMES

Just Games **G 9**

62 Brewer St W1. 01-437 0761. Plenty of playthings for adults and children. Enthusiasts will appreciate the shop's comprehensive range of Trivial Pursuit questions (including the Scottish set) and other trendy boardgames. More traditional games too: chess, backgammon and, if you want to emulate the denizens of Gerrard Street, mah-jong. Not cheap, but prices can be justified by the huge variety of games on offer. *Open 10.00–18.00 Mon–Sat (to 19.00 Thur).* Access, Visa.

LEFT-HANDED

Anything Left Handed G 7

65 Beak St W1. 01-437 3910. This shop offers salvation for those forced to fumble through life in a right-handed world. Left-handed scissors, fountain pens, playing cards are all stocked, along with propagandist T-shirts proclaiming the 'rights' of the left-handed. Staff helpful but a little earnest. *Open 10.30–17.00 Mon–Fri, 10.00–14.00 Sat.* No credit cards.

MAGAZINES

Vintage Magazine Centre J 9

39 Brewer St W1. 01-439 8525. Huge emporium of ephemera, which started out in 1976 as a small business in Earlham Street selling old magazines to enthusiasts. Now the shop's operations extend to picture research for advertising agencies and importing hard-to-find memorabilia from the States. One of Soho's best venues for browsing; the magazines can be removed from the cellophane covers for closer examination.

Range of magazines is pretty comprehensive: *Harper's* from the 30s, *Picture Post* from the 40s, *Spick* from the 50s, *International Times* from the 60s and the *Observer Magazine* from the 70s. (Historic girlie titles are available, but are kept to one side, away from the prying eyes of schoolboys who aren't interested in early editions of *The Eagle*). First editions are particularly prized and if you do have a copy of *Private Eye* No 1, or better still *Playboy* No 1, bring it here for a valuation. But be warned: the shop is a commercial operation, and they'll only offer you a maximum of two-thirds of what they feel they can sell the magazine for.

When the shop moved to these premises, owner Danny Posner started to buy in assorted T-shirts, posters and other nostalgic bits and bobs to complement the magazines downstairs. Some of this is overpriced tat (ghastly Marilyn Monroe figurines for instance) but occasionally you'll find the odd gem like a Man from U.N.C.L.E. lapel-badge or a Captain Scarlet

scrapbook. *Open 10.00–19.00 Mon–Sat, 14.00–19.00 Sun.* Access, Amex, Diners, Visa.

MUSICAL INSTRUMENTS

J. & A. Beare

J 5

7 Broadwick St W1. 01-437 1449. Beare's, violin sellers and restorers, have been established here since 1872 and their business belongs to that era. They even close for lunch. Musicians from all over Europe and beyond come here to buy antique instruments (including those made by Stradivarius), and Yehudi Menuhin is a regular customer. Service is polite, if a little diffident at times. The wood-panelled shop is an excellent example of how Soho's musical traditions and crafts-

manship live on in spite of the advent of the video jukebox. *Open 09.00–12.15 & 13.30–17.00 Mon–Fri.* No credit cards.

Chas E. Foote **G 9**

17 Golden Sq W1. 01-734 1823. Considerably more civilised than the chaotic and sometimes offhand instrument shops to be found in Tin Pan Alley, Foote's specialise in drums – cymbals, congas, snares and timpani – for pop and classical musicians. The staff are particularly helpful and will gladly give impartial advice even if you're not prepared to purchase so much as a single string. The basement offers a full range of stringed, woodwind and brass instruments. *Open 09.00–17.30 Mon–Fri, 09.00–17.00 Sat.* Access, Visa.

Soho Soundhouse **M 2**

18a Soho Sq W1. 01-434 1365. Bands with bookings in Soho might find this shop useful if they leave the guitar, spare strings or even the plectrum behind. Wide range of electric and acoustic guitars is complemented by a selection of electronic keyboard instruments. Cost-conscious managers could investigate the synthesisers and consider making their guitarists redundant. Synthesisers are much cheaper to run. Classic guitars such as Fenders and Gibsons always available. *Open 10.00–18.00 Mon–Fri, 10.30–18.00 Sat.* Access, Amex, Visa.

NEWSAGENTS (INTERNATIONAL)

Capital Newsagents **M 7**

48 Old Compton St W1. 01-437 2479. Although not quite in the same league as Moroni's, Capital still sells plenty of foreign newspapers and mags, mainly to the local Italian community. Arab and Greek titles are also popular. They are more tolerant of browsers than Moroni, but it is still inadvisable to regard this shop as an annexe to the library in Charing Cross Road. *Open 07.30–18.45 Mon–Fri, 07.30–18.30 Sat, 08.00–12.00 Sun.* No credit cards.

A. Moroni & Son

L 7

68 Old Compton St W1. 01-437 2847. Mr Moroni is not one of the square mile's most affable souls and browsing in his international newsagent's shop is actively discouraged. Nonetheless he provides an excellent selection of newspapers and magazines, although it's hard to obtain papers from the States. They usually arrive ten days late and cost about six times as much as they would in their country of origin.

Poseurs will appreciate the kudos value of being spotted in Valerie's or the Bar Italia with one's head buried in Brazilian *Vogue*, *The New Yorker* or *Vanity Fair*, the Moroni's price sticker having been removed from the front cover. However, *the* organ to be seen with must be the Italian sports paper, *Gazzetta della Sporta* which offers machismo as well as cosmopolitan cred. Who'd be seen dead reading a foppish fashion magazine when the *Gazzetta* can offer you style *and* the English football results? *Open 07.30–19.15 Mon–Sat, 08.00–13.00 Sun.* No credit cards.

PHOTOGRAPHIC

A1 Cameras

K 4

9–12 St Anne's Court W1. 01-437 8746. Seemingly chaotic shop which nonetheless offers an excellent repair service for cameras. Repair and return is usually very swift (most repairs are carried out on the premises) and A1 will give you an estimate before they start work. Rescue service also available if your film gets stuck in the camera. *Open 09.00–17.00 Mon–Fri.* No credit cards.

Joe's Basement

K 7

89–91 Wardour St W1. 01-434 9313. Primarily a processing lab for professional photographers, Joe offers probably the best deal on colour and black and white film in London. And he's open 24 hours a day, seven days a week. Bring your holiday snaps here. Processing and printing – which is carried out by hand – is of excellent quality, but since it is geared to the trade, much more expensive than at a high-street chemist. Service is very quick: Joe says he will develop transparencies in two hours and produce prints from trannies in six. Phone for details of delivery service. *Open 24 hrs Mon–Sun.* Access, Visa.

PRINTS

The Print Gallery — E 6

17 Newburgh St W1. 01-439 1530. Work from up-and-coming young artists. Most of their contemporary prints – mainly landscapes, portraits, floral still-lifes – are from limited editions which don't normally exceed 250. The gallery also retails a selection of hand-painted cards; expensive but attractive. Framing service takes about four days. *Open 09.00–19.00 Mon–Fri, 10.30–17.00 Sat.* Access, Visa.

RECORDS AND CASSETTES

Daddy Kool — K 2

93a Dean St W1. 01-437 4500. De only record shop in Soho specialising in de reggae music, mon. Daddy Kool's range encompasses secondhand rarities, new imports and mainstream catalogue stuff. Secondhand records bought and exchanged, but since this is a commercial operation, it is unlikely that your pile of ageing dub sounds will make you a fortune. *Open 10.00–19.00 Mon–Sat.* No credit cards.

58 Dean Street Records — M 7

58 Dean St W1. 01-437 4500. Cramped, sweaty shop specialising in movie themes. Re-live Francis Lai's *Un Homme et Une Femme*! Wallow in the original *West Side Story*! Pay three times as much as you'd expect for soundtrack albums! Five Eight's selection is comprehensive, but prices are high. However, the staff are knowledgeable and the atmosphere a good deal more civilised than the vinyl supermarkets on Oxford Street. *Open 10.00–19.00 Mon–Sat.* Access, Visa.

Groove Records N 5

52 Greek St W1. 01-439 8231. When this shop opened in the early 70s, stock was a catholic mix of glamrock, 60s soul and what contemporary DJs had termed 'progressive'. Now what's on offer is almost 100 per cent black – disco, jazz funk, hip hop and 80s soul. Groove is owned by Soho's most unlikely record-shop proprietor: Jean Palmer, a grandmotherly figure in her 70s who, like John Peel, has seen them all come and go and is still hanging on in there. Jean can usually be spotted behind the counter, keeping a watchful eye over her customers and occasionally ejecting the odd bopper who insists on treating her premises as a free-entry disco. *Open 10.00–19.00 Mon–Wed, 10.00–20.00 Thur–Sat, 14.00–18.00 Sun.* No credit cards *or cheques*.

Harold Moore's Records F 4

2 Great Marlborough St W1. 01-437 1576. Specialists in classical rarities, this is one of the friendliest and most helpful record shops in Soho. Harold and his partners offer expert advice and fair prices on any rare recordings. Stock is particularly strong on virtuosos, but their eclectic selection seldom disappoints. They often buy job lots from the estates of collectors who've passed away; these can yield some real finds and the odd bargain. *Open 10.00–18.30 Mon–Sat.* Access, Visa.

Hitman Records J 8

2 Lexington St W1. 01-437 8708. Specialist soul/hip hop/jazz funk and salsa record store. Most of stock is hard-to-find material imported from the USA. Deletions often available. Tiny selection of compact discs. *Open 10.30–21.00 Mon–Sat, 14.00–18.00 Sun.* No credit cards.

SEX SHOPS

Ann Summers J 8

26 Brewer St W1. 01-437 4016. Ann Summers' chain of sex

shops is by far the most reputable of the industry. They have a reputation for fair play, decent products and helpful service. This is one of their unlicensed shops; as a result the stock is mainly comprised of lingerie (peek-a-boo-bras, basques, see-through jockstraps etc) and novelties such as edible knickers (strawberry flavour) and wind-up plastic penises. As this shop does not have a licence only 10 per cent of its stock can be made up of sex aids such as dildos and vibrators, and it cannot sell even soft porn. Staff here are extremely obliging and a sign attached to the dildo rack suggests that they will be prepared to demonstrate the products if a customer so wishes(!). Women are frequent customers but members of the dirty raincoat brigade are nowhere to be seen. *Open 10.00–23.00 Mon–Sat, 10.00–18.00 Sun.* Access, Amex, Diners.

Ann Summers O 2

159 Charing Cross Rd WC2. 01-437 1886. Ann Summers' only licensed sex shop. The company pays Westminster City Council over £12,000 a year for its licence which entitles it to sell an unlimited amount of sex aids and a quantity of softish porn (newsagents generally sell stronger material). The shop is divided onto two floors; downstairs for sex aids and mags, upstairs for lingerie and bondage equipment. They also do a nice line in rubberwear. Staff members, who are exceptionally helpful, wear badges with their names on. Westminster insist upon this. *Open 10.00–22.00 Mon–Thur, 10.00–23.00 Fri & Sat.* Access, Amex, Diners.

Lovejoys O 5

99a Charing Cross Rd WC2. 01-437 1988. Upstairs is an ordinary remainder bookshop, downstairs a licensed sex shop selling the full range of very soft to almost hard-porn magazines. All tastes catered for including spankers and spankees. This seems to be the current hangout of the Soho Dirty Raincoat Club; worth taking a look on the offchance you might spot your boss stashing contact mags into his briefcase. Large range of sex aids including dildos, vibrators, assorted erection creams and strange rings which go over the tip of the penis. All items are discreetly wrapped in brown paper bags. *Open 10.00–22.30 Mon–Sat.* Access, Visa.

SHOES

Red or Dead L 11

22 Rupert St W1. 01-439 2408. Poseurs' shoe shop specialising in Doctor Martens. Apparently they are still *de rigueur* in many of Soho's trendier nightclubs, a fact borne out by this shop's success since it opened in the summer of 1987. Apart from DMs, there's also a selection of hip T-shirts and jogging-type wear (yawn). Staff can be standoffish. *Open 10.30–21.00 Mon–Fri, 10.30–19.30 Sat, 12.30–19.30 Sun.* Access, Visa.

Shoes K 7

8–9 Walker's Court W1. 01-734 4848. One of Soho's cheapest shoe shops, offering remarkable savings on 'sale' items. Beware, however, of the tat and be prepared to settle for something else if they don't have your size; Shoes sells mainly oddments. If you want something for the office and don't work in advertising, head towards Oxford Street. *Open 09.30–18.00 Mon–Fri, 10.00–18.00 Sat.* Access, Diners, Visa.

SPORTS

Lonsdale F 7

19 & 21 Beak St W1. 01-437 1526. Suddenly boxing is trendy again, as Messrs Honeyghan and Bruno (who used to work as a sales assistant here) inspire the nation's youth to put on gloves and beat the hell out of each other. Soho's boxing connections are well-established (in the 40s and 50s Jack Solomons ran a gym in Great Windmill Street) and this shop offers aspiring pugilists and lily-livered poseurs the opportunity to don the latest in trendy boxing attire. Choose from Lonsdale T-shirts, smart leather boots and those super headguards that can

transform a ten-stone weakling into a human dynamo. Also a range of general sporting equipment. *Open 09.00–18.00 Mon–Fri, 09.00–17.00 Sat.* Access, Visa.

Paolo Garbini

H 8

36 Great Pulteney St W1. 01-734 9912. No bicycles, but all the accessories a Sohoite would need to pedal around the square mile with aplomb. Saddles, toe-clips, water bottles and a huge range of safety equipment (including those useful but ugly plastic helmets) are available, together with a range of thigh-hugging shorts. Paolo is an Italian international, and when not serving in the shop still competes in top-level tourings. He also runs the Soho Cycling Club, an *ad hoc* gathering of enthusiasts who take their bikes out at weekends, and he and his staff are more than happy to dispense expert advice. *Open 09.00–19.00 Mon–Fri, 09.00–15.00 Sat.* Access, Visa.

Soccer Scene

D 5

24 Carnaby St W1. 01-439 0778. Replica team strips sold here by the dozen, but if you don't run a team of your own, they won't mind you buying just one or two. Prices are high, but that doesn't seem to bother the fathers, mothers and Continental tourists who snap up the snazziest strips. To encourage parents to part with more money, most teams make minor changes to their strip at least once a year. The changes, though cosmetic, are usually enough to convince little Johnny that he is no longer the proud owner of a Chelsea/Manchester United/West Ham kit and needs a new one. Also a range of trainers, running shoes and football boots. *Open 09.30–18.00 Mon–Sat.* Access, Amex, Diners, Visa.

TAILORS

A. Dometakis

G 6

47 Lexington St W1. 01-437 1075. Tiny bespoke tailors run by Greek-Cypriot Andreas Dometakis, his wife and sister,

specialising in shirts. Andreas opened his first shop in Soho in 1968 and moved to these premises in 1975. Choose from 1200 different patterns in cotton, silk, linen or wool/cotton. Most of the fabrics are made in England, plus a few imports from Switzerland. In comparison with Jermyn Street prices are reasonable. Service is friendly, without being obsequious. Minimum order two shirts, waiting time six to eight weeks. *Open 09.00–18.00 Mon–Fri, 10.30–13.00 Sat.* No credit cards.

TOBACCONISTS

Coleman & Cohen **N 7**

42 Frith St W1. 01-734 5482. A family firm of tobacconists established this shop in 1903. Although recently taken over by the Finlays chain, the shop has retained its individual charm and not become a victim of faceless corporatism. It sells cigars, cigarillos and cheroots from countries such as Holland and Indonesia as well as Cuba, along with a range of cigarettes. The staff are knowledgeable without being patronising and even if you don't want to buy anything, you can still drop in for a light from the gas flame which burns on the counter. *Open 09.00–18.00 Mon–Fri, 09.00–17.30 Sat.* No credit cards.

Inderwick's **E 6**

45 Carnaby St W1. 01-734 6574. Inderwick's, established in 1797 in Wardour Street, is still one of the best tobacconists in Soho. Within the dark confines of this small shop, you can choose from a vast selection of pipes, cigars, cheroots, tobaccos and even snuff. If you are really unadventurous, they will even stretch to 10 Silk Cut. Although Inderwick's made its name from selling high-quality Meerschaum pipes in the 18th century, in recent years it has diversified and it's now possible to purchase a wide range of accessories including cigarette boxes and holders and a small range of snuff boxes. *Open 09.00–18.30 Mon–Sat.* No credit cards.

TOOLS AND HARDWARE

Burgess & Galer H 9

51 Brewer St W1. 01-437 4989. This shop has been in the Galer family since it opened in 1896. Primarily architectural iron-mongers, they also stock Swiss army knives, general iron-mongery and tools. An emergency locksmithing service is also available during opening hours. *Open 08.30–17.30 Mon–Fri, 08.30–12.30 Sat.* Access, Amex, Diners, Visa.

House Bros (Cutlers) F 10

85 Brewer St W1. 01-437 3857. Family firm established in Soho in 1864 which specialises in DIY tools and knives for the catering trade. Full range of Sabatier chef's knives available, excellent quality but expensive. The shop is also useful for picking up odds and ends of general hardware – washing-up liquid, bleach etc and the bluff proprietor is happy to sell nuts, bolts and screws individually. Another, smaller branch at 49 Rupert Street. *Open 09.00–17.45 Mon–Fri, 09.30–15.00 Sat (Sat hours can vary).* Access, Visa.

MARKETS

Berwick Street Market

One of the best food markets in London, established here since the late 19th century. In 1778 the Committee for Paving, Cleansing and Public Works reported that 'brokers' living in the area were to be summoned for setting out their goods in the street. The market finally gained official recognition in 1906.

Berwick Street contributes a lot to Soho's raffish, village-like atmosphere. Although a number of stalls specialise in general market goods such as household cleaning materials, fruit and vegetables have always been Berwick Street's strong-point. However, the quality can be variable and unless you know that a particular trader's bananas, oranges or apples are always up to scratch, you may have to take pot luck. Most of the traders display better quality produce on the front of their stalls, but they won't sell you this, so keep your wits about you and watch carefully what is put in your bag. Resist the temptation to squeeze the produce; the traders have a reputation for rudeness and are masters of finely-honed sarcasm. They will not show any mercy, even to the women they insist on calling 'lovie'.

Prices, in general, are very reasonable although the produce sold here is never perfect. It's easy to come by unusual fruit and veg such as sharon fruit, papaya and okra, and the market is also a good source of root ginger; surprisingly, the latter is usually cheaper here than in Chinatown. Fresh flowers from the stall in the middle usually represent very good value for money as do the pot plants.

The best bargains are probably to be had at about 5pm on Saturday when the traders are preparing to pack up for home. At this point their patter reaches fever pitch and their prices rock bottom as they try to get rid of perishables which won't last the weekend. If you're not buying, the best time for rubbernecking is early in the morning when the traders are taking deliveries and opening up their stalls. This is noisy, hectic, barrow-boy Soho, much trawled in the 60s by photographers anxious to find robust images with which to contrast the effete posturing of Carnaby Street. (Marc Bolan worked here in the 60s on his mother's fruit stall.)

The stalls are set up remarkably quickly each morning, then the stallholders usually pop into Bar Bruno on Wardour Street for a cup of tea. (At lunchtime, pints of beer are brought out from The King of Corsica pub.) The produce is then sorted. The best fruit is placed at the front of the stall, the unsaleable discarded into the cardboard boxes which litter the pavements and will, by the end of the day, give Berwick Street the appearance of a shanty town thoroughfare despite the electric dustcart which patrols the street throughout the day heralded by cries of 'mind yer back'.

Berwick Street has a roguish charm which other street markets in London somehow lack. The spivs and shysters of 50s Soho were at home here and Berwick Street still has its share of rascals. Watch out for the pickpockets, and don't get involved in any of the (illegal) Find the Lady card games which

occasionally take place in Walker's Court. They are all rigged and although the dealers pay out occasionally, you can rest assured that the lucky winners are always stooges working with the dealers.

Rupert Street Market

Much smaller than Berwick Street, but also specialising in fruit and veg. Don't come here for the basics though; Rupert Street traders tend to sell unusual items which are difficult to find outside the posh food halls. Usually expensive, but most produce is very good quality. A number of Soho's restaurateurs buy here at wholesale prices. The old adage 'you get wot you pays for' rings very true in Rupert Street, and it is unlikely that you will be swindled. In general, traders are slightly more deferential than those in Berwick Street since they are dealing with what they regard as a better class of customer.

6 Entertainment

Although many tourists and newcomers will find what remains of Soho's sex scene oddly alluring, the area offers much more in the way of legitimate entertainment. In Soho there are at least half a dozen theatres, a handful of cinemas (not counting the preview rooms used by the film industry) and plenty of places in which you can enjoy yourself during the day. Try Marshall Street baths, for instance, if you want to reverse the kind of decline which is induced by too many visits to Patisserie Valerie.

It's at night, however, that Soho assumes its glow, with hordes of trendies and others flocking in for a taste of the night life. In summer, the pavements are packed with poseurs, but those in search of more conventional entertainment are seldom disappointed. At dusk, the area soon fills up with pre-theatre diners and drinkers before a hiatus once the performances have started. Curtain-down time, however, sends the audiences back onto the streets and into the restaurants. At this point, clubland Soho begins to stir.

While the antics of the clubbers may not be to everyone's taste, they provide a reminder that Soho is one of the noisiest, most exciting centres of entertainment in the capital. But don't be perturbed if you have no interest in salsa, hip-hop or funk; Soho offers a huge variety of entertainment of which the clubs are but a small part. Somewhere within this square mile, even the most finicky of visitors will find something to amuse.

CASINOS

You can only enter a gaming house as a member or the guest of a member. Generally speaking, in order to become a member you will be asked by the club to fill in a declaration of your intent to gamble, present some form of identification (passport, driving licence, bank card) and pay an annual fee. You will not then be permitted to gamble until 48 hours has elapsed from the time you signed the declaration form. Both the clubs listed below operate on this basis.

Charlie Chester

12a Archer St W1. 01-734 0255. **K 9**

Archer Street is without a doubt one of Soho's sleaziest streets, and Charlie Chester's is certainly Soho's scruffiest casino. However, it is still remarkably popular. On a Friday or Saturday night the roulette tables and blackjack schools are crowded with punters, and during the week a steady stream of gamblers ensures that the coffers of Brent Walker, Charlie Chester's owners (who took over the Trocadero in 1987), remain swollen.

The casino is on two floors, the ground floor offering roulette, punto banco, blackjack and craps. Downstairs the atmosphere is a little more refined, but by no means sophisticated. There is a naff little restaurant and bar at one end of the room. Far better to risk your money at the tables. The food, shall we say, is variable in quality.

Beginners shouldn't have any problem trying their luck at roulette, a game beloved by the bingo fraternity, moody-looking Chinese (the biggest spenders of all) and Asian businessmen. Before 9pm the minimum stakes here are very low, but they rise sharply later on. Should you attempt to place a stake which is below the minimum, it will be noticed and your money will be returned gracelessly by the croupier. Very noticeable here are the 'minders' who sit at the tables keeping an eye on the croupiers and the punters. Since the London casino fiddles of the 70s, casino owners have made it virtually impossible for their staff to cheat. Those who apply for membership receive a tacky plastic card which is valid for life and will also get you into Charlie Chester's sister casinos elsewhere in Britain.

Charlie Chester

Open: 14.00–04.00 Mon–Sun.
Admission: Members and guests only.
Membership: Essential. £5.
Dress: No jeans, men must wear jackets.
Credit cards: Not accepted.

Golden Nugget

22–32 Shaftesbury Ave W1. 01-734 6211. **K 10**

Although the Golden Nugget is by no means the kind of establishment that the likes of John Aspinall, Lord Lucan or Soraya Khashoggi would be seen gambling in, it's not too scruffy. The customers are predominantly Chinese though there's a sprinkling of tourists, Sohoites and middle-aged ladies who look as though they'd be more at home in a suburban bingo hall. In fact the ambience of the GN is not unlike one of the Ladbroke-run pleasure palaces that exist throughout London and beyond. The croupiers at the roulette tables call out 'No more bets' in accents more redolent of Mile End than Monte Carlo and they don't even use one of those little rakes to gather up the chips.

Newcomers to the tables should not feel intimidated if they want to have a flutter. The three games played at the club: punto banco, blackjack and American roulette are all conducted in English. A novice would be best to start on one of the roulette tables where minimum stakes are low and customers tolerant of amateurs. Ladies will not meet any moustachioed mystery men prepared to thrust high-value chips down cleavages, but at least they'll be able to have a taste of the action themselves. Absolute beginners can ask one of the gaming staff for advice about the rules of the game, and instruction leaflets are also dished out.

The Golden Nugget's small-time ambience belies the fact that at times big money does change hands. Most of it of course ends up in the hands of the owners (who run a string of casinos

including the wideboys' favourite, the Sportsman on Tottenham Court Road) but you never know your luck. And you needn't necessarily put any money down; just watching the expressions on the faces of the punters as they lose hundreds of pounds can be compelling enough to while away a couple of hours.

Golden Nugget

Open: 14.00–02.00 Mon–Thur & Sun, 14.00–03.00 Fri & Sat.
Admission: Members and guests only.
Membership: Essential. £1.15.
Dress: No jeans, men must wear a jacket.
Credit cards: Not accepted.

CINEMAS

Astral 1 & 2

5–7 Brewer St W1. 01-734 6387. **K 8**

Licensed cinema showing ludicrous soft porno movies with titles such as *Erotic Inferno*, *Hot Acts of Love* and *Warm Nights, Hot Pleasure*. Much of the material is heavily censored nonsense from abroad, the rest low budget home-produced stuff which first reached the cinemas here in the late 70s and early 80s. Most television dramas have a greater erotic content and the dialogue is a lot more polished. However, if stiffly acted, badly scripted movies are your wont, the Astral is about the best place in Soho to see them, and the management promise that relaxed licensing restrictions will soon allow them to show stronger material.

Prices are reasonable; for a flat fee you can stay all day. The cinema is clean, the seats are comfortable and small packets of Kleenex can be obtained from the booking office, which oddly enough doubles as an ice-cream kiosk. Chewing gum addicts who leave their Wrigley's Spearmint at home may find the Astral's liquorice-flavoured condoms (available from a vending machine outside the lavatories) an acceptable substitute. *Open 11.00–24.00 Mon–Thur, 11.00–01.00 Fri & Sat, 11.00–22.30 Sun. Continuous programmes.* No credit cards.

Curzon West End

93 Shaftesbury Ave W1. 01-439 4805. **N 8**

A good deal plusher than most cinemas in the West End, the Curzon offers serious movies which aren't too demanding: Merchant Ivory's *Room With A View*, which ran here for months, was a typical example. The CWE's programming is closely linked to its superior sister, the Curzon Mayfair. Films tend to open there and subsequently transfer. Not cheap. *Doors & box office open from 11.00 Mon–Sun. Occasional late shows Fri & Sat at 23.00.* Access, Visa.

Metro

11 Rupert St W1. 01-437 0757. **L 11**

Originally funded by the GLC, the Metro is the sole saving grace of the ghastly Trocadero complex. Smallish and cosy, the cinema specialises in intelligent, liberal-minded films which usually go down well with *Time Out* reviewers. No Rambo here. Staff, including usherpersons, are uniformly trendy film buff-types. As you might expect, the refreshments have a wholemeal slant: samosas, carrot cake, flapjacks etc. It is impossible to buy a hotdog. Ring for details of video presentations and the occasional Chinese programme on Sunday nights. Seat prices reasonable. *Open Mon–Sun. Late shows Fri & Sat at 23.15.* No credit cards.

Moulin

43 Great Windmill St W1. 01-437 1653. **J 10**

Sleazier than the Astral, the Moulin offers much the same material – censored, ageing soft porn – except here there are six different programmes to choose from. The only films shown here remotely worth seeing are the Russ Meyer 'Super Vixens' series in which Meyer's pneumatic heroines succeed in sending up the entire genre. Once you've paid your admission charge, you can stay as long as you like, but don't expect your eyes to be riveted to the screen. *The Sound of Music* was more erotic than most of the movies shown here. *Open 11.00–02.00 Mon–Sun. Continuous programmes.* No credit cards.

HEALTH CLUBS

Marshall Street Leisure Centre

Marshall St W1. 01-798 2007 **F 5**

Listed 1920s complex, recently trendified by Westminster City Council who seem anxious to cash in on the prevailing health and fitness boom. Much of the original architecture remains; the wall at one end of the pool, reopened in 1987, is particularly striking.

The centre represents excellent value for money. Weight training is available at a fraction of the price one would pay in a private club and it is possible to have a lunchtime game of ping-pong – ideal for the busy executive who can't muster the strength for a game of squash. Private classes in martial arts and keep fit can also be arranged. In addition, baths and showers are available for those who prefer to smell sweet before a night on the town.

Marshall Street Leisure Centre

Open: 08.30–19.00 Mon–Thur, 08.30–17.30 Fri, 09.00–17.00 Sat. Closed Sun.
Admission: Varies according to activity.
Membership: Not available.
Dress: Swimming costumes available for hire.
Credit cards: Not accepted.

Metropolitan Club

27–28 Kingly St W1. 01-734 5002. **C 6**

Yuppie enclave amid the utility shops, pubs and cafés of Kingly Street, which offers a complete physical overhaul for the tired businessperson. Aerobics, weight-training, dance classes, sun beds are all available, along with jacuzzis (mixed sex but no nudity please) in which executives can wind down after a busy day at the agency. Patrons are advised to bring waterproof coverings for their Filofaxes.

Ninety-eight per cent of those who use this health club work, rather than live, in Soho which probably accounts for the astronomical membership fees – presumably tax-deductible if you have the right kind of accountant. Unashamedly, the club panders to the needs of decaying admen, hacks and film moguls. Who needs a jog in the park when you can get fit and be trendy into the bargain?

Apart from using the Nautilus weight-training equipment, which bears an uncanny resemblance to medieval instruments of torture, clients can also take a dip in the club's plant-fringed pool. The latter is far removed from a standard municipal baths: nubile, leotard-clad ladies disport themselves around its 'shores' while waiting for the jacuzzi to empty. It can get very hot up there. The management maintain that this is due to the temperature of the water. Refreshments, including fruit juices, salads and wholemeal sandwiches are available from a small licensed restaurant whenever the club is open.

Metropolitan Club

Open: 09.00–23.00 Mon, Wed, Fri & Sat, 07.00–23.00 Tue & Thur, 09.00–22.30 Sun.
Admission: £15 day membership.
Membership: Essential. £450 per annum; £275 six months; £65 one month; plus £30 enrolment fee for all but day membership.
Dress: Designer tracksuits.
Credit cards: Access, Visa.

LIVE MUSIC

Astoria

157 Charing Cross Rd WC2. 01-434 9592. **O 2**

Formerly the Astoria Theatre, this new live music venue opened in the summer of 1987. While the present clientele is not as trendy as those who frequented the place in its earlier incarnation as a once-weekly nightclub, Delirium, a good range of modern bands play here regularly. There are usually two acts a night, the first featuring a British band, the second an American one.

The theatre auditorium has had its seats ripped out and replaced with a dance-floor. Capacity is about 1500, and on a popular night it can get very sweaty down there. Cool off first in the tastelessly-named 'Keith Moon Bar'. Prices are about half as much again as you'd expect to pay in a pub, and drinkers have to make do with plastic 'glasses'. Large signs in the foyer and lavatories emphasise that 'Drugs are not allowed'.

The Astoria is owned and run by John Gunnell, a veteran of the Soho club scene – he used to run the Flamingo and the Bag-O-Nails and also managed Cream. He issues 'Gold Cards' to selected members of the press, rock stars and people who he thinks will 'spend a few bob'. Everyone else must pay to get in.

Astoria

Open: 19.30–03.30 Mon–Sat (to 23.00 when no late show). Closed Sun.
Admission: £5–£10.
Membership: VIPs only; not required.
Dress: Smart casual except on punk and heavy metal nights.
Credit cards: Access, Amex, Diners, Visa.

The Marquee

90 Wardour St W1. 01-437 6603. **K 6**

A legendary Soho rock venue; some of Britain's most successful pop musicians cut their teeth in this sweaty little room. The Marquee started life as an Oxford Street jazz club in 1958 and moved to Wardour Street in 1964. At the time the country was in the grip of Beatlemania; the Mersey Sound had spawned a new, vibrant pop scene and London bands such as The Rolling Stones and The Kinks were after a piece of the action. Both bands played at the Marquee, which soon became as famous as the Cavern in Liverpool. It was here during The Who's regular Tuesday night residency that Pete Townshend perfected the group's guitar-smashing act which was to cost them dear in HP repayments but guarantee them masses of column inches.

Throughout the decade, the Marquee played host to some of the world's most promising young stars. An extraordinarily astute booking policy meant that the club could attract the cream of the world's musicians – Jimi Hendrix, Ten Years After, David Bowie – before they became too expensive and started performing in football stadiums. The Marquee missed out on the Beatles, however; by the time the club moved to Soho, the Fab Four were millionaires and their Pierre Cardin jackets were far too smart for this grubby little joint.

Yet those who'd played at the Marquee in the early days recalled the tremendous atmosphere of those first few gigs. Many of the greats, including Led Zeppelin, Yes and Genesis, returned to Wardour Street long after they'd installed the platinum-plated jacuzzis and bought up half of the Home Counties.

In the 70s, interest in the Marquee waned slightly but the post-77 punk explosion brought the fans back again. The Clash, The Damned, The Boomtown Rats all performed here and for a few months it seemed that the club was once again at the centre of musical innovation. The Jam, regulars at the Marquee, released a song called *A Bomb in Wardour Street* celebrating this golden age. (The *enfants terribles* of the new wave, The Sex Pistols, only played here twice, on both occasions as a supporting act; the management deemed them 'unmusical' and felt they did not warrant further bookings.)

Since those crazy, beer-and-phlegm-stained days the Marquee has failed to live up to its reputation; very few bands of note have emerged from the club in the last few years. The Marquee has in fact become positively unhip, attracting a clientele mainly composed of heavy metal freaks from the suburbs. Yet they behave themselves and it is possible to buy a drink (at pub prices) without being pushed around, abused or made to feel untrendy. The standards of musicianship vary wildly, but on a good night the music is exactly how rock and roll should be: fast, coarse and sweaty. And venues don't come much sweatier than the Marquee.

At the time of writing, it was likely that the Marquee would be moving out of Wardour Street into temporary premises (phone for details). The Club will return to this site in 1989.

The Marquee

Open: 19.00–23.00 Mon–Sat, 19.00–22.30 Sun.
Admission: £3.50–£5.
Membership: Not required. Privilege card (£2 for six months) entitles the holder to reduced admission price and advance bookings.
Dress: 'Anyway, Anyhow, Anywhere'.
Credit cards: Not accepted.

Ronnie Scott's

47 Frith St W1. 01-439 0747 **M 6**

Since Ronnie Scott opened his first club in Gerrard Street in 1959, he has booked virtually every big name in the business.

The present club, which opened in 1965, still enjoys a reputation as one of Europe's foremost jazz venues. Most of the greats, including Oscar Peterson, Count Basie, Sonny Rollins and Chick Corea have played here and Scott continues to attract big names such as Nina Simone and Sarah Vaughan.

Most of the action takes place in the main restaurant/bar area on the ground floor. The punters sit at ancient tables with little red table lamps, very close to the stage. (Arrive early if you want a good seat.) The main artistes perform here, but there is also a smaller bar and stage area upstairs which is used by up-and-coming young combos anxious for exposure. Two acts perform two hour-long sets each every evening.

The atmosphere at Ronnie's varies considerably, depending on the type of performer. A big draw will obviously pull the punters in and the club can become very hot and smoky. Many people like their jazz served like that, but those who prefer comfort and space should perhaps go along on Monday or Tuesday when the demand for tickets is not so great.

In recent years, the club has been attacked in print for its treatment of the punters. Entrance fees are very steep indeed and surly staff, overpriced drinks and poor food have been cited as examples of the club's cavalier attitude towards those who pay the rent. Certainly the food is expensive and very boring, but you don't have to eat here. Drinks, too, are priced way over the odds, but the tiny bar and slow service mean that most people just don't have time to get expensively drunk.

Yet after 27 years, Ronnie Scott's remains an important Soho nighterie. It's rare that one has the opportunity to hear such big-name jazz performing in such an intimate setting. Providing you don't mind crowds, don't eat and make do with a glass of squash all evening you should have a marvellous time.

Ronnie Scott's

Open: 20.30–02.30 Mon–Sat, 08.00–23.00 Sun.
Admission: £8. Reductions for members, students and Musicians' Union.
Membership: £30 per annum; not required.
Dress: No restrictions.
Credit cards: Access, Amex, Diners, Visa.

Soho Jazz Festival

Although jazz has reverberated in Soho for a good many decades, the annual Jazz Festival is a very recent addition to the district's cultural calendar.

The Festival, which began in 1986, was dreamed up by Peter Boizot, the colourful entrepreneur who founded the Pizza Express chain and now owns Kettners. A lifelong jazz enthusiast, Boizot publishes *Jazz Express* (a freebie magazine), and acts as Festival Director. He and his small team co-ordinate the Festival each year, booking venues for the multifarious performers. The venues he chooses are as diverse as Soho itself. Last year's eclectic mix included the Astoria, Groucho's, De Hems pub and the Trocadero. The artists who have appeared at the Festival include some of the biggest names in contemporary and trad jazz: Humphrey Lyttleton, Charlie Byrd and the New Orleans All Stars were just three of the 60 plus acts booked to appear in 1987.

The reasons for the success of the Jazz Festival in fact lie in its diversity. The acts playing the clubs certainly pull in the purists, but the foot-tapping combos performing in the streets also have an appeal. The Festival has now pretty much established itself as a regular feature on the Soho scene. It is a shame, however, that press interest is so lukewarm. Many of the events are under-publicised and it isn't until the Festival is over that most Sohoites find out about what's been on. This may be because Boizot himself is not fond of journalists. Instead of granting interviews, he prefers to issue his own puffs for the Festival, some of which deserve to be sent to the Carlisle Street offices of *Private Eye* for publication in 'Pseud's Corner'.

However, beneath the waffle he does convey one or two pertinent points: 'It has been the case for years and years that every night is jazz festival night in Soho, with its multitude of clubs and entertainment. The Soho Jazz Festival simply emphasises what already exists and we hope, brings joy to listeners old and new.'

The Festival is usually held in the first fortnight of October. For information, phone Kettners on 01-437 6437.

MEMBERSHIP CLUBS

Groucho Club

45 Dean St W1. 01-439 4685. **M 6**

The Groucho Club was set up in 1985, ostensibly to cater for those sections of the media – mainly publishers, literary agents and authors – who needed somewhere quiet and central in which to talk business, eat and, of course, drink. The club has now achieved 75 per cent of its intended full complement of 1500 members, and feels secure enough to turn its nose up at those working in the film and advertising industries.

The main focus of the club is the bar. This occupies a large room at the front and leads into the brasserie at the rear. The bar is usually cool and dark – in summer ceiling fans give the room an almost colonial feel, spoilt somehow by the mish-mash of furniture (soft comfy sofas, hi-tech plastic stools) and fittings. Most of the furniture was picked up in a job lot by Groucho's co-owner Liz Calder and the art deco lampshades are identical to those in her home. Although Groucho's is no longer as trendy as it was when it first opened, famous-face spotters will find plenty of material. Madonna chose to hold her birthday party here in 1987 during her first British tour.

Hacks use the bar in the afternoons to conduct interviews and in the evenings publishers can be seen treating their authors to the odd bottle of house champagne. Waiter and waitress service is perhaps too efficient; members who don't wish to drink and are content just to sit and read the papers are frequently cajoled by the staff into ordering their usual tipple. The drinks are probably overpriced, given the high membership fees, but Groucho's have got the sordid business of paying the bill off to a fine art. A member is not expected to part with money until the end of the evening, during which time he or she will have settled into the club's relaxed ambience, drifted into the brasserie (the Anglo-French cooking has improved since the early days) and strolled back to the bar for a nightcap.

The restaurant upstairs is grander than the brasserie, and in terms of ambience and style is remarkably similar to the upstairs restaurant at L'Escargot. The food is also similar, but

the emphasis here is on so-called New British Cuisine. The Club Room, also upstairs, is rarely used but is probably the most comfortable section of the establishment. Here you can watch remote control TV or video, write letters on ostentatious Groucho Club stationery or read review copies of trendy, middlebrow novels.

Those members who regularly fall asleep at Groucho's will be pleased to learn that the club will shortly be building a suite of bedrooms. One bathroom is already available, but patrons are advised to avoid using the solitary house towel, which doesn't seem to have been washed since the club opened.

Groucho Club

Open: 09.00–01.00 Mon–Fri. Closed Sat & Sun.
Admission: Members and guests only.
Membership: £200 per annum, plus £50 enrolment fee. Reductions for out-of-town members and under 28s. New members must be proposed and seconded by a current member.
Dress: No restrictions.
Credit cards: Access, Amex, Diners, Visa.

Moscow Club

62 Frith St W1. 01-437 0062. **M 4**

Moscow's opened in 1985 as Soho's answer to Zanzibar, the once-fashionable Covent Garden haunt of media moguls and aspiring media moguls. Not as refined as Groucho's and cheaper to join, Moscow's somehow seems a trifle parvenu. Most of Moscow's 650 members work locally in films, magazines or advertising and would probably love to belong to Groucho's if the latter would let them in.

The smallish interior is decked out in cool chrome and black, giving the club a hi-tech atmosphere. During the day, members place their cocktails and personal organisers on Moscow's eerie green glass tables (very 70s) and talk business. Music is uncomfortably loud pre-recorded tapes. In the evenings, it is possible to go to Moscow's for a drink after work and still see EastEnders – a large television has been installed in one corner. American/international food is available at the bar.

Moscow Club

Open: 12.00–15.00, 17.30–01.00 Mon–Fri. Closed Sat & Sun.
Admission: Members and guests only.
Membership: £120 per annum. New members have to be proposed by a current member.
Dress: No restrictions but it helps to look trendy.
Credit cards: Access, Amex, Diners, Visa.

SAUNAS

Mishuko Sauna

64 Frith St W1. 01-434 2569. **M 4**

Very different from the dubious saunas and massage parlours which once abounded in Soho. Mishuko is a clean, well-run establishment aimed at busy executive types. And it's not just a sauna: also on offer are alternative treatments such as Japanese shiatsu and aromatherapy. A wide variety of massage treatments including Swedish and Finnish are available. The centre is very popular with Japanese businessmen, who can obviously afford the high charges, but it is open to both sexes (women may use the facilities until 14.00 every day). *Open 10.30–01.00 Mon–Fri, 10.30–22.00 Sat. Closed Sun.* Access, Amex, Diners, Visa.

Windmill Sauna

17 Great Windmill St W1. 01-437 8552. **K 10**

Men-only enclave consisting of sauna, plunge pool and massage facilities beneath what used to be the Windmill Theatre and is now Paramount City. The building looks extremely insalubrious from the outside, but in fact is very comfortable. The clientele is predominantly gay, often theatrical. *Open 10.30–23.30 Mon–Sat, 12.00–22.00 Sun.* Access, Amex, Diners, Visa.

STRIP SHOWS

Twenty years ago, Soho was full of strip clubs and strippers would dash between venues, performing at perhaps a dozen different establishments. Now that so few remain, the professional strippers are feeling the pinch. Many have switched to the pub/working men's club circuit, leaving Soho to the amateurs. However, the remaining clubs have been granted licences by Westminster City Council which indicates, at least, that they are well run and represent reasonable value for money.

Carnival Revue Club

12 Old Compton St W1. 01-437 8337. **O 5**

Discerning voyeurs would certainly favour the Sunset Strip (punters are much closer to the stage and binoculars are not required) but the Carnival has a seedy charm of its own. The first three rows of the auditorium are usually chock-a-block with regulars, the last three empty. (The police sit here when they drop in from time to time to ensure that girls and punters are not getting carried away.) The girls gyrate in time with standard middle-of-the road pop, plus a few golden oldies; The Rolling Stones' *Let's Spend the Night Together* is a favourite.

Carnival Revue Club

Open: 12.00–23.00 Mon–Sat. Closed Sun.
Admission: £4–£5.
Membership: Not required.
Dress: Raincoat.
Credit cards: Not accepted.

Raymond Revuebar

Walker's Court, off Brewer St W1. 01-734 1593. **K 7**

Paul Raymond opened his Revuebar in 1958, on the site of a meeting place/eating house known as the Doric Rooms. Before arriving in Soho, Raymond had taken a series of revues around Britain and Europe, providing theatregoers with what, in those days, was a very risqué evening of entertainment.

Until 1968, the Lord Chamberlain's office was responsible for licensing shows and local watch committees would be appointed to scrutinise them. If the members of the committee felt that the local community would be outraged by a particular show, its run would be cancelled. The stuffy standards of the day did not allow naked women to move on stage, and shows which included fat women or women with sagging breasts stood little chance of reaching the public. The Lord Chancellor also insisted that pubic hair should be shaved and pudenda covered with sticking plaster. In 1968, however, the Theatres

Act was introduced. Apart from ensuring that shows such as *Oh! Calcutta* and *Hair* could be presented on the West End stage, the change in law meant that the shows at the Revuebar could become more explicit. Even so, the show here has never been shocking or crude.

Raymond has long enjoyed a reputation as Soho's most respectable sex king. He is involved in straight theatre, night clubs, girlie mag publishing and also owns a substantial chunk of Soho real estate. He supports the Soho Society's clean-up campaign and they in turn give their tacit approval to his activities; they are very keen to make the distinction between Raymond, who owns a legitimate business, and the fly-by-night operators who run the hostess bars.

Although the Revuebar is not a rip-off, undoubtedly many of the Japanese tourists and European businessmen who flock to the front rows every night find the show a little disappointing. There seems to be little in the way of serious titillation, largely because the dancers spend so much of their time on stage naked. The dance routines are very slick, if a little passé (the naked girl-on-motorbike cliché is dusted off in the first act of the show each evening) and the girls are certainly very attractive. Yet there is nothing faintly erotic about the show; perhaps the girls are too perfect, too unreal. Each has a uniformly nubile figure and a delicately trimmed triangle of pubic hair.

The show changes about once every six months. At present there are no male dancers (they were taken off after complaints from serious voyeurs who felt they weren't seeing enough female flesh) but they may return. There is usually a smattering of women in the audience at the Revuebar and a few well-hung hunks might make the show a little more appealing for them. Otherwise, the audience is composed of standard Soho smut-goers; businessmen, tourists and groups of men out on stag nights.

Raymond Revuebar

Open: 19.00–23.00 Mon–Sat. Closed Sun. Two shows a night at 20.00 & 22.00.
Admission: £10–£12.
Membership: Not required.
Dress: No restrictions.
Credit cards: Access, Amex, Diners, Visa.

Sunset Strip

30a Dean St W1. 01-437 7229. **L 5**

One of only two straightforward strip clubs in Soho which have been granted 'sex establishment' licences by Westminster City Council. Sunset Strip has been here since 1960, and offers much better value for money than the peep shows and near-beer bars which the council has been attempting to drive out.

For a reasonable entrance fee, punters can watch up to a dozen women remove their clothing in the space of an hour. Each woman appears on the small stage for between five and ten minutes. The hurried schedule means that there is little scope for considered choreography and most of the women are naked within about three minutes. They spend the rest of the act cavorting around the stage wobbling their breasts in time with the music and staring at the audience who seem to become more uncomfortable by the minute.

Not one of Soho's most sophisticated nightspots, the Sunset Strip attracts a mixed clientele of local businessmen, football supporters and lads on stag nights. There is keen competition for the seats at the front and at busy times it's standing room only. In theory, it is possible to stay in the club all day and evening – the shows are continuous – but this is not encouraged by the management.

The punters do not utter a word to each other throughout the proceedings, concentrating their minds on the activities on stage. Occasionally one of the girls may stroll naked among the audience for a chat but the policy here is strictly hands off. Raunchier strip shows can often be had in suburban pubs.

Overall, the atmosphere is somewhat sleazy. The punters are jaded, the girls are often past their prime and some of their costumes (body stockings, leotards, schoolgirl outfits etc) look as though they might have been picked up in Marshall & Snelgrove's closing down sale. But you get more than a glimpse of naked flesh, which, in Soho these days, is pretty unusual.

Sunset Strip

Open: 12.30–23.00 Mon–Sat. Closed Sun.
Admission: £5.
Membership: Not available.
Dress: No restrictions.
Credit cards: Not accepted.

THEATRES

Apollo

Shaftesbury Ave W1. 01-437 2663. **K 9**

Shaftesbury Avenue, which separates Soho proper from Chinatown to the south, was only created just over a hundred years ago, in 1887. With much of the area's original slum property destroyed by the construction of the road, there was great scope for new building and six theatres opened on the Avenue between 1888 and 1907.

The Apollo was built by Lewen Sharp in 1901 and intended as a venue for musicals. However, by the 1920s it had switched to presenting serious drama and sophisticated comedy. It now stages a variety of productions including musicals, comedy and drama. *Box Office open 10.00–20.00 Mon–Sat.* Access, Amex, Visa.

Boulevard

Walker's Court W1. 01-437 2661. **K 7**

Dinky theatre owned by Paul Raymond and adjacent to the famous Revuebar. Formerly a venue for alternative cabaret, the Boulevard now presents serious plays and comedies, most of which have transferred from other fringe theatres. On a good night some of the best theatre in town; on a bad night pretentious nonsense which should have remained in Islington. *Box Office open 10.30–20.30 Mon–Sat.* Access, Amex, Diners, Visa.

Globe

Shaftesbury Ave W1. 01-437 3667. **L 9**

Designed by prominent turn-of-the-century theatre architect W. G. R. Sprague, the Globe is one of Shaftesbury Avenue's cosiest and most attractive theatres. It opened in 1906 as the Hicks Theatre, named after one of its founders: in the last 40 years its successes have included Christopher Fry's *The Lady's Not For Burning*, Noël Coward's *Nude With Violin* and Robert Bolt's *A Man For All Seasons*. Today light comedies seem more popular with the Globe's management than serious drama. *Box Office open 10.00–20.00 Mon–Sat.* Access, Amex, Visa.

Lyric

Shaftesbury Ave W1. 01-437 3686. **K 10**

One of five major theatres on the northern side of Shaftesbury Avenue, the Lyric was designed in 1888. It spent its early years presenting comic opera, later moving on to serious drama including productions of Shakespeare's tragedies. In 1933 the theatre was refurbished by Michael Rosenauer, giving the interior an odd mixture of styles. Eclectic range of productions these days include small-scale musicals, low-budget drama and comedy. *Box Office open 10.00–20.00 Mon–Sat.* Access, Amex, Visa.

Palace

Cambridge Circus WC2. 01-434 0909. **P 6**

The Palace, originally known as the Royal English Opera House, opened its doors for the first time in 1891, but rapidly changed its name and style of productions in 1892 when it became the Palace Theatre of Varieties. Well established as a venue for big-name musicals, *The Sound of Music*, *Jesus Christ Superstar* and now *Les Miserables* have all achieved phenomenal success and record-breaking runs.

Though not likely to rival the Soho Brasserie as one of the area's trendiest meeting places, the Palace has its own brasserie downstairs. Open to the public 10.30–15.00 Mon–Sat, theatregoers only 18.30–21.15 Mon–Sat. *Box Office open 10.00–20.00 Mon–Sat.* Access, Amex, Diners, Visa.

Palladium

8 Argyll St W1. 01-437 7373. **C 3**

Enormous theatre from which the TV series *Sunday Night At The London Palladium* was broadcast to the nation in the 60s. The programme was revived in the 70s, but audiences no longer found the mixture of song and dance, stand-up comedy and audience participation quite so compelling.

Built in 1910, the theatre stands on the site of what was the home of a circus presented by impresario Charles Hengler. It enjoyed a heyday in the 1920s, when extravagant revues were presented and box-to-box telephones installed, before becoming a cinema in the 1930s. Nowadays, although the Palladium is still regarded as the home of variety, recent presentations (musicals in particular) have had a habit of closing prematurely. *Box Office open 10.00–20.00 Mon–Sat.* Access, Amex, Visa.

Piccadilly

Denman St W1. 01-437 4506. **H 10**

Attractive theatre built in the 1920s of Portland Stone, which contrasts with the shoddiness of the rest of Denman Street. The interior lost some of its original mock-Edwardian character after a revamp in the 1950s, but the exterior is well preserved. Productions are very much a mish-mash of mainstream drama, musicals and comedy. *Box Office open 10.00–20.00 Mon–Sat.* Credit card bookings 01-379 6565. Access, Amex, Diners, Visa.

Prince Edward

Old Compton St W1. 01-734 8591. **N 6**

This ugly, harshly designed theatre dominates the Cambridge Circus end of Old Compton Street. It was designed by Edward Stone in the 1930s; after a number of incarnations as cinema and cabaret/restaurant, the Prince seems set to spend at least the next few decades as a venue for live entertainment. Andrew Lloyd Webber and Tim Rice's *Evita* opened here in 1978 and was a phenomenal success. It was followed by *Chess* in 1986 which seems destined for an equally long run. Tickets are sold out months in advance and the touts who block Old Compton Street's pavements immediately before a performance can be a nuisance. *Box Office open 10.00–20.00 Mon–Sat.* Access, Amex, Visa.

Queens

Shaftesbury Ave W1. 01-734 1166. **L 9**

Queens was built in 1907. Designed by W. G. R. Sprague and intended as a twin for the Globe, it has enjoyed an illustrious history from very humble beginnings. In 1913, Tango Teas were introduced; patrons could dance, watch a fashion parade and take tea in the stalls. The Edwardian foyer was destroyed during German bombing raids in 1940 and the theatre was rebuilt in 1959 to designs supervised by Sir Hugh Casson. The modern frontage is an intriguing design which does not clash unduly with what remains of the original interior. Mostly sophisticated comedies or serious drama. *Box Office open 10.00–20.00 Mon–Sat.* Access, Amex, Visa.

NIGHTLIFE

Nightlife in Soho doesn't really start until about 10pm. By then the best tables in the best restaurants have been commandeered and the smart set are weighing up their choice of clubs for the night. An important decision indeed: what's in can become out within a matter of days.

Soho's first 'night clubs', grand houses which held masked balls frequented by the aristocracy, were established at the end of the 17th century. As the aristocracy moved away from the area a more bohemian atmosphere prevailed, much of it centred around coffee houses of the day. Coffee drinking was to provide the focus for another great Soho era with the arrival of the coffee bars of the 1950s. This is when Soho discovered cappuccino, drainpipe jeans and rock 'n' roll.

The most celebrated Soho coffee bar was the 2 i's at 59 Old Compton Street (now the Bistingo bistro next door to Fratelli Camisa). London's equivalent of Liverpool's Cavern Club, this was a steamy, dark little enclave in which the sound of skiffle would reverberate throughout much of the night.

The Swiss Hotel, now Comptons, was another key venue during the Soho beat boom, and the young Adam Faith was often to be found at Russell Quay's Skiffle Club on Old Compton Street. The 50s also saw the establishment of the Marquee Club and Ronnie Scott's; two venues which have endured the ravages of time and trend and have played a key role in the musical heritage of the area. Both clubs thrived in the 60s. Yet in the early part of the decade a very different club was attracting attention.

The Establishment Club at 18 Greek Street presented what would now be called 'alternative comedy' – sharp little sketches performed by the post-Cambridge 'Beyond the Fringe' crew. Dudley Moore, Peter Cook, Eleanor Bron and David Frost all appeared here. Their acerbic wit was to send shock-waves across the bows of the Macmillan Government and guarantee the performers jobs in television for at least 20 years. Bill Stickers' restaurant, a triumph of bad taste, now stands on the site of the club.

The pop clubs also took off in the mid-to-late 60s with Wardour Street emerging as the centre of clubland. Every night super-cool establishments such as the Whisky à Go-Go (now The Wag and still trendy) and the Flamingo would attract the groups of the moment plus their adolescent entourages. The Flamingo started life as an R & B venue which brought in young blacks in pork pie hats who came to listen to Georgie Fame, and then became a favourite with the mods. Presently its followers expanded to include big-name groups like The Beatles and The Rolling Stones who would whizz around Soho from club to club in souped-up Mini Coopers. Halcyon days indeed, and a golden age for the club owners who'd rub their hands with glee whenever a Beatle, a Stone or a Small Face staggered through their door.

Although the 60s saw Soho clubs such as the Bag O' Nails (Kingly Street), The Scene (Ham Yard) and the Jack of Clubs (Brewer Street) enjoying a boom, the 70s ushered in an altogether more elitist phenomenon: the cult club. The punks were the first to stake their claim and for a few years dominated venues like the Marquee and the Vortex, later the Ritzi. Throughout the late 70s and early 80s all the cults had their clubs, most of which seemed to be in Soho. The New Romantics, typified by Adam Ant, began their assault on the national consciousness in a dingy little club called St Moritz in Wardour Street.

The success of the cult clubs like St Moritz, the Batcave and Foobert's encouraged a number of opportunist DJs to realise the potential of setting up an exclusive nightspot. The rule is that a successful club should make a big show of rejecting the drongos, the Next-suited bank clerks and the tourists when they arrive at the door. A fashionable club, thrown open to all and sundry, will soon cease to be so.

Many club organisers recognise the transitory nature of the business and open up 'one-nighters'. These are hastily arranged clubs within clubs which set very strict dress codes and operate on a here today, gone tomorrow basis. Soho's poseur element is told of the club's whereabouts by word of mouth or, as a last resort, via the London listings magazines. Unfortunately the customer must take pot-luck; some of these evenings, held in shabby warehouses or far from fashionable central London discos, can be truly dire. Others, as long as you are prepared to succumb to the sartorial and musical dictats of the organisers, may be just about tolerable.

However, if we are to believe those who monitor Soho's clublife for *NME*, *The Face*, *I-D* and *Blitz*, the real fun is to be had at one of these pop clubs. Not that the word 'pop' should ever be uttered once you step, correctly dressed, beyond the portals of these haute-cool establishments. Consider yourself fortunate that you're in, look dark, trendy and mysterious and buy plenty of drinks.

NIGHTCLUBS

Le Beat Route

17 Greek St W1. 01-734 6308. **N 5**

Long-established Soho nightspot which, in terms of trendiness, has never quite made it. Caters mainly for the tourists, plus a large contingent of medallion men from the suburbs. The gentlemen's lavatories always reek of naff aftershaves. Paco Rabanne seems to be a favourite, but not among the women.

Naffness apart, the club offers a reasonable deal. Service at the bar is prompt and the admission price usually includes one drink. There is a small dance floor, complete with disco unit, multi-coloured beams and pulsating strobes. From here, the Paco Rabanne enthusiasts eye up the talent – mainly the white stiletto brigade – who promptly ignore their efforts.

Le Beat Route offers a relatively tame introduction to London clubland – music is mainstream soul and golden oldies – but overall, guys and gals, the place is redolent of a set for a 1973 edition of *Top of the Pops*.

Le Beat Route

Open: 21.00–03.30 Mon–Sat. Closed Sun.
Admission: £7.
Membership: £25 per annum; not required.
Dress: Suburban chic; no jeans or trainers.
Credit cards: Not accepted.

Café de Paris

3 Coventry St W1. 01-437 2036. **K 11**

Although the Café de Paris is situated in Soho's nether regions, it is a crucial local landmark which first opened as a dance hall-cum-society rendezvous in 1926. Noël Coward, Marlene Dietrich and David Niven all came here.

During the Second World War the Café became famous as a

place of entertainment for the Allied forces based in, and passing through, London. Many of the comedy acts from the Windmill Theatre such as the Goons and Jimmy Edwards appeared here and it became affectionately known as the Café Khaki. It offered the troops and their girls a temporary respite from the tension of war. Unfortunately, all that went awry on 8 March 1941 when two 50-kilo German landmines crashed through the Rialto cinema above and killed 80 people, including Ken 'Snakehips' Johnson, who was leading the band that night. The attack was a major disaster but the Café was soon rebuilt and reopened.

After the war, the club won back some of its former glory and Princess Elizabeth even held her 23rd birthday party here. Nowadays the club is a rather faded facsimile of its former self – the gold and scarlet-trimmed decor gives the appearance of an enormous provincial curry house. In the foyer we are told that Elizabeth Taylor, Maurice Chevalier and Elizabeth Welch all came here, but that was when the Café was in its heyday.

Yet the Café has an incredibly loyal following, particularly among the afternoon tea dancers. Usually in their 40s or 50s, they are expected to be able to foxtrot, waltz and, on occasions, gyrate to a spot of jazz funk. Young Sloane girls can also be seen joining in at the tea dances, no doubt secure in the knowledge that their soulmates are too busy in the City to disturb them. Although tea dances have been held here since the Café opened, they never attracted much attention until 1980 when the plump Conservative MP Geoffrey Dickens was found to be an aficionado. Dickens, a vociferous defender of Victorian family values, regularly used to meet his mistress here.

In the evenings the Café attracts a mixed clientele. Most people are in their late-20s/mid-30s and the music – easy listening soul, rock 'n' roll and pop standards – is to their taste. The Café only becomes trendy, and the door policy discriminatory, on Tuesdays and Wednesdays. Tuesday night is The Whip; on Wednesdays a young entrepreneur called Nick Fryer takes over and runs the Club Parisienne. Dress should be as stylish as possible, music is straightforward classic soul. Membership is compulsory, but you may be able to charm your way in if you're a pop star.

Café de Paris

Open: Tea dances: 15.00–17.45 Wed, Thur, Sat & Sun. Closed Mon, Tue & Fri. Evenings: 19.30–01.00 Mon & Thur, 10.00–03.00 Tue & Wed, 19.30–03.00 Fri & Sat, 19.30–24.00 Sun.
Admission: Tea dances: under £3. Evenings: £2–£6.
Membership: Not required except for Wednesday night.
Dress: Smart casual (Tue & Wed evenings smart trendy).
Credit cards: Not accepted.

Limelight

136 Shaftesbury Ave W1. 01-434 0572. **P 7**

Seriously trendy nightspot which opened in 1986, taking over a disused Victorian-Gothic church. The labyrinthine corridors and numerous dancefloors make this one of London's most unusual venues. The main stage is in the centre of the club, bang opposite the enormous bar. Service is prompt, measures large and prices steep. Make sure you visit one or two pubs beforehand.

Live bands perform here most evenings, pretentious DJs the rest: style of music depends largely upon prevailing trends. If you loathe dancing, it's possible to sit and pose while still watching the band from one of the four balconies overlooking the dance floor.

Ambience is fashionable, but not oppressively so, particularly downstairs, where jazz bands perform to a yuppie audience which is too old and straight to be deemed even remotely trendy. It is surprising how so many of these types manage to get through the normally harsh vetting procedure carried out at the door. Limelight habitués scorn this section of the club, but it is popular nonetheless and at least you can hear yourself speak. If you prefer not to lean against the bar, you can sit down on comfy, 60s-style sofas and trendy little waitresses will bring you your drinks. Food is typical, uninteresting club fare such as burgers and salads and is not cheap.

Most people who go to the Limelight are inveterate poseurs; the notion of spending an evening at one of London's trendiest clubs and talking about it at work the next day can be very attractive. Additional kudos can be garnered by wangling an invitation to the revolting, but compelling, VIP suite. Here genuine pop stars – not just the second-rate flotsam and jetsam who seem to dominate the rest of the club scene – such as David Bowie, George Michael and Boy George drink cocktails with their lackeys, the smooth-talking record company PRs. The bar is also infested with hungry, camera-laden paparazzi, all competing to snatch a shot of a plunging neckline or that indiscreet peck on the cheek.

The Limelight is certainly unusual in that it offers a truly trendy night out; but given that clubland's hordes are notoriously fickle and fashions in nightclubs are as unpredictable as the traffic crossing Cambridge Circus, get there soon.

Limelight

Open: 21.30–03.00 Mon–Sat. Closed Sun.
Admission: £5–£10.
Membership: VIPs only.
Dress: Trendy.
Credit cards: Access, Amex, Visa.

Madame Jo-Jo's

8–10 Brewer St W1. 01-734 2473 **K 7**

High camp Soho nighterie owned by Paul Raymond and run by the irrepressible Madame Jo-Jo. She/he presides over the Bar-bettes, a team of pretty young men decked out in lipstick, tights and high-cut leotards who fetch drinks and perform a song-and-dance act as part of the club's nightly revue.

An extraordinary place for an after hours drink and well worth a visit; the atmosphere is particularly friendly and not in the least intimidating. Although Jo-Jo's obviously appeals to gay/transvestite clubgoers, women and straights are not made to feel unwelcome. The Bar-bettes offer a professional, efficient drinks service ('Here's your change, daahling') and the drag acts can be very amusing, even if some of the jokes do border on the misogynistic. The first half of the cabaret starts at midnight, the second at 01.30.

Madame Jo-Jo's

Open: 22.00–03.00 Mon–Sat. Closed Sun.
Admission: £5.
Membership: Not available.
Dress: Smart casual.
Credit cards: Access, Amex, Diners, Visa.

Shaftesburys

24 Shaftesbury Ave W1. 01-734 2017. **K 10**

Billed by the management as 'London's stylish disco-diner', the club has little to recommend it, apart from a friendly, obliging bouncer on the door and low-to-medium prices depending on which night of the week you choose to go. Midweek, the atmosphere is rather like that of a New York singles bar particularly if you are a woman who decides to take a seat at the bar. You'll soon be flanked by a pride of pre-prandial piranhas. This is the time and the place to get chatted up by Continental businessmen who may offer to whisk you off for something to eat.

Later on things become more lively with a standard pop/rock/disco and sometimes live soul acts. Shaftesburys scores zero on the trendiness rating but it obviously appeals to some people. On Thursday nights, a small segment of Soho's self-appointed arty set take the club over and hold their own little gathering which they call Sacrosanct. Gay scene on Sunday nights.

Shaftesburys

Open: 22.00–03.30 Mon, 23.00–03.00 Tue, 21.00–03.00 Wed & Thur, 21.00–03.30 Fri & Sat, 17.00–24.00 Sun.
Admission: £5–£7.
Membership: £20 per annum; not required.
Dress: Smart casual.
Credit cards: Access, Amex, Diners, Visa.

Studio Valbonne

62 Kingly St W1. 01-439 7242. **D 8**

A fading 60s nighterie, which desperately needs an infusion of trendiness if it is to attract the devotees of Soho's current club scene. A vast, often empty building with lavish lighting and a large dance floor, the Valbonne has clearly seen better days. In 1966 members of the England football team came here to celebrate their victory in the World Cup Final.

Now a predominantly wideboy clientele dominates the dance floor and the Valbonne has become a favourite venue for stag and hen parties. Most nights the music is standard jazz/funk soul but occasionally the place is taken over by outside entrepreneurs for bizarre one-offs which are a throwback to the punk era. The Valbonne's greatest blessing, however, is that it is handy for an early breakfast/late supper at Harry's late-night restaurant.

Studio Valbonne

Open: 21.00–03.00 Mon–Sat. Closed Sun.
Admission: £5–£8.
Membership: £100 per annum for men, £25 for women; not required.
Dress: Smart casual.
Credit cards: Access, Amex, Diners, Visa.

The Wag

35 Wardour St W1. 01-437 5534. **L 9**

The Wag, one of Soho's hippest hot spots, regularly attracts a mixture of languid young blades, comatose existentialists, and out-and-out poseurs. For men, flat top haircuts are *de rigueur*, for women anything in black. Both sexes go out of their way to dance solo; the key to success at the Wag is to look cool, distant and interesting. Conversation is irrelevant.

Music (loud) varies each evening, according to the whim of the owners and whatever the street-wise hacks on the music/

style papers deem to be the prevailing trend: it could be hip-hop, jazz, soul, funk or 70s glam. Aspiring Wag-ites should digest *The Face*, *Blitz* and *I-D* before attempting to make an entrance, particularly if they're planning to try their luck on a Friday or Saturday when it's very difficult to get in.

Although admission prices are reasonable, drinks are pricey. True trendies should eschew the glasses. Drinking straight out of a can will almost certainly secure points on the street cred scale, but make sure none of those super-cool hip-hoppers mistake your lager for an ashtray.

Decor is garbage-dump chic, very dark with lots of graffiti. There is a large bar at the back of the club which tops up the dancers, and a small one at the front which caters for those who wish to scrutinise Gerrard Street from the discomfort of their seats. The venetian blinds give this part of the club the faint air of a Parisian caveau. Astonishingly, no-one seems to smoke Gauloises.

The Wag

Open: 22.30–03.30 Mon–Sat. Closed Sun.
Admission: £3–£6.
Membership: List closed.
Dress: Trendy.
Credit cards: Not accepted.

7 Sex and Soho

Since the 1930s, when the first French prostitutes began to ply their trade here, minded by the pimps who'd brought them across the Channel, Soho has been known as the capital's sinful square mile. Its reputation has attracted generations of voyeurs from all over the world, yet most of the time sexy Soho fails to deliver. Those in search of titillation usually go home unsatisfied, lighter in wallet but wiser in mind. In comparison with the fleshspots of Europe such as the Reeperbahn in Hamburg, the Leidseplein in Amsterdam and even the scraggy rue St Denis in Paris, 'sinful' Soho is about as sexually exciting as a wet weekend in Wigan. And a lot more expensive.

Until recently, the general view of the authorities towards the Soho sex scene was that if it were left alone it would go away. This mentality proved of great advantage to the sleaze merchants controlling Soho's sex industry, enabling them to extort vast sums of money from those who came into the area. It is true that Soho has one or two reputable striptease clubs and revues but the vast majority are just old-fashioned clip joints.

By the mid-70s things had really got out-of-hand. The number of prostitutes in the area may have been decreasing (there'd been a big exodus to Shepherd Market in Mayfair) but near-beer bars, bed shows and nude-encounter parlours were proliferating. Soho had become an enormous sex supermarket, albeit one offering very few bargains.

For years, Westminster City Council, under whose jurisdiction Soho falls, had distanced itself from the area, showing a marked reluctance to get involved in the environmental problems that the sex industry had brought. However, all this began to change when the local residents association, The Soho Society, started to get involved. The Society has always insisted that theirs is not a moral crusade, but one based on concern for the environment in which its members live. They accept that Soho has always had its more raffish inhabitants and are also prepared to accept the sex industry in moderation, but felt it was necessary to put pressure on the Council to tighten up their planning controls in order to ensure that Soho remained a proper community.

In spite of energetic lobbying by the Society, by now monitoring every single planning application, Westminster seemed deaf to the problems. The Council did refuse planning permission in a number of cases after the Society had objected, but still weren't taking them seriously. It took the loss of two seats on the Council to independents, one in Soho and one in Mayfair, to convince Westminster that the Society merited a better hearing.

Those who controlled the sex scene in Soho were nobody's fools; their lawyers had enabled them to dart round the planning laws from the moment the Society and, to a lesser extent, the Council began to keep an eye on their activities. Years of meetings between the Soho Society, the Council and the police followed before the clean-up campaign began in earnest. Finally, in 1986, government legislation gave Westminster the power to grant licences to so-called 'Sex Establishments' in the area. Each licence costs £12,300 and if this wasn't enough to discourage the fly-by-night entrepreneur, the application form certainly would. The applicant was required to supply his home address, details of his employment history and his income. He was also expected to provide details of the people he intended to employ. Inevitably, this probing was enough to scare off any mobster worthy of the description and as a result many of the dodgier establishments have since closed down.

Thanks to the new licensing system, the effects of the clean-up campaign in Soho have been considerable. A few hostess bars and porn shops still operate without a licence but it won't be long before they're raided and their premises taken over by legitimate businesses. In the meantime, seedy Soho is still worth a look and a laugh. Catch it while it's still there. . . .

HOSTESS BARS

Many of the men who come into Soho in search of some action are tempted by the so-called 'hostess' or 'near-beer' bars which arrived in the 40s and proliferated in the 70s. Thanks to the admirable clean-up campaign spearheaded by the Soho Society in the early 80s, they have diminished in number, but touts of dubious appearance still sit in doorways trying to persuade passers-by to part with their money. They are frequently successful. Once a ticket has been bought, the gorilla on the door will press a concealed buzzer which signals to his colleagues downstairs that business is coming their way. The punter will step uneasily down the staircase to a dimly-lit basement in which a coterie of young and not-so-young ladies dressed in body-stockings, leotards or micro-skirts with fishnet tights, are lounging around. He then takes a seat, usually a plastic-covered armchair which wouldn't look out of place as a stage prop in a Joe Orton play.

While the punter is waiting for the show, a girl will come across and ask him if he would like a drink. If he is a businessman he might order a gin and tonic. If he is a lad down from the north for a cup match his tipple is likely to be lager. Neither drink will contain any alcohol, since these premises are unlicensed. (Those who own and run these establishments have able lawyers who ensure that their clients never fall foul of the law.) Instead the businessman will be served a syrupy soft drink with a whiff of juniper berries and the football fan will get a glass of alcohol-free lager. Cheers!

It is possible that the cannier punter might at this point decide to sup up, pay the bill and withdraw. Yet few do. Before he has finished his drink, one of the young 'hostesses' will proffer a wide smile and approach him. She will ask him if he would like her to sit next to him. When he agrees, she will ask him if he would like to buy her a drink. Invariably he does and she orders champagne. Together they finish the bottle, by which time he has lost his patience. Their conversation has been banal, his 'show' has consisted of half a dozen fuzzy slides projected on the wall and he is completely sober. It is time to go, but first he must pay the bill.

A bottle of 'champagne', usually fizzy grape juice, in one of these establishments would normally set you back about £40. In addition to this you will have to pay a service charge of £5–£10 and a 'hostess fee' of £30. A 'gin and tonic' normally costs about £10 and a half-pint of 'beer' £5. On receiving a bill of this magnitude, many punters protest, yet they have no recourse to the law. The girls, usually well-clued-up barrack-room lawyers themselves, will point to the price list which is always displayed in these bars. Although the list may be difficult to read in the dim light, it does set out the prices and a hand-written note in the corner of the list states that all the drinks are 'de-alcoholised'. If the punter continues to object, the girls will become very stroppy indeed, and sure enough, the gorilla on the door who sold the man his ticket in the first place will be summoned to sort the matter out. These gentlemen are not normally known for their diplomacy, and their appearance downstairs is usually enough to have the customers reaching for their wallets. However, the truly recalcitrant visitor will probably be punched in the face. And it's no good pleading poverty. Many of the apes who mind these establishments will escort you to the nearest bank or cash dispenser.

In the summer months in particular the local police receive dozens of complaints from tourists and businessmen who have lost money in near-beer bars. Unfortunately, there is little they can do, since the hostesses always stay within the law. If a member of the staff hits, or even threatens a client, he has reasonable grounds for complaint but there are rarely any witnesses to these incidents. If the police are called to a near-beer bar, the girls and the apes will, of course, swear blind that nothing untoward has occurred. It is up to the punter to press further charges, and few do. How many respectable businessmen would admit to having patronised a sleazy hostess bar in the depths of Soho?

In the unlikely event of this happening to you, it is probably worth contacting the police. Approach one of the Home Beat constables who can usually be found walking around Soho. While they can do very little in law to help, it is possible that if they go back to the bar with you, their presence may encourage the hostesses to acknowledge that you were in fact over-charged. It is unlikely that you will get a full refund, but the hostesses may, grudgingly, give you some of your money back. The near-beer bars are such an obvious rip-off that it is perhaps surprising that so many people fall prey to them every year; the less-than-salubrious exteriors of these places usually indicate the calibre of the establishment. Be on your guard.

Over the years these bars succeeded in collectively dragging Soho down. When they first opened, they used teams of young runaways to attract custom. The girls would approach likely-looking punters and say they were looking for a dancing partner to take them to a club. Of course, the 'club' would turn out to be a hostess bar wherein the punter would be systematically fleeced in the time-honoured fashion. Once they got wise to this trick, the Clubs Squad based at what was then Savile Row police station (it's now called West End Central) raided a number of these bars and although the bars remain, the girl touts have since disappeared.

The new Sex Establishment licensing system operated by Westminster City Council has put paid to the activities of many of the near-beer bars. In the 70s there were getting on for 100 of these bars in the area; now there are probably less than a dozen. Although the Council is prepared to grant licences to reputably-run sex shops and strip clubs, it is unlikely that a near-beer bar would receive the authority's stamp of approval. The service and facilities they offer would not, in the Council's opinion, merit a licence.

At the time of writing, most of the near-beer bars still in existence were concentrated around the Tisbury Court/Walker's Court/Winnett Street/Rupert Street area, traditionally Soho's sleaziest quarter. Many of the bars advertise a show, but to conform with the law their placards and signs must not promote any form of entertainment which may involve sexual titillation. The words 'Pussy Show' for instance would probably provoke the police and the local council to take action; these signs are considered to be a vulgar blot on the environment.

In spite of the new laws, the slimy touts on the door are still trying to tempt the punters in, their fingers jumping to their buzzers as soon as they manage to sell a ticket. The council and the police may never succeed in flushing out the hostess bars completely, but their success to date in closing down so many has made Soho a less expensive place for the thousands of naïve visitors who come into the area every year.

PEEP SHOWS

In the early 1980s, Soho's peep shows, bed shows and 'nude-encounter parlours' enjoyed an unfettered boom. The peep shows were probably the most popular, largely because they offered the punter in search of flesh a relatively good deal. For a pound or two he could walk into a small booth and, through a peephole, observe a naked, bored-looking girl or a couple cavorting on a bed. The pound would normally last about 30 seconds, the flap on the peephole closing up as soon as the cash ran out. There were reports of some girls being prepared to masturbate if the punter pushed more notes through the peephole, but police raids with marked notes, and the advent of the pound coin with its tendency to roll away, have forced the girls to call it a day. The remaining, unlicensed, peep shows now feature girls dressed in leotards working out on exercise machines – it's hardly worth the time, let alone the money.

Some disreputable nude-encounter parlours would give the punters the opportunity to touch the girls, but the police kept a weather-eye on their activities and most, if not all, have closed down. Like the bed shows and the peep shows, the parlours have fallen victim to the new legislation. At the time of writing, none had been granted Sex Establishment licences from Westminster City Council. One bed show on Wardour Street, run reputably by a women's collective, stood a reasonable chance of getting a licence but went bust before the owners had a chance to apply. The rent demanded of the women by the landlord amounted to around £500 a week.

Some of the hostess bars advertise bed shows as part of their 'service' but these should be avoided. The sole purpose of their hoardings is to lure the punter down for an extremely expensive drink. Once he has started drinking, he finds himself waiting, perhaps several hours, for the 'show' and gazing at an empty stage (usually a grubby mattress pushed into the centre of the room). He will finally make an exit when he realises that his bill has ballooned out of all recognition.

The hostess bars don't usually bother to put on a show unless they know the police have dropped in to take a look at their activities. And since it is illegal to present an unlicensed show which involves sexual titillation, the officers are usually treated to the highly erotic spectacle of a man and a woman sitting on the bed, fully clothed, having a banal conversation about the time of day or the state of the weather – riveting stuff!

PROSTITUTES

Prostitutes have been based in Soho since the early 17th century. Young ladies of this calling would tout for business in taverns, coffee houses and some of the less salubrious places of entertainment. However, the mid-19th century was to prove the boom-time for prostitution. In the 1860s it was estimated that there were around 80,000 prostitutes living in London; most barely scratching a living. Many were aged under 13 and had few prospects of obtaining more 'respectable' work. At about the same time, a new breed of high-class prostitute had begun to emerge. They would frequent the night clubs favoured by the aristocracy – the Argyll Rooms on Shaftesbury Avenue was a particularly popular venue – and were suitably well dressed and well mannered. Many of the prostitutes lived in lodging houses in Soho, mainly in Great Windmill Street. Rents were usually expensive, but the girls were prepared to put up with this; it was worth paying a bit more to live in such proximity to the gentry's places of pleasure.

Prostitution in Soho today bears little resemblance to its 19th-century heyday. Numbers have dwindled, and many of the girls walking the streets are not prostitutes at all, merely con-artists or 'clippers' as they are known locally. Like the hostess bars, they are concentrated in the alleys around Rupert Street Market but can also be found in the smaller streets, such as Carlisle Street and Bateman Street. Since 1959 when the Street Offences Act became law, it has been illegal for prostitutes to solicit for trade in a public place. The clippers, however, flagrantly flout the law, risking arrest if one of the men they proposition turns out to be a plain-clothes policeman.

The clipper's con works like this: she will approach a likely-looking man and ask wearily 'Fancy a nice time, darling?' or 'Looking for business?' If he's interested, the girl will chat to him for a few minutes before discussing the price. He will be expected to pay cash, in advance and once he has got out his £50 or so (Soho clippers don't come cheap) the clipper will say that she has got some business to attend to, would he be kind enough to meet her at her flat in 10 minutes' time. The punter usually agrees, and when the girl hands him a key he is convinced that everything is on the level. Then perhaps he pops into a café or a pub before making his way to the girl's flat.

When he arrives at the address she has given him, it transpires that he's been sent to the National Westminster Bank on Wardour Street or one of the offices on Soho Square. He waits nearly two hours, but never sees the girl again. She has decided to lie low for a few days, or has left Soho in the hope of finding more mugs elsewhere, perhaps in Sussex Gardens, Paddington or Westbourne Grove, Bayswater. Every year hundreds of frustrated men are rolled in this way. The police can take action against the clippers, but if they proceed with charges and the case comes to court, the punter will have to give evidence – the main reason why most men who are ripped off in this way prefer not to make a complaint to the police.

There are, however, some genuine prostitutes in Soho and they probably represent the best value for money that 'sinful' Soho can offer. They don't, in general, rip people off; unlike some prostitutes in London, they are not 'protected' by muscular pimps who jump out of the wardrobe to steal the punter's wallet as soon as he drops his trousers. As one policeman based in Soho said: 'At least the punter will get his leg over.'

Immediately after the war, many of the prostitutes in Soho were French. Most now are English or West Indian and of an uncertain age. They can be as old as 70. The 'girls' are usually professionals who have been on the game for much of their working life; in Soho there are no part-timers; the 'have-it-away-day' housewives who come to London on cheap return tickets from the provinces for a day's work tend to stick to the districts around main-line railway termini.

The Soho girl sets about her work quickly and clinically and will probably get annoyed if the punter takes too long; while she is with him, her next client will be waiting on the stairs or handing over his money to the elderly maid who has probably been sitting in a chair in the doorway of the flat for years. A professional Soho prostitute will guard her territory jealously; woe betide anyone who encroaches upon her pitch or clips one of her clients. (Since the rise of the clippers, many pros have taken to posting signs warning punters not to part with any money on the stairs.)

These prostitutes will operate in one of the many small flats which can be found in unlikely places; on the floor above a travel agency, or next door to a sweet shop. They advertise their services by placing a small sign marked with their name and the word 'Model' underneath a buzzer in the doorway. For about the cost of a meal for two at a medium-priced Soho restaurant a punter will have the opportunity to have sex, wearing a contraceptive (something the prostitutes are now most particular about since the advent of AIDS) for up to half an hour. This does not seem a bad deal, given that so much of 'sinful' Soho is geared up to fleecing the frustrated visitor and leaving him as unsatisfied as when he arrived.

CRIME

'. . . in Soho, all the things they say happen, do: I mean, the vice of every kink, and speakeasies and spielers and friends who carve each other up, and, on the other hand, dear old Italians and sweet old Viennese who've run their honest, unbent little businesses there since the days of George six, and five, and backward far beyond. And what's more, although the pavement's thick with tearaways, provided you don't meddle it's really a much safer area than the respectable suburban fringe. It's not in Soho a sex maniac leaps out of a hedge on to your back and violates you. It's in the dormitory sections.'

Colin MacInnes, *Absolute Beginners*

In the early 50s, when MacInnes wrote *Absolute Beginners* – part of his trilogy of London novels – Soho's unofficial entertainment industry was dominated by two-bit gangsters. They ran the clubs, some of the pubs and a number of dodgy gambling joints. They also pimped for the prostitutes. The general public, however, were not normally affected. The mob kept their nefarious activities to themselves; although the odd murder would, from time to time bring the police and the press into the village, the citizens of Soho were able to go about their daily business without disruption.

The spivs and the spielers (gambling clubs) had been here since the Second World War; Berwick Street Market had always attracted sharp-suited gentlemen with brilliantined hair who sold 'hot' cases of whisky or organised impromptu card games. In general, they were tolerated; the spivs were not the sort who would mug an old lady for her pension book. As MacInnes says, the Soho of the 1950s was safe for those who didn't dabble.

Soho is still one of the safest areas in the capital. The mugging and sexual assault rate is very low and it is one of the few areas in which a woman still feels safe walking around after dark. Handbags and wallets should be watched however. Gangs of pickpockets operate at all times in Oxford Street and sometimes feel tempted to make the occasional foray south into Soho. Restaurants and pubs are a favourite haunt of these thieves, so either deposit your bag with the management or keep it close by you; never leave it on the floor.

The chances of getting mugged, raped or murdered in Soho are pretty remote these days. The most common offences committed in the district are those involving the illegal parking of cars; traffic wardens pound the streets of Soho from morning to night and the Metropolitan Police clamp patrols are ever-vigilant. If you can't find a parking meter, find a car park; better still come to Soho by tube or bus. The crazy parking in some of Soho's streets makes it difficult for pedestrians to negotiate the area, let alone other cars.

Yet Soho wasn't always so safe. Since the 19th century, a number of unpleasant murders have occurred, lending a veneer of truth to the sensational stories about London's Den of Vice that some newspapers insist on printing even today. Probably the first recorded Soho murder occurred in 1843 in Broadwick Street (then Broad Street). Michael Stoltzer, a German immigrant, shot dead his friend Peter Keim, a boot-maker. He did this calmly and in full view of the rest of the street. The Prussian Kaiser intervened on his behalf, and Stoltzer was eventually spared the rope on a plea of insanity.

Many of the murders which have taken place in Soho have involved prostitutes. This is partly because in the early 1920s and 30s, the mob realised how rich the pickings could be if they set the girls up in flats and took a substantial cut of their incomes. It was necessary, of course, to intimidate the girls from time to time and this sometimes ended in bloodshed.

But the pimps didn't always have it their own way. In 1936 a middle-aged pimp called 'Red Max' Kassel was shot in a flat in Little Newport Street, rented by a prostitute called Suzanne Bertron. Kassel had had an argument over money with Bertron's live-in ponce, one George Lacroix, and the landlord of the flat, Pierre Alexandre. They dismembered and disposed of the body and Suzanne was left to clean up the flat. This she did with her maid, Marcelle Aubin. Unfortunately, in their zeal to rid the flat of evidence, the pair cut off the bottom of the blood-stained curtains – a detail which was noticed by detectives who later made routine calls on Red Max's associates. This was the seedy, fog-enveloped Soho that provided a melodramatic backdrop to a number of contemporary B movies, such as *Greek Street* (1930), *Murder in Soho* (1939) and *The Soho Murders* (1942).

In the early 40s, four brutal murders cast a long shadow across Soho. These were dark days indeed; Soho had already been bloodied by the Blitz and news was now filtering out that a mass murderer was on the loose. On 10 February 1942, an ex-actress called Nita Ward was found dead in her Wardour Street flat, her throat slashed and her body mutilated. The day before, Evelyn Hamilton, a schoolmistress, had been found strangled with a stocking in an air-raid shelter in Marylebone and on 11 February, Florence Lowe, 43, was found murdered at her home, also in Marylebone. Within a few days, another victim of strangulation, Doris Juannet, was found at her home in Paddington.

Two of these women were found to be prostitutes, and the girls on the game in Soho were, unsurprisingly, extremely worried. Painstaking enquiries led the police to the billet of a young airman, Gordon Cummins, in St John's Wood. He had taken a girl to the Trocadero in Piccadilly and then attempted to strangle her outside a pub. Interrupted by an off-licence delivery man, Cummins fled, leaving his gas mask case (with his service number on it) behind. Cummins was hanged on 25 June 1942 during yet another bombing raid. Although Cummins posthumously became known as the 'Ripper of the Blitz', his crimes received very little publicity at the time; reports of an outrage of this sort would not have been terribly good for wartime morale.

No such reticence was shown later in the decade when the killing of Margaret Cook in 1946 was written up in graphic detail by the contemporary crime reporters. Cook, an ex-borstal girl, was found shot dead outside a club called the Blue Lagoon, in a passageway running off Carnaby Street. Although Cook had no connection with the club, the case, which remains unsolved to this day, was always known as the Blue Lagoon Murder.

The following year, 1947, two prostitutes 'Black Rita' Barrett and Rachel Fenwick were found murdered. Rita at her flat in Rupert Street, Rachel at hers in Broad (now Broadwick) Street. Their murderers have never been found, but police have always believed that they may have become the victims of organised crime. You don't say no to a pimp.

The most recent killing of a prostitute in Soho occurred in February 1987. Colleen Weller, a drug addict and clipper, was found dead in a yard off Rupert Court, having been stabbed repeatedly. At the time of writing, no suspect had been found, but police were convinced that Colleen was the victim of someone she had clipped.

Although many of the clippers, like Colleen, are addicted to heroin, Soho is no longer a major drug-trafficking centre. Soft drugs are peddled on street corners and at certain cafés, but heroin, cocaine and the new menace, crack, are more likely to be sold in the suburbs. In the 60s, however, a lot of junkies used to buy and sell around Piccadilly Circus; many registered addicts would take their prescriptions to the all-night branch of Boots, now no longer a 24-hour chemist.

For many decades, Soho was also very much at the centre of the illegal gambling trade. Until casinos were licensed in 1954, hardened gamblers who lacked the wherewithal to fly to Monte Carlo or Le Touquet were forced to patronise the spielers which the mobsters had set up all over town. There was a high concentration of these establishments in Soho. As fast as the boys in blue could close them down, new ones would spring up, often in private residential premises.

These premises would be vacated for the night by their wealthy owners or tenants who would be paid to take a suite at one of the grand West End hotels. The organisers would then set up roulette tables or blackjack schools, run games until daybreak and walk out hundreds, if not thousands, of pounds richer.

Marked cards, bent wheels and crooked croupiers were standard practice. Yet still the punters were prepared to risk large sums on the baize. Winnings were, of course, tax free and refreshments complimentary. However, this aspect of crime in Soho largely disappeared with the introduction of the Gaming Act – most of the spielers cashed in their chips and moved on to other things.

Soho is now virtually Vice-free; most of the prostitution rackets having been flushed out in a series of police raids in the 70s and early 80s. That part of the pavement outside the Wimpy Bar on Piccadilly Circus no longer attracts lone males looking for a pretty young boy for the night; the 'Meat Rack' has been done away with. And Playland, the amusement arcade in Great Windmill Street which was the centre of a vice-ring based on male prostitution in the 70s, is also long gone. Other arcades, however, still make vast amounts of money, but employ security guards on the door to ensure that nothing untoward occurs.

Soho certainly has been cleaned up; organised crime is no longer powerful. Those sections of the Vice which remain are more interested in how far they can push the Obscene Publications Act than in putting out a contract on a club owner. The police, meanwhile, have put bobbies back on the beat; constables from West End Central, Vine Street and Bow Street stations patrol on foot. In short, unlike the majority of inner city areas, Soho is safer, more respectable and more attractive than it was 10 or even 20 years ago.

8 Chinatown

Soho's Chinatown is concentrated in a small area to the south of Shaftesbury Avenue centred on Gerrard Street and encompassing Lisle, Macclesfield, Leicester and Newport streets. Only really established in the 1960s, many hundreds of Chinese people now live and work here, yet to most outsiders, Chinatown remains largely a mystery.

The dozens of restaurants attract thousands of hungry visitors from London, Britain and Europe, but the glimpse they get of this fascinating quarter reveals little about the day-to-day lives of the people who work here. Occasionally the press has a stab at Chinatown, concentrating on such nefarious goings-on as Triad-inspired murders, illegal gambling dens and attacks involving cleaver-wielding gangs, but by and large the shutters are firmly down. Most Western observers find the area truly impenetrable and as difficult to comprehend as Chinese characters on a menu.

Most Chinese people working in Soho are involved in the restaurant trade, although a sizeable Chinese professional class comprising accountants, solicitors and engineers has taken shape in the last few years. It's impossible to place an accurate figure on the number of people who work in the Chinese restaurants locally since many of the employees are paid cash in hand and are not registered with the authorities. Similarly, since many of the Chinese people living in the area have never bothered to complete census forms nor place their names on the electoral roll, population figures are also unreliable. However, the community is certainly thriving, and in the last 10 to 20 years more and more of the businesses, shops and restaurants in the area have gone over to Chinese ownership.

Westminster City Council, the local authority responsible

for Chinatown, has not been slow to acknowledge the importance and rateworthiness of the area. Local councillors enjoy good relations with the leaders of the Chinese community; in 1985 the Council provided the money to turn Gerrard Street into a pedestrian precinct, complete with pagoda-style telephone boxes, street signs in Chinese and ornamental gateways at either end. It also funds half the salary of a full-time social worker based at the Chinese Community Centre in Gerrard Street. Much of the social worker's time is spent helping with enquiries about form-filling, welfare rights and grants, organising events for pensioners and running the community's youth club.

Although Soho's tradition of providing a refuge for immigrants was established in the 17th century when the Huguenots came over from France, the Chinese are relative newcomers to the area. The first Chinese immigrants arrived in Britain in the 18th century at a time when the tea trade with China was very important. Ships would unload their cargos at the port of London which stretched at that time from Tower Bridge to the Plaistow Marshes. The crews had usually made the gruelling journey from China for little reward and many of them decided to jump ship, putting down roots in the Limehouse area of London's dockland. The Chinese instinct for business has always been well developed and some of these seamen saw great opportunities here. A combination of hard graft and good fortune enabled many of them to set up Chinese laundries which were to become highly successful small businesses.

London's docks were devastated during the Blitz. Many of the businesses which the Chinese had established were razed and the community was forced to look for somewhere else to live. From about 1952 they began to settle in and around Gerrard Street, a down-at-heel thoroughfare which had more than its share of prostitutes' parlours and dubious nightclubs. However Gerrard Street also had a reputation as something of a gastronomic centre; London's first European restaurants were established here in the 19th century. It didn't take long for the Chinese to set up their own restaurants; within two decades the community had built up another thriving business area, based this time on catering. (The advent of the domestic washing machine had seen off many of the laundries.)

The 60s and 70s attracted new waves of Chinese immigration, mainly from Hong Kong and the New Territories. Many of the Chinese who moved here were able to take advantage of the UK's liberal immigration and nationality laws which gave Hong Kong residents automatic British citizenship. As the population of Chinatown began to swell, more and more of the small shops and restaurants in the area were taken over by the Chinese. Apart from offering an enormous range of restaurants and shops, Chinatown also provides the community with a number of Chinese-run businesses and services. Two Chinese newspapers are published from the area, a number of Hong Kong-based banks have set up branches in Soho and, at one end of Gerrard Street, there is even a Chinese barber.

There is, however, a darker side to Chinatown. While Gerrard Street is not by any means overrun by cleaver-happy gangsters working for the Triads, the police do acknowledge that organised crime has an influence in the area. Similarly, while Chinatown is no longer such an important cocaine and heroin trafficking centre as it was in the 70s, small-time drug dealers have managed to find a niche here.

The general crime rate in Chinatown is in fact abnormally low for an inner city area. The police believe that this is because the Chinese have a tradition of sorting out their disputes amongst themselves. They are reluctant to inform the authorities if they believe they have been wronged, preferring instead to exert their own pressure on miscreants. This may amount to no more than getting a few cousins to have a 'word', and most of the time this form of self-policing allows the residents of Chinatown to go about their business in a quiet, trouble-free way. Occasionally, however, an unresolved feud can have devastating repercussions: in 1982, for instance, seven people died in a firebomb attack on a Chinese gambling den below a supermarket in Gerrard Street.

Such cases are thankfully very rare. But there is no doubt that within Chinatown a number of restaurateurs and shopowners have, over the years, faced petty blackmail threats, protection rackets and other attempts to interfere with their businesses. There is some debate over whether these activities are inspired by the Triads (the Mafia-like secret societies based in Hong Kong) or merely the work of local ne'er-do-wells on

Gerrard Street

the lower rungs of a ladder to a criminal career. In 1982 an all-party House of Commons Home Affairs Sub-Committee, which had made a study of Britain's Chinese community, concluded that there was no evidence to suggest that Hong Kong-based Triads were controlling criminal operations in London. The committee's report stated that: 'Our witnesses unanimously agreed that the so-called Triads are simply gangs using Triad nomenclatures to inspire fear.'

For the most part, it seems that the gangs are engaged by unscrupulous local businessmen. The high concentration of shops and restaurants in the area has led to fierce competition which isn't always fair. Often the gangs will employ petty, niggling tactics in an attempt to put pressure on a restaurateur or shopkeeper deemed too successful by one of his rivals. Those involved in the video trade (big business in Chinatown, given the local community's penchant for imported movies) have also been involved in business disputes which have occasionally erupted into petty violence initiated by the gangs. In 1987 one local video distributor was stabbed in the buttock as he walked down Shaftesbury Avenue. In its report, the Commons Committee made it clear that it believed that many of Chinatown's gambling dens are run and used by these gangs: 'Criminal elements are to be found there, the street membership of gangs usually consists of croupiers and bouncers from the clubs and the clubs are closely involved in drug dealings.'

Few Westerners, with the exception of raiding police officers from the Clubs Squad based at Savile Row, have set foot inside the clubs, and would not be welcome if they did. The cry 'members only – get out' normally precedes a forcible ejection; Chinese gamblers do not appreciate voyeurs. In the 70s there were at least ten clubs in the area, now there are five. Most are situated in basements on Gerrard Street, but are not easily visible to Western eyes.

The Chinese passion for gambling is legendary. Although the legitimate betting shops (there are at least four in Chinatown) and the Golden Nugget and Charlie Chester casinos have their share of Chinese punters, most serious Chinese gamblers in the area use the clubs. They usually open at about 3pm each afternoon (there is no point opening any earlier as many of the waiters and cooks who patronise them will have worked long into the night). They offer a range of games and an atmosphere which is not dissimilar to that of a brightly-lit betting shop. Chinese tea is available, often served with slices of orange, melon or pineapple, and in the summer soft drinks and cans of beer are sold from fridges stocked by the backers of the game. (Usually a syndicate will get together to fix the odds and fund a bank.) Each club has a prominent statue of Kwandia, the Chinese god of war which adds a slightly sinister touch to the proceedings. However, these effigies are available, in bronze, porcelain or plastic at any of the Chinese gift emporia clustered around Gerrard Street.

Croupiers, usually young women, preside over the plastic-topped tables while nervous punters shuffle around, anxiously eyeing the game. One of the most popular games, and the one requiring the least skill is fan tan. The croupier has a bucketful of buttons which she empties out upon the table once the punters have made their bets, in cash or chips. With a plastic fan-like instrument she draws off the buttons in groups of four until only one, two, three, or four remain on the table. The punter has a choice of odds depending on where he places his chips on the table. If he covers a single number he has a one-in-four chance of receiving three times his original stake. If he covers three numbers he will only receive one third of the odds as he has a three-in-four chance of winning.

Most clubs also offer pai-kau, a game similar to dominoes and played with only four people, although spectators are encouraged to make side bets. At the start of the game, each player receives four 'dominoes' from the banker. The player must then arrange his dominoes in two pairs. The object of the game is to put down pairs which have a higher value than the banker's.

If a restaurant worker's appetite for gambling is still not sated after a visit to one of the clubs and a flutter on the horses he can always join one of the impromptu mah-jong schools which thrive in the basements or upstairs rooms of certain restaurants. In the evening the clatter of the mah-jong tiles can often be heard from the street. Occasionally it's possible to have a peek at one of these games, providing you make it clear that you are a diner looking for a loo rather than a police officer seeking a conviction.

Every so often Soho's gambling joints are raided by the Clubs Squad, and their managers duly taken to court. The fines they receive can run into thousands, but the managers always pay up phlegmatically, regarding them as a form of income tax (which they wouldn't otherwise pay). In recent years, the police have adopted a softly softly approach to the clubs. They fear that closing them down would merely drive the gamblers underground; at present they serve as a useful observation post, allowing the police to keep an eye on known villains.

Although the dens are still very popular among the older Chinese, the young (many of whom were born and went to school in this country) aren't particularly interested in them. Their command of English gives them social and economic opportunities which their parents may not have had; the gambling clubs are therefore less of a draw. The clubs, however, are the sole source of relaxation for many of those who work unbelievably long hours in Chinatown's restaurants. A typical day would start at 11am and finish at 12pm, during which time the worker might have only a single hour-long break which he would normally spend in a gambling club.

In general, the Chinese are not enamoured of Western drinking habits, and it is rare to find them popping out for a pint between shifts. Before it was tarted up, De Hems on Macclesfield Street used to attract some Chinese custom; the King's Arms (Gerrard Street) and the Polar Bear (Lisle Street) still do, but not very much. Most Chinese are happy either to drink in the clubs (most provide cold beer) or at home.

The younger Chinese spend a lot of their leisure time at the cinema. The Hong Kong Cultural Centre on Gerrard Street shows movies from Hong Kong and Taiwan every day, and on Sundays there is usually a late-night bill of Cantonese films at the Odeon in Leicester Square. The Metro on Rupert Street also shows the occasional film from Hong Kong.

Outsiders wanting a taste of authentic Chinatown should come here on a Sunday afternoon when Gerrard Street is stuffed to the gills with Chinese families shopping and promenading. The narrow streets leading off Gerrard Street are crammed with cars and light vans; many of the Sunday afternoon shoppers run takeaways and restaurants in the provinces and are here to take advantage of the wholesale trade in Chinese vegetables and groceries. Sunday is also the traditional day for taking dim sum. The half dozen or so restaurants which offer these filling, inexpensive snacks are usually packed with Chinese families from all over the country and it can be difficult to secure a seat, particularly in the middle of the afternoon.

The Chinese New Year celebrations, held about a month after our own, are also well worth seeing. For at least a week, the shops and restaurants in Gerrard Street and thereabouts are bedecked with paper lanterns, streamers and coloured lights. Many of the restaurants put on special 'banquet menus' which offer unusual Chinese delicacies at an excellent price. Throughout the festivities, Chinatown throbs with activity.

Chinese New Year has only been celebrated in earnest here for about 15 years. The carnival started when a group of young architectural students managed to persuade local businessmen that a Chinese festival would help to bring trade into the area. Now the Chinatown Association has stepped in to organise the festival (which grows bigger and bigger every year) and the customary whip-round. The amount contributed to festival funds varies wildly, but in a good year a large restaurant such as the Chuen Cheng Ku or the New World would be expected to chip in about £500 apiece.

Apart from stumping up what amounts to an annual 'subscription' to the festival, businesses are also expected to donate 'Hung Poa' or 'Luck Money' when Chinatown's New Year celebrations reach their climax on the Sunday afternoon. An enormous, garish dragon in search of Hung Poa is trailed around the streets (usually by students and members of local martial arts clubs) against a backdrop of clashing cymbals and drums. The money, which represents a sort of insurance premium against misfortune in the forthcoming year, is dangled out of upstairs windows by local businessmen anxious to be seen to be doing their bit for the carnival. The cash (always in notes) is either attached to a line on a makeshift 'fishing' rod, or tied, at intervals, along a length of string. It is sometimes even wrapped in cabbage leaves. The money is apparently donated to local Chinese charities.

The New Year celebrations and the extent to which they have grown over the years are an indication of the robust economic health of the community. The years leading up to 1997, when Britain's lease on Hong Kong expires, will see a further growth in the population. More and more small entrepreneurs will bring their money and businesses over here in an attempt to escape what they believe will be economic disaster once the Chinese regain control of the colony. Their passage may be trickier than it might have been in the 60s or 70s (Britain's nationality laws are much stricter now) but, with acumen like theirs, there is little doubt that they will find a way.

EATING IN CHINATOWN

There's been a real explosion of interest in Chinese food in recent years. The wok is now as much a part of trendy English middle-class life as the cafetière. Soho's restaurateurs in particular, have responded to this new awareness of Cantonese food with new, improved speciality menus and unusual items which you wouldn't normally find outside Hong Kong.

The first Chinese restaurants to open in Soho were the chop suey houses of the 1940s. They served up a curious Sino-American cuisine, based largely on beansprouts and noodles, which won no prizes for culinary invention, but was always very cheap. However, Soho's chop suey houses were not destined to last long. Many of their owners sold up after the war and moved out to the suburbs to open restaurants and take-aways, introducing the British palate to the delights of monosodium glutamate, tinned lychees and numbered menus.

The Cantonese moved into Gerrard Street in earnest in the late 1960s and began opening their own restaurants, which were far superior to the original chop suey houses. Since then, Chinatown has established a reputation for providing some of the best and cheapest food in London, and while some restaurants do offer a selection of Pekingese and Szechuan dishes, most remain resolutely Cantonese.

Dim sum is the real speciality in Chinatown and is normally available from noon to around 6pm. Dim sum comprises a range of snacks: dumplings stuffed with barbecue pork, chicken or prawns, along with spare ribs, stuffed mushrooms, yam croquettes and rice dishes. Unless you have an enormous appetite, five or six items should prove more than sufficient.

Chinese restaurants seem to be undergoing much the same transformation as that of the Indian restaurants a few years ago. Some establishments in and around Gerrard Street have even engaged interior designers to create a look which may be appealing to the Europeans, but could well end up alienating the Chinese. In spite of this, Soho's Chinese restaurants are amongst the best in the Western world. There's an enormous range to choose from and you can eat Chinese food virtually round the clock if you've got the stamina.

RESTAURANTS

Chuen Cheng Ku

17–24 Wardour St W1. 01-437 1398. **L 9**

The best signposted Chinese restaurant in Soho; a totem-pole dragon guards the main entrance in Wardour Street, giving passers-by a taste of the garish yet authentic Cantonese decor they'll find inside. This vast establishment opened in the 1970s to rave reviews, but has recently been in decline. The food – standard Cantonese – can err towards the greasy and the waiters are occasionally surly and rude. That said, service is swift and the food is generally very good value. Dim sum here is a treat, served in the traditional manner by young trolley-pushing waitresses who speak scant English. If your Cantonese is a little rusty, ask for one of the CCK's picture menus and point.

The restaurant usually has a very noisy, lively atmosphere, with waiters rushing to and from the kitchens at top speed. Customers range from local media trendies for whom dim sum is all the rage, to well-behaved football supporters down from the north for a big match. Sundays see a big influx of Chinese who come here for dim sum. The CCK is often the venue for local wedding parties as their banquets are reasonably priced. The manager is extremely accommodating and if you'd like to have a set meal here, tell him how much you want to spend, and he will come up with a suitable menu.

> ### Chuen Cheng Ku
> *Open:* 11.00–23.45 Mon–Sun.
> *Food:* £7.00. *House wine:* £4.90.
> *Credit cards:* Access, Amex, Diners, Visa.

The Diamond

23 Lisle St WC2. 01-437 2517. **N 9**

Worthwhile Cantonese restaurant whose finest attribute is its late licence. On the whole the food is average, but the menu contains the occasional gem, which will almost certainly make your meal a memorable one. The steamed fish in tomato sauce is superb, but market price is charged for this dish and it could turn out to be expensive.

The customers at The Diamond are an interesting mix; mainly people who work in the restaurant trade locally or those appearing at one of the West End theatres. For years, this restaurant has enjoyed the patronage of some of London's top chefs, which obviously serves as some kind of endorsement for the food, even though they are probably attracted chiefly by the restaurant's convenient hours. Given their long hours, the staff remain remarkably chirpy and complimentary pieces of fresh orange are dispensed at the end of your meal.

The Diamond

Open: 12.00–02.00 Mon–Sat, 12.00–24.00 Sun.
Booking: Advisable.
Food: £6.50. *House wine:* £5.50.
Credit cards: Access, Visa.

Dumpling Inn

15a Gerrard St W1. 01-437 2567. **M 9**

Long-established restaurant which is altogether more classy and refined than many of the dubious establishments on Gerrard Street. The Dumpling Inn is much favoured by bigwigs of the Chinese community, who use it as an unofficial HQ and meeting place. It's also popular with free-spending tourists, who don't baulk at the exceptionally high prices.

The restrained, cool decor suggests that Dumpling Inn may have been the model for many of the Chinese restaurateurs who 'went upmarket' in the early 1980s; the owner dispenses business cards bearing the legend 'A touch of class', and decorates each table with fresh flowers.

The food is consistently good here and predominantly Pekingese, although the menu also reflects influences from other Chinese regions. Jellyfish is available as a starter and other 'banquet'-style dishes such as fresh shark's fin with whole chicken and fresh abalone are worth trying. Sample, also, the fish in pepper and vinegar soup (virtually a complete meal) and the deep-fried duck.

> *Dumpling Inn*
>
> *Open:* 12.00–23.45 Mon–Sat, 12.00–23.30 Sun.
> *Food:* £20.00. *House wine:* £5.50.
> *Credit cards:* Access, Amex, Visa.

Fung Shing

15 Lisle St WC2. 01-437 1539. **O 9**

One of the few restaurants in Chinatown which attracts the business lunch set. As a result, prices are higher than most, but the wide range of Cantonese dishes available – including hot pots and seasonal specialities – are usually of a very high standard. The owners of the Fung Shing have set out to offer authentic Cantonese cuisine in an environment which 'sophisticated' Westerners will find to their taste. The decor is delightful, and makes a change from the usual gold and scarlet fittings, but the air-conditioned atmosphere seems a little antiseptic. The Chinese tend not to come here, preferring the more traditional restaurants and cafés clustered in and around Gerrard Street.

Nonetheless, the Fung Shing is well worth a visit, particularly if you are a newcomer to Chinese food. As prices are high, the restaurateur is less dependent on a high turnover of diners and the waiters usually have time to explain the food and make suggestions. Avoid the set meals which don't represent particularly good value (you can find most items elsewhere at half the price) and choose one of the day's specialities.

> *Fung Shing*
>
> *Open:* 12.00–23.30 Mon–Sun.
> *Food:* £20.00. *House wine:* £6.80.
> *Credit cards:* Access, Amex, Diners, Visa.

Lee Ho Fook

15–16 Gerrard St W1. 01-734 9578. **N 9**

One of Chinatown's longest established restaurants, now sadly in decline. Even a wider than usual range of dim sum items does not seem to attract custom and Lee Ho Fook is often empty at lunchtimes. The problem is that it is not different enough from the countless cafés and restaurants on Gerrard Street which serve food of an equal standard but at cheaper prices. The long menu offers few surprises. However, the take-away cake section at the front sells excellent pastries.

> **Lee Ho Fook**
>
> *Open:* 12.00–23.30 Mon–Sat, 12.00–22.30 Sun.
> *Food:* £8.00. *House wine:* £4.80.
> *Credit cards:* Access, Amex, Diners, Visa.

Lee Ho Fook

4 Macclesfield St W1. No phone. **M 8**

Altogether more interesting than its Gerrard Street parent, this branch of Lee Ho Fook is an authentic little eaterie much patronised by the Chinese and the local cognoscenti. Very difficult to find as the name appears above the entrance only in Cantonese script and there is no number on the door. There is no written menu, since only a handful of dishes are available; pork and rice, duck and rice, pork and duck and rice. Occasionally soup and choy sum will be served as well, but don't count on it. Despite this, lunching here can be quite an experience, and not one which will cause much of a dent in your bank balance.

> **Lee Ho Fook**
>
> *Open:* 12.00–20.00 Mon–Sun (but closes earlier if the duck runs out).
> *Food:* £4.00.
> *Credit cards:* Not accepted. Cash only (no cheques).

Ley-Ons

56 Wardour St W1. 01-437 6465. **L 7**

Formerly a Lyons tea shop and, before the war, a chop suey establishment. In common with many Chinese restaurants in Soho Ley-Ons has recently been tarted up. Much of the kitsch wallpaper and uncomfortable seating has been removed; the restaurant now seems larger and airier and attracts a more business-like clientele.

A good bet for lunch, particularly if you are shopping in Old Compton Street and don't want to make the trek south to Chinatown proper. Dim sum is excellent and there is always a large range of savoury and sweet dishes available. The steamed char sui pork buns are delicious, and more adventurous eaters may wish to sample the steamed shark-fin's dumplings or chicken's feet. Dim sum is ordered from a pictorial menu, so you shouldn't run into trouble. Main menu is standard Cantonese fare; no great shakes but adequate for the price. Service can be erratic, but has improved of late.

> *Ley-Ons*
>
> *Open:* 11.30–23.15 Mon–Sun.
> *Food:* £8.00. *House wine:* £6.00.
> *Credit cards:* Access, Amex, Diners, Visa.

Luxuriance

40 Gerrard St W1. 01-734 0262. **M 9**

Another of Soho's new-wave Chinese restaurants, Luxuriance is a plush, upmarket establishment. The huge and varied menu is particularly strong on Peking cuisine and seafood. Set menus consisting entirely of fish courses are available, and many of the dishes are unobtainable elsewhere. Quick-fried eel, for instance, is a Luxuriance favourite and you should not miss out on the jellyfish either.

Although the menu is exciting, the atmosphere is rather subdued. The decor and style of this beautifully designed restaurant is aimed squarely at the affluent Westerner; as a result, few Chinese bother to come here. While service is exemplary, the ambience is redolent of an international hotel's coffee shop. You could be anywhere but Chinatown.

Luxuriance

Open: 12.00–23.30 Mon–Thur & Sun, 12.00–24.30 Fri & Sat.
Food: £8.50. *House wine:* £5.50.
Credit cards: Access, Amex, Diners, Visa.

Mr Kong

21 Lisle St WC2. 01-437 7341. **N 9**

A superb restaurant and an excellent example of what a Cantonese restaurateur can do if he puts his mind to it. Edwin Kong, who is head chef and senior partner here, left the Diamond to set up Mr Kong in 1984. His menus are inventive, unusual and varied enough to give diners plenty of choice. The speciality menu is changed every two months; choose from a wide range of sizzling dishes, such as lamb with ginger and spring onions or unusual seafood dishes; steamed scallops and king prawns in a noodle 'bird's nest' is particularly popular.

Most dishes are Cantonese in origin, although some display Peking and Szechuan influences. Others, such as sliced beef with mango, indicate that Mr Kong is prepared to draw on a number of international cuisines, including nouvelle French and Creole. When in season, game such as quail and venison will also appear on Mr Kong's speciality menu. The emphasis throughout is on very fresh ingredients and the choy sum in particular is always crisp and very tasty.

Mr Kong is more upmarket than most Chinese restaurants in the area and his prices reflect this. However, given the standard of food, they are not unreasonable. Decor is designed to appeal to Western tastes; nonetheless more than half the diners are Cantonese – always a good endorsement. Service is friendly, if not fast, and there is a comprehensive wine list.

Mr Kong

Open: 12.00–01.45 Mon–Sun.
Booking: Advisable.
Food: £10.00. *House wine:* £4.80.
Credit cards: Access, Amex, Diners, Visa.

New World

1 Gerrard Pl W1. 01-734 0677. **O 8**

Currently the hottest ticket in town for dim sum. Excellent selection (including delicious crispy fried wun tun and spare ribs which have some meat on them) served from trolleys by waitresses who speak very little English. If he's not too busy, the head waiter will try to explain some of the dishes, but otherwise point and take pot luck. The New World is very large and the staff sometimes have difficulty coping with all the covers, let alone offering a translation service as well.

Enormous menu includes range of Szechuan and Peking specialities and is very strong on seafood, including steamed scallops (available individually as a starter) and softshell crab which the owners import from the United States. These are extremely tasty, very easy to deal with and caused a stir in the foodie press when they were first introduced here in the mid-80s.

The decor is traditional Hong Kong kitsch, but the service rather more genteel than in some establishments. This is probably what attracts the Chinese families, especially at weekends, when you will almost certainly have to queue. Bookings are only accepted for the evening.

New World

Open: 11.00–23.45 Mon–Sun.
Booking: Advisable for the evening.
Food: £7.00. *House wine:* £4.90.
Credit cards: Access, Amex, Diners, Visa.

Poon's

4 Leicester St WC2. 01-437 1528. **N 10**

Poon's is a phenomenally successful chain of three Cantonese/ Pekingese restaurants, and of them all, this branch probably offers the best deal. The Covent Garden establishment is outrageously expensive, while the pokey little café-like branch on Lisle Street offers only a limited range of dishes.

Specialities here include sweet and sour fish, wind-dried meats and sausages, and the 'hot-pot' dishes: casseroles of pork, eel, oyster and wind-dried meats. Poon's Chinese clients are very keen on these, but Europeans tend to ignore them, preferring the more familiar dishes such as lemon chicken or crispy-fried beef. The hot-pots are certainly an acquired taste; if you do plump for one of them, it's probably best to order just plain boiled rice as an accompaniment – the sauces in which these dishes are cooked can be very powerful.

Poon's also serves what is arguably the best Peking duck in Chinatown. It may not be cheap, but it is delicately flavoured and never fatty. Unlike some Chinese restaurants, Poon's does not require 24 hours' notice to serve this dish and also offers proper pancakes in which to wrap your duck; far superior to the dainty little gone-in-one-mouthful discs served elsewhere. Another bonus is that once you've finished your pancakes, the waiters will bring out what they call 'the remains of the duck' in a vegetable stir-fry. Order only a half duck if you want to sample anything else on the menu – it can be extremely filling.

Although the food here can seldom be faulted for either quality or value, the service is erratic and it is not one of Soho's most comfortable restaurants. Tables are packed closely together, and the lighting is far too bright. The waiters are rarely interested in explaining the menu and it is usually impossible to attract their attention if you want to change your order. Nevertheless, Poon's is still one of the very best, most reasonably priced Chinese restaurants in Soho. Booking is advisable, particularly at weekends. Get there on time, as the staff are not inclined to hold tables for very long. At most you'll be allowed five minutes' grace.

Poon's

Open: 12.00–23.30 Mon–Sat. Closed Sun.
Booking: Advisable for the evening.
Food: £5.00. *House wine:* £4.30.
Credit cards: Not accepted.

Soho's Friend

4 Meard St W1. 01-437 1316. **L 6**

Charming little restaurant offering a curious mix of Pekingese and Indonesian food. Soho's Friend has been open since 1978 and in that time Meard Street has been transformed from one of Soho's most unpleasant little alleyways into a very desirable residential thoroughfare. The transvestite brothel next door, which used to discourage families from eating at the restaurant, is long gone and trade is now flourishing. It's not difficult to see why. The food here is imaginative and reasonably priced and the service, surprisingly for a Chinese restaurant, is first-class.

The decor, however, is stuck firmly in the 1970s. Record company executives with burgeoning bellies place considerable stress on the hi-tech chairs and the small dining area is bathed in a strangely depressing half-light. The shabby paintwork and ceiling fans also contribute to give the place a down-at-heel colonial feel. Not to worry, the shell-on prawns in hot sambal sauce more than make up for the lack of comfort. Try also the shredded pork with vegetables and pancakes, a poor man's Peking duck and a rarity on Chinese menus.

Soho's Friend

Open: 12.00–15.00, 17.30–23.30 Mon–Sat. Closed Sun.
Booking: Advisable for the evening.
Food: £6.50. *House wine:* £4.30.
Credit cards: Access, Amex, Diners, Visa.

Wong Kei

41 Wardour St W1. 01-437 8408. **L 9**

Immense, sprawling Cantonese caff, much patronised by Chinese locals. Service is appalling, conditions extremely uncomfortable but food excellent value for what it is. Arguably Soho's cheapest and rudest Chinese, the staff make Norman Balon, landlord of the Coach & Horses and self-styled 'rudest publican in Soho' seem a model of genial charm.

Shrill cries of 'upstairs' 'downstairs' or 'sit here' reverberate around the room as the waiters make a snap judgement about where they feel you should sit. If you are in a respectable-looking party of four or more, you will probably be shown to one of the upstairs floors. Here the atmosphere is civil, but by no means refined. If you're a couple, it's likely you'll be sent downstairs, where the service is just about acceptable. Roughest ride is reserved for those who dare to dine here alone; they are manhandled into a seat at the back of the ground floor – Wong Kei's very own Skid Row.

At some point you will be given your free pot of Chinese tea and the menu. Ignore the chicken and cashew nut/sweet and sour pork-style items and stick to the rice and noodle dishes which the Chinese themselves favour. The choy sum with oyster sauce (not on the menu) is also a good bet as is the (very) hot and sour soup and Singapore fried noodles. Servings of wun tun soup are enormous and have the added interest that you may have watched your wun tuns being prepared by the two nimble-fingered lads by the front door.

Although the Wong Kei has enjoyed considerable success over the last few years and soon grew out of its previous premises in Rupert Court, prices have remained remarkably stable. It continues to attract customers in their droves; presumably they don't come here for the ambience.

Wong Kei

Open: 12.00–24.00 Mon–Sun.
Food: £4.00. *House wine:* £4.00.
Credit cards: Not accepted. Cash only (no cheques).

SHOPS

Atoz Martial Arts Centre
M 8

3 Macclesfield St W1. 01-734 4142. The martial arts groups in Chinatown play an important part in the New Year celebrations and many of them come here to buy their equipment. Some of the stuff looks truly menacing (Ninja masks and kendo staves, rice flails and clubs made of wood and metal), while the rest (jackets, sashes and slippers) would not look out of place worn in one of the local restaurants. If you are interested in joining a martial arts group, the helpful staff will usually be able to point you in the right direction. *Open 11.00–18.00 Mon–Sat.* Amex, Diners, Visa.

China Beauty Centre
O 9

3 Lisle St WC2. 01-734 7302. This is an essential stopping-off point during the Chinese New Year celebrations. A huge variety of traditional, brightly coloured Chinese costumes and accessories can be bought or rented and the Beauty Centre will even produce souvenir Polaroid prints of the revellers they dress. Take a look at the prints from previous years which the owners have placed on the wall at the back of the shop. A make-up service is also available; very popular with local Cantonese brides who come here to be made up on the morning of the wedding. *Open 11.00–19.00 Mon–Sun.* No credit cards.

Chinatown Fish & Meat Market
O 8

14 Newport Pl WC2. 01-437 0712. The Chinese have a high regard for fresh, high-quality seafood. It is perhaps surprising, therefore, that this is the only proper Chinese fishmonger in the area since the sudden demise of Peter the Fisherman on Peter Street. David Lam, who owns and runs this shop, is an expert and will always take time to explain how to cook some

of the more exotic fish and seafood he sells. The centrepiece of his display is a large freshwater tank, full of massive carp and long, thick eels. David's assistants will kill the fish you choose on the spot, as quickly and humanely as possible.

Fish which arrive on David's slab already dead include pomfret from China and Bangladesh, the beautiful, multi-coloured parrot fish from the Mediterranean, grouper from the Seychelles and the yellow croaker from Argentina. There's not a fish finger in sight. David also makes efforts to ensure that those who pine for oysters when there isn't an 'R' in the month don't do so for long; his fat, juicy specimens are imported from France and are available throughout the year.

The shop also has a well-stocked freezer cabinet wherein you will find that elusive ingredient (abalone, cuttle fish, scallops) for the stir-fry that looked so mouthwatering in Kenneth Lo's cookbook. The meat counter, however, will only appeal to the more adventurous. Solidified pig's blood is an ingredient favoured by the Chinese and stocked here in large quantities. *Open 11.00–20.00 Mon–Sun.* No credit cards.

Golden Gate Grocers O 8

16 Newport Pl WC2. 01-437 6266. The new Chinese shopping precinct at the eastern end of Gerrard Street offers some excellent shopping facilities. Golden Gate is one of the best Chinese supermarkets in the area and a good starting point for someone wanting to experiment with authentic Chinese food. The staff are overwhelmingly helpful, the shop's layout is less chaotic than in the bigger establishments on Gerrard Street, and it never seems to be crowded. The green vegetable selection is pretty comprehensive and the assistants will advise if you are confused by the wide array on show. Choy sum is probably the most popular Chinese vegetable. It should be rinsed, chopped up, stir-fried and served with oyster sauce (also available here). Other green vegetables on sale at Golden Gate include guy lau (similar to broccoli), and bor choy (similar to spinach). *Open 10.00–20.00 Mon–Sun.* No credit cards.

Hong Kong Cultural Service O 8

46 Gerrard St W1. 01-734 5037. Chaotically-run general store, which has a particularly wide selection of books, records and periodicals from Hong Kong, Taiwan and mainland China. Students of Cantonese would do well to invest in some of the pulp thrillers and romances that are popular with the local Chinese or perhaps a Cantonese translation of Shakespeare, Conan Doyle or Dickens. Interesting array of cookbooks too; most are imported from Hong Kong and explain, in English and Cantonese, how to make dim sum, wun tun soup or Peking duck. If these disappoint, however, Mr Chung, owner of the shop since 1970, will be more than happy to advise. His English is perfect and his knowledge comprehensive. The handicrafts on sale represent excellent value for money: the HKCS has perhaps the best selection of cork sculpture in the whole of Chinatown, and the wind chimes and wall hangings are enough to render the suburban plaster duck redundant. *Open 11.00–20.00 Mon–Sun.* No credit cards.

Loon Fung Supermarket N 9

42–43 Gerrard St W1. 01-437 7332. Probably the largest Chinese supermarket in London if not Britain, Loon Fung has an enormous range of fresh and frozen food (including meat), prepared foods imported from the Far East and oriental cooking utensils. Much patronised by the owners of provincial and suburban takeaways, Loon Fung is an excellent source of everyday Chinese ingredients such as monosodium glutamate, fresh choy sum and root ginger. Since much of the fresh produce is sold loose, you will be able to buy just a small amount. This is also one of the best places in Chinatown to buy a wok. Prices are very reasonable. Loon Fung is also one of the few shops in Chinatown with a licence to sell alcoholic drinks. Try sake from Hong Kong or Japan, Chinese beer or Wan Fu (a light French table wine produced especially for consumption with Chinese food – well that's what the label says anyway). *Open 10.00–20.30 Mon–Sat.* No credit cards.

New Oriental **O 9**

4–8 Newport Pl WC2. 01-434 2989. Handicraft shop selling high-quality products. No tat here, but prices are not as low as you might find elsewhere in Chinatown. The New Oriental has probably the best cloisonné collection of any shop in the West End: jugs, plates, bowls and vases are available individually or in pairs. Given the standard of the workmanship involved they represent excellent value for money. Also a range of sculpture in jade and cork imported from China and some Chinese chic in the shape of decadent-looking quilted jackets and bathrobes. *Open 11.00–19.00 Mon–Sun.* Access, Visa.

Sound of China **O 8**

6 Gerrard St W1. 01-734 1970. A thriving pop music industry has evolved in the Far East over the last few years and shops such as the Sound of China do a good trade in records and tapes from Hong Kong and Taiwan. The first pop records to gain favour with young Chinese were merely Cantonese versions of American and British Top 20 hits, but now a much wider range is available. Many of the discs on sale here are of music written and recorded in Hong Kong by local bands. They are probably too shrill for Western ears, but sell like hot char sui pau in Gerrard Street. This well-run shop also has a good selection of Chinese magazines and newspapers. *Open 12.00–20.00 Mon–Sun.* No credit cards.

Ying Hwa **N 9**

14 Gerrard St W1. 01-439 8825. Unusual emporium which retails a very odd mixture of oriental tat. Ying Hwa's multifarious lines include tapes of Chinese folk music, cookbooks (recipes translated from Cantonese into unorthodox English) and soft, spongey old-fashioned table tennis bats. If you decide to pay Ying Hwa a visit, allow plenty of time. The shop seems in utter disarray so it is unlikely you will find what you want immediately. But browsers are welcome and the staff helpful. *Open 11.00–19.30 Mon–Sun.* No credit cards.

9 Soho Services

Adult Education

Central London Adult Education Institute **J 9**
Piccadilly Branch, 23 Great Windmill St W1. 01-437 2736 (after 18.00). Housed in the Soho Parish School, this branch of the Institute offers inexpensive courses in languages, wine appreciation, singing and other subjects. For further information consult the ILEA publication *Floodlight*, available at public libraries, bookshops and newsagents.

Advice Centres

Central London Community Law Centre **H 6**
13 Ingestre Pl W1. 01-437 8746. Free legal advice on any subject to people who live or work in the area. Donations very welcome. *Open 15.00–19.00 Tue, 12.00–14.00, 15.00–19.00 Wed.* Telephone advice available *10.00–17.30 Mon–Fri.*

Electrical Association for Women **E 5**
25 Foubert's Pl W1. 01-437 5212. Set up in 1924, the Association offers free advice on electrical appliances to members of either sex. Regular courses are held (learn how to wire a plug or change a fuse) and there are plenty of free pamphlets available. *Open 09.00–17.00 Mon–Fri.*

Banks

National Westminster **K 5**
110 Wardour St W1. 01-439 1861. *Open 09.30–15.30 Mon–Fri.*

Barclays **N 3**
25 Soho Sq W1. 01-439 6851. *Open 09.30–15.30 Mon–Fri.*

Both banks have foreign exchange facilities, but it is usually best to order currency in advance. Commission rates are much cheaper than at commercial bureaux de change. Both banks also have external cash dispensers for obtaining money outside banking hours.

Betting Shops

To place a bet in one of these establishments you need to be over 18. Cheques are accepted if supported by a bank card. Most bookmakers are ex-directory but telephone bets will be accepted from account holders.

Coral **O 9**
1–3 Newport Pl WC2. *Open 10.00–17.30* (*to 18.30* if evening racing begins before then) *Mon–Sat.*

Ladbrokes **M 10**
33–37 Wardour St W1. *Open 10.15–17.30 Mon–Fri, 10.00–17.30 Sat* (*or ½ hr before last race, whichever is later*).

Mecca **C 6**
31 Kingly St W1. *Open 10.15–17.30 Mon–Fri, 10.00–17.30 Sat.*

William Hill **J 8**
33 Brewer St W1. *Open 10.15–17.30 Mon–Fri, 10.00–17.30 Sat.*

Bureaux de Change

Bureaux de change offer foreign exchange facilities and will also cash cheques and Eurocheques if supported by a cheque card. Commission is negotiable but always more than a bank would charge.

Chequepoint
7 Shaftesbury Av W1. **J 11**
01-409 1122. *24 hrs Mon–Sun.*
37 Coventry St W1. **L 11**
01-839 3772. *24 hrs Mon–Sun.*

Deak International **J 11**
15 Shaftesbury Av W1. 01-734 1400. *Open 24 hrs Mon–Sun.*

Eurochange **H 11**
2 Sherwood St W1. 01-437 2139. *Open 08.00–22.00 Mon–Sun.*

Car Parks

APCOA **G 4**
51 Poland St W1. *Open 08.00–24.00 Mon–Sat.*

NCP **J 8**
Brewer St W1. *Open 08.00–24.00 Mon–Sat, 11.00–18.30 Sun.*

NCP **J 10**
6 Denman St W1 (exit Ham Yard). *Open 24 hrs.*

NCP **O 8**
Gerrard Pl W1. *Open 24 hrs.*

NCP **C 7**
Kingly St W1. *Open 08.00–24.00.*

NCP **M 11**
Leicester Sq WC2 (entrance Leicester St). *Open 08.00–02.00 Mon–Fri, 08.00–03.00 Sat, 08.00–24.00 Sun.*

Chemists

Boots **J 11**
44 Piccadilly Circus W1. 01-734 6126. *Open 08.00–20.00 Mon–Sat.*

Broadway Pharmacy **G 5**
18 Broadwick St W1. 01-437 3846. *Open 08.30–19.00 Mon–Fri, 09.00–19.00 Sat.*

Compton Pharmacy **L 8**
32 Wardour St W1. 01-437 7329. *Open 08.30–18.30 Mon–Fri, 09.30–18.00 Sat.*

Underwoods **E 6**
36 Carnaby St W1. 01-734 6217. *Open 08.30–19.00 Mon–Fri, 09.00–19.00 Sat.*

Dry Cleaners

These are good general dry cleaners. Anything that can't

be dealt with on the premises will be sent to a specialist.

Celebrity Dry Cleaners **J 4**
155 Wardour St W1. 01-437 5324. Also suede and leather cleaning. *Open 08.30–17.30 Mon–Fri.*

De Luxe Cleaning **J 8**
30 Brewer St W1. 01-437 8541. Evening gown specialists; invisible mending also undertaken. *Open 08.30–17.00 Mon–Fri and some Sats.*

Perkins **K 5**
102 Wardour St W1. 01-437 4846. Suede cleaning and a tailoring service. *Open 08.30–18.00 Mon–Fri, 08.30–12.00 Sat.*

Emergency Accommodation

Centrepoint Soho **M 8**
65a Shaftesbury Av W1. 01-434 2861. A charity which provides emergency accommodation for young people down-and-out in the West End. There is usually a queue of young hopefuls by about *20.00*. Admission by interview at the gate. *Night shelter open 20.00–08.00 Mon–Sun.*

Employment

DHSS **H 7**
Colquhoun House, 50 Broadwick St W1. 01-734 7010. This is not a benefit office, although you can obtain general advice about Supplementary Benefit and National Insurance here. *Open 09.30–15.30 Mon–Fri.*

Job Centre **H 2**
195 Wardour St W1. 01-439 4541. *Open 09.00–17.00 Mon–Thur, 10.00–17.00 Fri.*

Estate Agents

There are no estate agents in Soho, but those listed below handle properties in the area. Property prices have risen rapidly since Soho became fashionable again. Realty specialises in grand homes, suitable for very wealthy foreign businessmen, while Sweby has smaller properties, including studios and one-bedroom flats, on their books.

Realty
1e Palace Gate SW1. 01-589 8899. *Open 09.30–18.00 Mon–Fri.*

Sweby Cowan
73 Monmouth St WC2. 01-631 5313. *Open 09.30–17.30 Mon–Fri.*

Family Centre

Soho Family Centre **J 8**
Island Block, St James's Residences, 23 Brewer St W1. 01-439 1578. Drop-in centre for parents and children comprising child-minding and playgroup facilities, a toy library and health education classes. Mainly for those who live in the area. The Family Centre, which is a charitable trust, is also hoping to set up family planning and Well-woman health clinics. These will be available to all. *Open 09.30–16.30 Mon–Fri.*

Hairdressers

Alan Oliver **D 7**
7 Kingly St W1. 01-734 2429. Basic haircuts by girl stylists in this men-only salon with a distinctly 70s atmosphere. *Open 09.00–18.00 Mon–Wed & Fri, 09.00–18.30 Thur, 09.30–15.00 Sat.* Access, Visa.

Cuts **N 6**
23a Frith St W1. 01-734 2171. One of Soho's fashionable unisex hairdressers which shares its premises with a traditional Italian barber's shop called Nino's. *Open 10.00–19.00 Mon–Sat.* No credit cards.

Haircutting Room **N 6**
53 Greek St W1. 01-434 1056. Shabby premises that evokes a 1960s box room. Very alternative. Be prepared for a long wait as they only cut one at a time. *Open 11.00–20.00 Mon–Fri, 11.00–17.00 Sat.* No credit cards.

Demop **F 8**
7 Upper James St W1. 01-734 1050. Club-like atmosphere catering for those who consider themselves at the forefront of Soho's avant garde. Adorned with depressing 'sculptures' by the Mutoid Waste Company. *Open 10.00–18.00 Mon–Fri, 10.00–16.00 Sat.* Visa.

Gavin Hodge **K 8**
29 Brewer St W1. 01-437 2301. A more mainstream West End salon. Prices are high but service is generally good. Sunbed and beauty treatments, including manicure, are available for men and women. *Open 10.00–20.00 Mon–Sat.* Access, Visa.

Rough Cut **J 8**
97 Berwick St W1. 01-734 2912. Super-trendy haircuts for men and women, generally unsuitable for those over 30. *Open 10.00–19.00 Mon–Fri, 09.00–18.00 Sat.* No credit cards.

Health Services

Great Chapel Street Medical Centre **K 2**
13 Great Chapel St W1. 01-437 9360. Walk-in medical help for the homeless and those without a doctor in London. However, the centre does not have huge resources; minor ailments can often be dealt with by a pharmacist. A psychiatrist is on duty on *Mon & Tue*, a chiropodist on *Mon & Thur*. *Open 12.45–16.00 Mon–Fri, 11.00–12.00 Sat.*

Hospital for Women **M 4**
Soho Sq W1. 01-636 8333. Hospital which specialises in gynaecological disorders. Patients must live in Soho or Bloomsbury and be referred here by their GP.

Margaret Pyke Centre **M 4**
15 Bateman's Buildings, Soho Sq W1. 01-734 9351. Free condoms and other forms of contraception for those who live anywhere within the Greater London area and Essex. This is London's largest NHS family planning clinic, dealing with over 900 patients a week. There is a three-week waiting

list for appointments, but service is usually swift and efficient. Morning-after pill and abortion referral also available, along with an emergency clinic at noon each day. *Open 09.30–19.00 Mon–Thur, 09.30–17.00 Fri.*

P & G Advisory Service **E 5**
26 Foubert's Pl W1. 01-439 8640. Private equivalent of the Margaret Pyke Centre, offering pregnancy testing, contraception and abortion advice. Appointments within two or three days of booking. *Open 09.00–17.30 Mon–Fri,* (phone lines open to *19.30*), *09.30–12.30 Sat.*

Housing Association

Soho Housing Association **K 9**
9a Archer St W1. 01-437 9141. Housing trust which develops and restores low-cost housing for local people. If you want to go on their waiting list, you must be recommended by Westminster City Council or your own local authority, you cannot apply to the Soho Housing Association in person. A points system is applied, which normally rules out single people who are without dependants. *Open 09.30–17.00 Mon–Fri.*

Launderettes

Petit Laundrette **P 9**
6 Little Newport St WC2. 01-437 7249. Service washes available. *Open 07.00–19.00 Mon–Sun.*

Sussex Wash Laundry Services **E 5**
10 Marshall St W1. 01-734 5818. Service washes available. *Open 08.00–19.00 Mon–Fri, 08.00–15.00 Sat.*

Library

Charing Cross Library
4 Charing Cross Rd WC2. 01-798 2058. Adult and music lending library run by Westminster City Council. Borrowers may join the library once they have provided proof that they live or work in Westminster. People living or working outside Westminster may also join but need to provide a library card from another London borough, plus proof of residence in that borough. Borrowing of books is free but there is a charge for records and cassettes. *Open 09.30–19.00 Mon–Fri, 09.30–13.00 Sat.*

Magistrates Court

Great Marlborough Street Magistrates Court **D 4**
21 Great Marlborough St W1. 01-434 5383. Cases are heard (and the public admitted) between *10.00–16.00 Mon–Fri, 10.00–13.00 Sat.*

Petrol

Since the closure of the Brewer Street garage, no petrol is available in Soho. The nearest garages selling petrol are in St Martin's Lane or at Selfridge's in Orchard Street.

Places of Worship

Church of Our Lady of the Assumption **E 9**
Warwick St W1. 01-437 1525. Masses: *Sun 08.00, 10.00 & 11.00; Mon–Fri 08.00, 12.45 & 17.45; Sat 08.00 & 12.45.*

French Protestant Church **N 3**
8 Soho Sq W1. 01-437 5311. Services *Sun 11.00* (French), First *Tue* of every month *12.30* (Bilingual).

St Anne's Church Chapel **M 8**
57 Dean St W1. 01-437 6727. Sunday service *10.00.*

St Patrick's Catholic Church **N 3**
Soho Sq W1. 01-437 2010. Sunday services *08.00, 09.00, 11.00, 14.00, 18.00.* (Cantonese *14.00*), (Spanish *15.00*).

West End Great Synagogue **L 4**
21 Dean St W1. 01-437 1873. Synagogue office *open 09.00–17.00 Mon–Thur, 09.00–12.00 Fri & Sun.* Services *19.30 Fri, 09.30 Sat.*

Police

Soho is covered by three police stations, although none of them are actually in Soho itself. They are:

Vine Street
10 Vine St W1. 01-434 5212.

Bow Street
28 Bow St WC2. 01-434 5212.

West End Central
27 Savile Row W1. 01-434 5212.

Post Office

Broadwick Street **J 5**
15 Broadwick St W1. 01-437 6842. *Open 09.30–17.30 Mon, 09.00–17.30 Tue–Fri, 09.00–12.30 Sat.*

Public Lavatories

Broadwick Street **J 5**
opposite the Post Office. Ladies and gents with attendant. In 1966 these conveniences were used for the filming of a Peter Cook and Dudley Moore television special in which John Lennon played a lavatory attendant. *Open 08.00–18.00 Mon–Fri, 10.00–18.00 Sat & Sun.*

Great Marlborough Street/Carnaby Street **D 5**
intersection. Underground ladies and gents with attendant. *Open 07.30–10.30 Mon–Sat, 08.30–10.30 Sun.*

There is also a French-designed automatic **'Superloo'** at **Cambridge Circus**, *open 24 hrs*, you will need 10p. **P 6**

Public toilets are also available in **Piccadilly Circus Underground station**. **J 11**

Schools

Soho Parish School **J 9**
23 Great Windmill St W1. 01-437 2736. Church of England Primary School for children aged 5–11. Many of the pupils live in the area. Parents who work in Soho and who would like to send their children here should contact the Headmaster.

Shoe Repairs

George's Shoe Repairs **J 7**
26 Peter St W1. 01-734 0417. Invaluable Soho institution which moved last year from Silver Place. Shoe repairs and key-cutting undertaken, plus accessories such as polish and brushes on sale. *Open 08.30–18.00 Mon–Fri, 09.00–14.00 Sat.*

Soho Society **M 8**

St Anne's Tower, 57 Dean St W1. 01-439 4303. This admirable organisation has done much to preserve the character of Soho and reverse the Vice-inspired decline of the 60s and 70s. The Society produces *The Clarion* (a monthly newspaper), organises the annual Soho Festival and runs a very active local history group. Membership is open to firms as well as to individuals. For more information contact the Secretary at the above address.

Transport

Buses
No buses are routed through the middle of Soho, but plenty travel along Shaftesbury Avenue, Charing Cross Road, Oxford Street and Regent Street. All-night buses are available from Trafalgar Square. For London Transport Travel information, phone 01-222 1234, *24hr service.*

Underground
Soho is served by four Underground stations, Oxford Circus, Tottenham Court Road, Piccadilly Circus and Leicester Square. Last trains leave at around midnight on weekdays, earlier on Sundays.

Taxis
Plentiful during the day, but can be impossible to find late at night, particularly on Fridays and Saturdays. There may be a chance of finding one in Soho's smaller streets where people are being dropped at clubs or restaurants. Best to go into Shaftesbury Avenue, Regent Street, Piccadilly or Charing Cross Road.

Mini-cabs
Avoid using the 'mini-cab' drivers who lurk around Cambridge Circus touting for business. The chances are that they are unlicensed, uninsured and if anything goes wrong, untraceable. Lone women should not get into one of these cars.

Old Compton Mini-cabs **O 6**
23–24 Old Compton St W1. 01-434 1213/3354. Reliable *24 hr* service, but negotiate the price first.

Westminster City Councillors

David Avery (Conservative).

Lois Peltz (Independent).

Write to them with any queries, complaints or suggestions at the Members' Office, Westminster City Hall, Victoria Street SW1.

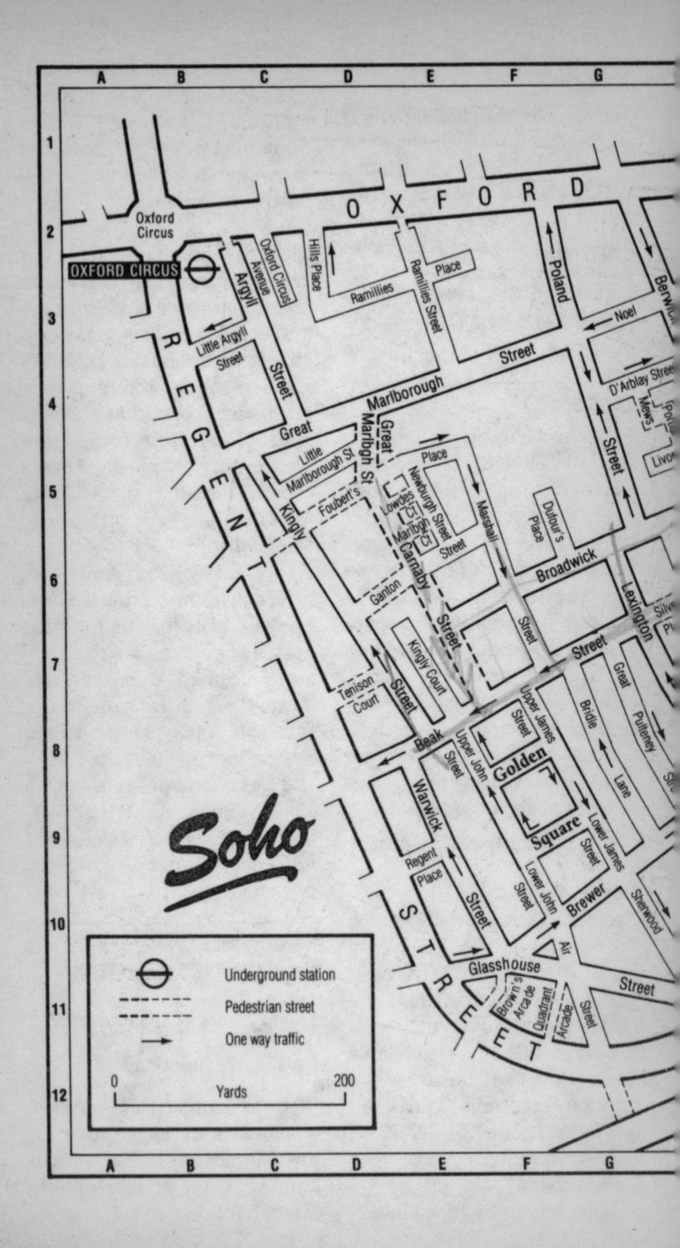
Soho
OXFORD CIRCUS
Oxford Circus
OXFORD
REGENT STREET
Argyll Street
Little Argyll Street
Oxford Circus Avenue
Hills Place
Ramillies Place
Ramillies Street
Poland Street
Noel Street
D'Arblay Street
Berwick
Great Marlborough Street
Little Marlborough St
Great Marlbgh St
Foubert's
Kingly Street
Lowndes Ct
Marlbgh Ct
Newburgh Street
Marshall Street
Dufour's Place
Broadwick Street
Lexington Street
Carnaby Street
Ganton Street
Kingly Court
Tenison Court
Beak Street
Upper James Street
Upper John Street
Golden Square
Bridle Lane
Great Pulteney Street
Warwick Street
Regent Place
Lower James Street
Lower John Street
Brewer Street
Sherwood
Air Street
Glasshouse Street
Brown's Arcade
Quadrant Arcade
Underground station
Pedestrian street
One way traffic
0
200
Yards

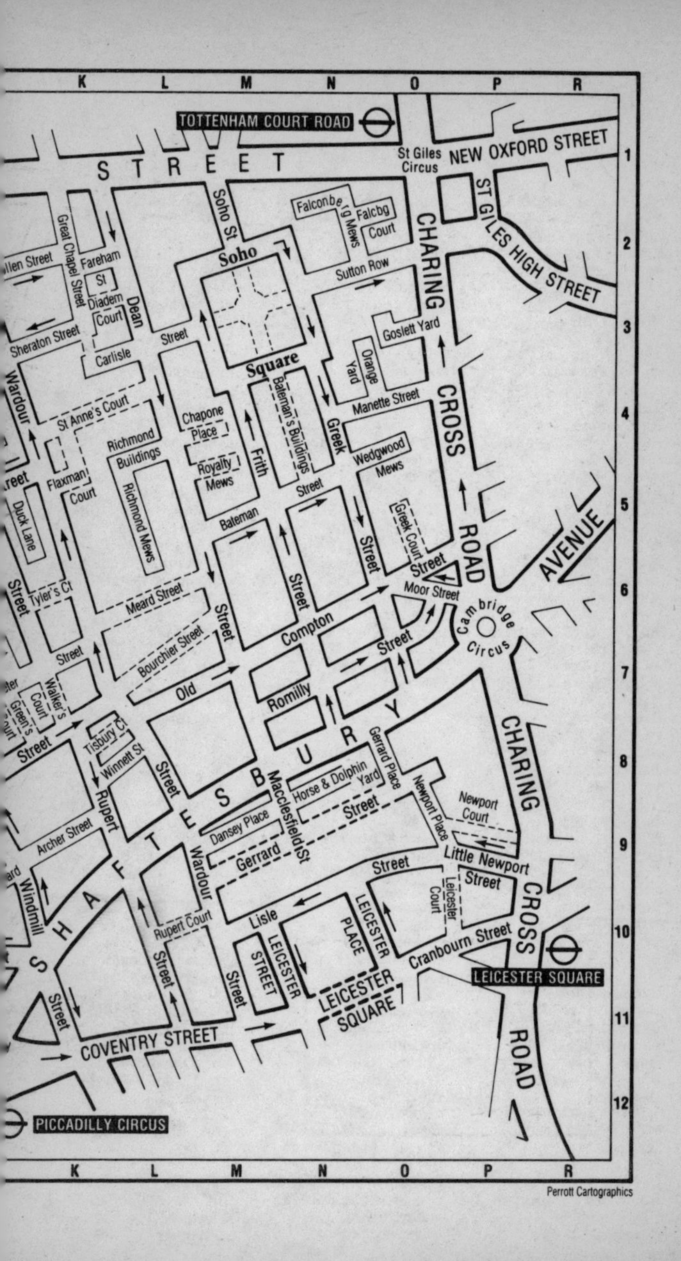

Perrott Cartographics

Index

Al Cameras 166
Academy 144
Accum, Friedrich 30
Admiral Duncan 99
Adult Education 245
Advice Centres 245
Alan Oliver 248
Algerian Coffee Stores 152
Alistair Little 46
Amalfi 47
American Retro 144
Andrea Doria 47
Andrew Edmunds 133
Angelucci, A. 152
Ann Summers 168
Anything Left Handed 163
Apollo Theatre 195
Argyll Arms 100
Argyll Street 16
Artists' materials 159
Ashley's 48
Astoria 183
Astral 1 & 2 180
Atoz Martial Arts Centre 241
Au Jardin des Gourmets 49

Bahn Thai 50
Baird, John Logie 21, 30
Banks 245
Banks, Sir Joseph 30
Bar Italia 91
Barocco Espresso Bar 92
La Bastide 50
Bath-House 100
Beak Street 6, 11, 16
Beare, J. & A. 164
Le Beat Route 202
Beau Monde 145
Beckford, William 31
Behan, Brendan 7, 15
Benedetto 144
Bengali Spice 52
Berwick Street 18
  Market 173
Betjeman, John 26
Betting Shops 245–246
Bill Stickers 53
Le Bistingo 54
Blackout 145
Blake, William 25, 31
Blue Posts
  (Berwick St) 101
  (Ganton St) 102
  (Rupert St) 103
Bookshops 159
Boswell, James 31
Boulevard Theatre 196
Boy Soho 145
Braganza 54
Brasseries 91–97
Brewer Street 6, 18
Broadwick Street 11, 18
Bureaux de Change 246
Burgess & Galer 173
Burke, Edmund 7, 21, 32
Buses 251
Butchers 151–152
Buttons shop 160

Café de Paris 15, 202
Café Loire 55
Cafés 91–97
Camisa, I. & Son 155
Canal, Antonio (Canaletto) 32
Capital Newsagents 165
Car parks 246
Carlisle Arms 103
Carlisle House 12, 19, 27, 28
Carlisle Street 19
Carnaby Street 19
Carnival Revue Club 192
Carwardines 153
Casanova, Giovanni Giacomo 32
Casinos 176–179
Cassettes 167–168
The Cavern 146
Central London Adult Education Institute 245
Central London Community Law Centre 245
Centrepoint Soho 247
Charing Cross Library 249
Charlie Chester 177
Charlotte Robinson Second Hand & Rare Books 159
Chemists 246
Chez Victor 56
Chiang Mai 57
China Beauty Centre 241
Chinatown 7, 222–244
Chinatown Fish & Meat Market 241
Chinese Community Centre 223
Chinese New Year 228–229
Chivers 162
Cho Won 58
Christopher New 146
Christy's Healthline 59
Chuen Cheng Ku 231
Church of Our Lady of the Assumption & St Gregory 20, 250
Churches 250
Cinemas 180–181
The Clachan 104
Clarkson, Willy 33
Clothes shops 144–151
Clowns 134
Coach & Horses (Great Marlborough St) 104
  (Greek St) 105
Coffee shops 152–153
Coleman & Cohen 172
Colony Room 7, 8, 15, 140
Compton Green 60
Comptons 7, 107
Cornelys, Theresa 12, 19, 33
Cowling & Wilcox 159
Cranks 61
Crime 217–221, 224–226
The Crown 108
Crown & Two Chairmen 109
La Cucaracha 61
Cult clubs 201
Curzon West End 180
Cuts 248

Daddy Kool 167
Dalli, J. & J. 151
De Hems 109
De Quincey, Thomas 7, 34
Dean Street 6, 14, 20
Dean's 134
Del Monico's 157
Delhi Brasserie 62
Delicatessens 153–156
Demop 248
Desaru 63
Designer clothes & accessories 144–151
Devonshire Arms 110
DHSS 247
The Diamond 231
Dickens, Charles 14, 17, 19, 22, 24
Direct Electronics 160
Dog & Duck 111
Dog & Trumpet 112
Dometakis, A. 171
Dress to Kill 146
Drinking 98–141
Drinking clubs 140–141
Dry Cleaners 246–247
Dryden, John 7, 21, 34
Duke of Argyll 112
Duke of Wellington 113
Dumpling Inn 232

Eating 41–97, 230–240
Ed's Easy Diner 92–93
Electrical Association for Women 245

Electrical shops 160–161
Emergency
Accommodation 247
Employment 247
Entertainment 176–208
L'Epicure 64
L'Escargot 65
Estate Agents 247
Eye Tech 147

Fabric Studio 161
Fabrics 161–162
The Falcon 114
Family Centre 247
Fans 147
F. FWD (Fast Forward)
148
Fauconberg House 12, 28
Film Industry 8–9
58 Dean Street Records
167
Fishmongers 156–157
Flowers 162
Foote, Chas. E. 165
Fratelli Camisa 153
The French House 7, 98,
114
French Protestant
Church 15, 20, 250
Frith Street 6, 21
Frith's 67
Fuji 68
Fung Shing 233
Furniture 162

Galsworthy, John 9
Gambling 176–179,
226–228, 245–246
Games 162
Gavin Hodge 248
Gay Hussar 69
Gerrard Street 7, 14, 21,
222, 223
Gerry's (Club) 141
Gerry's (Off-licence) 157
The Glassblower 115
The Glasshouse 116
Globe Theatre 196
Golden Gate Grocers 242
Golden Lion 116
Golden Nugget 178
Golden Square 12, 14, 22
Grahame's Seafare 70
Great Chapel Street
Medical Centre 248
Great Marlborough
Street 22
Magistrates Court 249
Greek Street 6, 7, 23
Green Man 117
Groove Records 168
Groucho Club 8, 188

Haircutting Room 248
Hairdressers 248
Hardware 173
Harold Moore's Records
168
Harry's 93
Hazlitt, William 7, 21, 34
Health Clubs 181–183
Health Services 248–249
Historic Soho 11–40
Hitman Records 168
Hong Kong Cultural
Service 243
Hospital for Women 23,
248
Hostess Bars 211–214
House Bros (Cutlers) 173
House of St Barnabas 16,
23
Housing Association 249
The Huguenots 12, 142
Hunter, John 35

Inderwick's 172
Intrepid Fox 118

Jimmy's 70
Job Centre 247
Joe's Basement 166
John, Augustus 7
John Milroy 158
John Snow 18, 118
Just Facts 148
Just Games 162

Kauffman, Angelica 35
Keats, John 8
Kemble, Fanny 35
Kettners 41, 71
Kettners Champagne Bar
135
King Charles II 24
King George II 24
King of Corsica 119
King's Arms 25, 120
King's Head 121

LMV Electrical Services
161
Laline 72
Last Days of the Raj 73
Last Resort 136
Launderettes 249
Lavatories 250
Lee Ho Fook
(Gerrard St) 234
(Macclesfield St) 234
Leicester Arms 121
Leoni's Quo Vadis 74
Ley-Ons 235
Library 249
Limelight 204
Lina Stores 155
Literary Soho 7–8
London College of Music
24
Lonsdale 170
Loon Fung Supermarket
243
Lovejoys 169
Luxuriance 235
Lyric Tavern 122
Lyric Theatre 196

MacInnes, Colin 15, 217
Madame Jo-Jo's 205
Magazines 163
Magistrates Court 249
Maison Bertaux 93
Maison du Pantalon 148
Map reference 45
Marat, Jean-Paul 13, 36
Margaret Pyke Centre
248
Markets 173–175
The Marquee 184, 200
Marshall Street Leisure
Centre 181
Marvelette 148
Marx, Karl 14, 20, 30, 36
Matono 75
Melati 75
Membership Clubs
188–190
Metro Cinema 181
Metropolitan Club 182
Mini-cabs 251
Minton, John 7
Mishuko Sauna 191
Monmouth House 12, 28
Morgan's 137
Moroni, A. & Son 166
Moscow Club 190
Moulin Cinema 181
Mozart, Wolfgang
Amadeus 21, 37
Mr Kong 236
Musical instruments
164–165
Mykonos 77

Nairn, Ian 6
'Near-beer' bars 211–214
Nellie Dean 123
New Oriental 244
New Piccadilly 94
New Rupert Executive
Club 141
New World 237
Newsagents
(International)
165–166
Nightclubs 202–208
Nightlife 199–208
Nollekens, Joseph 20, 37

Oddbins 158
Off-licences 157–159
Old Coffee House 123
Old Compton Street 6,
14, 15, 25
Onslow, Arthur 38

P & G Advisory Service
249
Palace Theatre 197
Palladium 197
Paolo Garbini 171
Pasta Fino 77
Pasticceria Cappucetto
94
Patisserie Valerie 94

Pavilion 78
Peep Shows 214–215
La Perla 79
Peter Hoggard 149
Petrol 249
Phil Rabin's Salt Beef Bar 95
Pho 95
Photographic shops 166–167
Piccadilly Theatre 198
Pillars of Hercules 124
Pizza Express 80
Poland Street 25
Police 250
Pollo 96
Pombal, Marquess of 38
Poon's 238
Post Office 250
Prince Edward Theatre 198
The Print Gallery 167
Prints 167
Prostitutes 215–217
Public Lavatories 250
Pubs 99–133
Pure Fabrication 149

Quartet Bookshop 160
Queen's Head 124
Queens Theatre 198

Randall & Aubin 156
Ransome, Arthur 7
Rasa Sayang 81
Raymond Revuebar 192
Records 167–168
Red Fort 81
Red Lion
(Great Windmill St) 125
(Kingly St) 126
Red or Dead 170
Restaurants 44–90, 231–240
Richards 156
Richmond Cornejo 149
Rimbaud, Arthur 14, 25, 38
Ronnie Scott's 185, 200
Rough Cut 248
Roy, William 39
Rugantino 82
Rupert Street Market 175

Saigon 83
St Anne's Church 11, 15
Chapel 250
Tower 25
St Patrick's Catholic Church 16, 27, 250
Satay & Wine 84
Saunas 191
Schools 250
Sex & Soho 208–221
Sex shops 168–170
Shaftesburys 206
Shakespeare's Head 126
Shampers 138
Shelley, Percy Bysshe 7, 25, 39
Sheraton, Thomas 39
The Ship 127
Shoe repairs 251
Shoe shops 170
Shoes 170
Shopping 142–175, 241–244
Slater & Cooke Bisney & Jones 151
Smith, John Christopher 40
Snow, Dr John 19
Soccer Scene 171
Soho 162
Soho Brasserie 6, 97, 98
Soho Electrics 161
Soho Jazz Festival 187
Soho Pizzeria 85
Soho Society 210, 251
Soho Soho 85
Soho Soundhouse 165
Soho Square 12, 15, 27
Soho's Friend 239
Sound of China 244
Spice of Life 127
Sports shops 170–171
Staël, Anne Louise de 40
Star & Garter 25, 128
Star Cafe 96
The Store 129
Strip Shows 191–195
Studio Valbonne 207
Sun & Thirteen Cantons 130
Sunset Strip 194
Swank 150
Synagogue 250

Tailors 171–172
Taxis 251
Taylor's 160
Thackeray, William 12
Theatres 195–199
This Address 150
Thomas, Dylan 7, 15, 99
Three Greyhounds 130
Le Tire Bouchon 86
Tobacconists 172–173
Tools 173
Topo Gigio 87
Tracks 139
Transport 251
Triads 224–226

Underground 251

Van Long 88
Verde Valle 89
Verlaine, Paul 14, 25, 38
Vinorio 156
The Vintage House 158
Vintage Magazine Centre 163

Wag, The 200, 207
Wagner, Richard 40, 108
Wardour Street 6, 29
West End Great Synagogue 250
West One 131
Westminster City Councillors 251
Wheeler's 90
White Horse
(Newburgh St) 132
(Rupert St) 132
William R. Barnes 160
Windmill Sauna 191
Wine Bars 133–139
Wong Kei 240
Woolf/Soho 150
Workers for Freedom 150
Worship, Places of 250

Ying Hwa 244

Zeitgeist 151